THE WORLDS OF WOLF MANKOWITZ

The Worlds of Wolf Mankowitz

Between Elite and Popular Cultures in Post-War Britain

ANTHONY J. DUNN

VALLENTINE MITCHELL
LONDON • PORTLAND, OR

First published in 2013 by Vallentine Mitchell

Middlesex House,
29/45 High Street, Edgware,
Middlesex HA8 7UU, UK

920 NE 58th Avenue, Suite 300
Portland, Oregon,
97213-3786, USA

www.vmbooks.com

First published in North
America in 2016

British Library Cataloguing in Publication Data

Dunn, Anthony J.
The worlds of Wolf Mankowitz : between elite and popular cultures in post-war Britain.
1. Mankowitz, Wolf. 2. Jewish authors--Great Britain--Biography. 3. Authors, English--20th century--Biography.
I. Title
828.9'1409-dc23

ISBN 978 0 85303 865 8 (cloth)
ISBN 978 0 85303 906 8 (paper)
ISBN 978 0 85303 994 5 (Ebook)

Library of Congress Cataloging in Publication Data
Catalogue record has been applied for

Printed by CMP (UK) Ltd, Poole, Dorset BH12 4NU

For my Mother and Father,
who always had faith in me

Contents

Plates

Acknowledgements

My most profound thanks go to the Mankowitz family, and especially to Daniel and Gered, who have given me unfettered access to the hoard of books, scripts, press-cuttings, letters, tapes and photographs which constitutes the Mankowitz Family Archive. Without their generosity in allowing me to quote at length from their Archive this book could have been no more than a brief memoir. They have given most selflessly of their time and expertise to ensure that this is a biography of scholarly substance. Any errors of detail or infelicities of expression and structure are, of course, my responsibility alone.

My sincere thanks also go to the following: Chris and Jane Bolger for introducing me to the Wedgwood Museum in Stoke-on-Trent and for life-long friendship; Els Boonen of the BBC Archives at Caversham who helped me tame their fiendish copying machine; the staff at the British Film Institute Library, Stephen Street, London; Maggie Chrystal for her professional expertise and her invaluable friendship; Katharine Deans for her heartfelt encouragement at a crucial stage; the Film History seminar at Senate House, London, with special thanks to Professors James Chapman and Jeffrey Richards for their support and advice; James Hogan, publisher of Oberon books, for putting me in contact with the Mankowitz family; Drs Alison and Aaron Kahn for delightfully recuperative family weekends in Oxford; Stephen Massil for commissioning my first Mankowitz article and for life-long friendship; my family who spurred me on to finish; my interviewees for their patience and insights; Alan Shelston who notated successive drafts with patient acuity, and for his life-long friendship; Sarah Westwood, sometime librarian of Downing College, Cambridge, who sleuthed out the Mankowitz tutorial file.

My thanks also to my editor, Heather Marchant, who steered me towards completion with professional aplomb.

Introduction

In the summer of 1997, one year before his death at the age of 73, Cyril 'Wolf' Mankowitz was interviewed about his life and work, over a number of sessions, by Gerald Davis of The Davis Gallery, Dublin. Mankowitz had relocated to Ireland in the early 1970s for tax reasons. His voice, preserved on some six hours of audio-cassette tape, and kindly made available to me by his son, Daniel, is not the voice of a man near death. Throughout this interview[1] his is a confident, bass voice, undercut by a sardonic edginess, as when, for example, he describes the financial machinations of the film industry; or his and his elder sister's creation of an American market for Wedgwood china; or his escapades with Orson Welles. By 1997 he knew he was just holding at bay his pancreatic cancer, first diagnosed some twelve years before. But his account of a haemorrhage and an out-of-body experience at London Airport, some years before, is jaunty and secular. He had no spiritual exaltation but he does recommend a haemorrhage for anybody who is in a state of great tension.

Mankowitz, then, is no misery memoirist. At six foot and with a fighting weight of sixteen stone he was a big and imposing man, a Jew, according to Frederic Raphael, who had decided he wasn't going to be ashamed of anything, and one who loomed large in the post-war cultural life of London. Mankowitz makes a significant revision in the Davis interview, for example, of the received history of the early years of the English Stage Company. He points out that the Royal Court might not have long survived its reincarnation as a radical theatre had it not been for the financial and management expertise of Oscar Lewenstein and himself, whose joint company supported a number of important shows at the Court, as well as fellow-Jews Neville Blonde and Lois Sieff. There was, therefore, an important Jewish presence, unacknowledged by all its official historians, at the birth of this new Royal Court.

In the 1950s and the 1960s, Mankowitz was ubiquitous in popular media, old and new. He was a frequent guest on 'Woman's Hour' and appeared on TV programmes such as 'What's My Line?' and 'Juke Box Jury'. He turned out numerous short stories for the *Evening Standard*, and wrote the original novellas and film scripts for *Make Me an Offer* and *A Kid for Two Farthings*. He produced two scholarly works on Wedgwood china and wrote both the theatre and film scripts of his short story *Expresso Bongo*. He was an East-Ender, loved the metropolis, and had a lifelong engagement with Dickens, scripting the very successful musical *Pickwick* (1963), a BBC TV series of the same name in 1969, and a series, 'Dickens of London', for Yorkshire TV in 1976. He was a founder-member of a dining club, the Pickwick Club in Great Newport Street, which opened at the same time as the musical, and became the preferred haunt of a new generation of actors and producers such as Michael Caine, Terence Stamp and Harry Salzman. He was one of the scriptwriting team for *Dr No*, the first James Bond movie. He promoted a generation of new Jewish actors, with lead roles for Sid James and Miriam Karlin in his series 'East End, West End' for Associated Rediffusion; the lead for Laurence Harvey in the film of *Expresso Bongo*; and amusing bit parts for Sid James and Alfie Bass in, respectively, *Trapeze*, starring Burt Lancaster and Tony Curtis, and *The Millionairess*, whose star leads were Sophia Loren and Peter Sellers.

One consistent thread throughout Mankowitz's very varied career is, in fact, a concern for and interrogation of his Jewish cultural inheritance. His family was secular in that, according to Helen Legg, his younger sister, their mother kept a very kosher household without being religious. They observed Passover and lit candles every Friday but Mankowitz's father, Solomon, only started to attend the synagogue in Manor Park late in his life in order to swell the diminishing congregation.[2] Mankowitz himself had no belief in a God nor in an afterlife, and in the Davis interview declares himself a Marxist and a Freudian. He was, briefly, a member of the British Communist Party while at Cambridge, although, as recently released MI5 documents show, it was his wife, Ann Seligmann, whose communism caused the authorities early concern. But he admired the ingenuity and beauty of the stories in the Old Testament and produced witty, modern versions of several of them for stage and television. He didn't speak Yiddish but he used the characteristic inflections and reversals of Yiddish English for many of his short-story characters and he was attracted by the wry cynicism and trickster figures in Yiddish writing.

Whatever else he was doing in the various periods of a busy writing life, he always wrote at least one work that linked him back to his Jewish inheritance. *The Samson Riddle* (1972) and *The Hebrew Lesson* (1972) are masterly dramatizations of the complex interfaces between myth, history and politics. *Almonds and Raisins* (1983) is an historical documentary of Yiddish cinema, and *A Night with Casanova* (1991) imagines a night-long encounter between Casanova, in his last days, and The Wandering Jew. Mankowitz put his professional skills to political use when he co-produced, with John Schlesinger, *Israeli*, aka *Israel, A Right to Live* (1967), a post-Six Day War documentary which places the conflict in its historical setting and features spokespeople from all sectors of Israeli society. The older sector of English, particularly English Jewish, society is the subject of the 1969 documentary *Cast Us Not Out*, which focuses on the care-home provision for senior citizens. Mankowitz wrote and speaks its commentary and the camera director is Walter Sushitzky, lighting cameraman for the very popular 1955 film version of Mankowitz's stage play, *The Bespoke Overcoat*.

But Mankowitz's name does not now loom large in the long roll call of distinguished Jewish writers in post-war Britain. Bernard Kops suggests, in interview,[3] several reasons for this. Success, he considers, came too early and in too many diverse forms for Mankowitz. Kops, although only two years younger than Mankowitz, saw himself in the 1950s as part of a still younger grouping, that of Wesker and Pinter, which wrote its way out of poverty and was quickly perceived as part of the new cultural vanguard in late-1950's Britain. 'None of us went to University', he points out. 'We had to be very clever and deft at what we were doing because we weren't educated.' By the late 1940s, Mankowitz, by contrast, had already graduated from Downing College, Cambridge, and was a co-editor, with Raymond Williams and Clifford Collins, of the important left-wing journal *Politics and Letters*, and a frequent contributor to the *Evening Standard* and the *Sunday Pictorial*. He was an East-Ender like Kops, Pinter and Wesker, but his father was a book-seller, not a fishmonger or a leather-seller; his office was in the West End, in Piccadilly Arcade; and his popular 1950s stories of conmen and tricksters were as likely to be set in Soho as in the East End.

A Kid for Two Farthings (1953), it is true, is set in Whitechapel and its Petticoat Lane and Club Row markets. But the East End Mankowitz depicts is, as he says in the Davis interview, an East End recalled from his childhood in the 1930s, and the child protagonist's delusion that the goat he has befriended is a unicorn is in the tradition of Yiddish tale-tellers such as Sholom Aleichem. Kops, too, sees himself as continuing this mix of fantasy and naturalism but his cultural comrades were Pinter and Wesker, despite their differences of technique and subject matter. For Kops they were all part of a great new wave of writers whose oppositional politics cohered around CND (Campaign for Nuclear Disarmament) and the Royal Court, which was for Mankowitz more an entrepreneurial base than a cultural collective. Kops admired Mankowitz as a Jew who had proved that a Jew could make it in the larger cultural world of London, one who had moved beyond the proletarian realism of Simon Blumenfeld and William Goldman. But he also sensed that his group was going to move beyond Mankowitz. They had a solidarity born by the chance combination of the time and their talent. Mankowitz, by contrast, seemed fragmented, pulled in too many directions at once. Frederick Raphael, in interview, recalls a man of frantic energy and imposing presence but insufficient focus.[4] He was, for Raphael, a kind of Jewish De Quincey.

Raphael also comments on Mankowitz's connoisseurship of Wedgwood china and interprets this as a bastion of value to set against his attraction for and involvement with the meretricious activities of popular culture. Mankowitz himself, in the Davis interview, acknowledges the lifelong impression made upon him as a young student by what he calls the 'Puritan verbal ethic' of his English tutor at Cambridge, Dr F.R. Leavis. Leavis thought well enough of Mankowitz to commission reviews from him for that select journal *Scrutiny*; but Mankowitz, married and with a growing family, couldn't earn a living as a literary critic and was temperamentally attracted to the popular cultural worlds of Fleet Street and film scripting, milieux despised, but not ignored, by the elitist Leavis. Mankowitz was thus spokesman for several different worlds, as the tale-teller of Yiddish ancestry, the connoisseur from high-minded Cambridge, and the media-savvy man about town.

Each of these cultural zones had its own definition of 'the people', a concept of great importance to the Marxist in Mankowitz and one that was undergoing radical revision in post-war Britain. The People's War had been won, but, in the cultural field, the question was: who would win the People's Peace? Yiddish speakers and their traditions of tale-telling were rapidly dying out, and Kops published his *The World is a Wedding* in 1963 as his memorial to that dying culture. Leavis had been redrawing the map of English Literature as a set of hierarchies of talent since the 1930s, but his post-war drive was to encourage his students to enter secondary-school teaching and establish English as the crucial discipline for a civilized populace. His concern was to revalue

English studies away from lazy 'appreciation' and, through close textual readings, towards a use-value in society at large. *Revaluation* was the title of his second book, published in 1936, which offered his evaluative map of English poetry from the seventeenth to the early nineteenth centuries. Mankowitz understood Leavis's argument about values, but, unlike Leavis, he also found value in the now interrelating media worlds of radio, television, the press, film and theatre. Most of his plots privilege the value of exchange over that of productive use, a most unusual stance for a self-confessed Marxist.

Wolf Mankowitz, therefore, is a particularly complex example of the long debate in British culture between populism and elitism. Bernard Kops is probably right when he argues that Mankowitz, to his disadvantage, made his name just too early to benefit from the innovations of the New Wave. A mere half-dozen years or so separate him, born in 1924, from Pinter, Wesker, Raphael, Lionel Bart and Michael Codron; but an age seems to separate him from them with his depiction of Jewishness in, for example, *The Bespoke Overcoat*. Kops thought it nearer Gorki's *Lower Depths* than contemporary London. But there are advantages in Mankowitz's Janus-like position. It enables the artist to mix past and present in new combinations. His Jewishness could be more confidently asserted in the more racially tolerant climate of post-war London; the writer could be both a London East-Ender and a London West-Ender.

A less confident and less energetic writer than Mankowitz might have been paralysed by the contradictions of his position. But Mankowitz was game. This study argues that he was not only the linkman between the 1930s generation of Jewish proletarian writers and the New Wave of the late 1950s, but was as committed as his near-contemporaries to elucidating the opaque contours of post-war Britain. The medley of styles and modes that is Carol Reed's 1955 film version, with Mankowitz's script, of Mankowitz's 1953 novella *A Kid for Two Farthings* is an outstanding example of this two-way pull between past and present. This, after all, is a film where Diana Dors as a seamstress is played against David Kossoff as a clichéd old Jewish tailor, and where rock 'n' roll shares a soundtrack with a traditional lament at Passover. In-between, however, is not a secure position, especially if you are a proud and talented man. There were times, as Kops recounts, when Mankowitz could be bitter and contemptuous of the next generation of Jewish writers. But he had not much time to spare for rancour. He was writing, writing, writing, and this first literary biography of Wolf Mankowitz aims not only to place him within the cultural currents of his times but also to retrieve and evaluate that voluminous output for the general reader. The surrealist collages created at the end of his life, late affirmations of the value of modernist parataxis, will also receive critical attention.

This critical biography, however, traces the life and works in conventional sequence, from birth to death. In one of its principal sources, the Davis interview, Mankowitz claims that he had no plan for his life. Everything happened by accident, and the content of the interview, which darts back and forth in time and records a varied cast of artists and personalities, mimics a life of chance. The opening section recalls friends and colleagues from the 1950s such as Alfie Bass, Peter Sellers and Jack Clayton; swings forward to his current interests in Dada and Surrealism, then back to his Cambridge days in the 1940s; then forward to his Wedgwood enterprises, then broadens into an encomium of the work of James Joyce. Elsewhere, he recalls his close associations with Orson Welles, Laurence Harvey and Alexander Korda; his involvement in an organization smuggling Jews out of Eastern Europe to Israel in the late 1960s; and working with Milos Forman in Rome on the eve of the Russian invasion of Czechoslovakia. But, overarching this episodic life, is the disciplined, cumulative, professional life of writing. By the time of the Davis interview, Mankowitz was too ill to write and knew his death was imminent. He therefore talks a numerous cast of selves into being, a last outburst of creative life before his own self sinks into nothingness. This biography tells the story of his furious creativity.

NOTES

1. Hereafter referred to in the text as 'the Davis interview'.
2. Helen Legg, interviewed by Daniel Mankowitz, September 2006.
3. Bernard Kops, interviewed by the author, 24 November 2003.
4. Frederick Raphael, telephone interview by the author, 11 August 2009.

CHAPTER ONE

Family, Cambridge and War Service (1924–46)

Cyril Woolf Mankowitz was born on 7 November 1924. He was the first child born to his mother, Rebecca Mankowitz (née Brick), whose family was originally from Matzov in Imperial Russia and who arrived in England, aged 2, in 1896. His father, Solomon Mankowitz, was born in Lutzin – then in Russia, now Latvia – in 1895. He arrived in England in 1908, aged 13 and, like Rebecca Brick, spent his childhood and adult years in London's East End.[1] Some six months before Cyril's birth the couple had moved into 45 Fashion Street, Whitechapel, which he remembers, in the Davis interview, as a two-room flat with a tap on the floor below, a lavatory on the ground floor at the bottom of a yard, and a deserted factory opposite, surmounted by Moscow-like cupolas. His maternal grandparents lived in nearby Slater Street, at number 104, which served as a cap shop, run by the grandfather, with living quarters above. Mankowitz describes his grandfather as a typical Southern Russian Jew, with an interest in animals, who always kept a goat in his backyard and would have kept a horse there if he could. Grandparents and parents spoke good English but, as Southern Russians and Northern Europeans,[2] were very different types. Mankowitz's milieu was entirely Jewish until the family moved to East Ham.

Mankowitz was 5 when Helen was born in 1929. Her elder sister, Barbara, was born in 1927. In her interview, Helen recalls a brother who could be kind and thoughtful, who gave her a Conway Stewart pen for her birthday, introduced her to classical music and took her in when she quarrelled with her family over her fiancé. But he was also the dominant child in the household – 'always a king' – says his sister, a boy who couldn't bear to be contradicted and who detested the succession of girls whom his mother employed to look after the children while she helped her husband on his stalls in East Ham market. He kept a snake in his room where he also had a chemistry set on a trestle table. He devised a walkie-talkie system for communication with other boys down the street, and Helen remembers how exciting the Edith Road house was, with the arguments and ambitions of her adolescent brother and his friends. 'They were a group of very bright boys', she remembers, and she recalls Clifford Collins in particular and how his cigarette trembled in the dark as the air raids sounded overhead. He went to Clifton public school and would team up with Mankowitz after Cambridge as a joint-editor, along with Raymond Williams, of the influential left-wing journal *Politics and Letters*.

The East Ham market had been local to the Mankowitz family for some time. They had moved east from Fashion Street in 1928, living first at 10 Cowper Avenue, E6, with an aunt, his mother's sister, who had a greengrocer's business in the market; and then, in 1933, to their own house in nearby Edith Road. Helen grew up in this house and she has other happy memories of it, as an environment where there was the usual bickering between the children, but also a great emphasis on reading and education. There was, Mankowitz remembers in the Davis interview, never any talk about business at home because his father was very bad at it. His father insisted that the answer to every problem was to be found in a book and he sold off his entire stock of books to finance his son for his first term at Cambridge. But he was always broke and often had only a strip of chewing gum to get him through the day.

As a boy, Mankowitz had a little stall in East Ham market where he sold stamps at weekends and on holidays. He would remain, throughout his career, attracted by markets and exchange, but, rather like his father, not very competent at handling money. His father, however, could see that he was very deft with words and, according to Syd Mould, his long-time friend from school and after, Mankowitz's father gave his son a complete set of the works of Bernard Shaw when he was 12 and sent books to him when his school, East Ham Grammar, was evacuated to Swindon in 1939.[3] Helen recalls their father had told his son, when he came next to bottom of his class at the age of 14, that he could either work or leave and get a job. His ambition at that stage had not extended beyond running a stall. But his father opened his horizons. He worked and became the first pupil from his school to get to Cambridge.

It was Mankowitz Senior whom Syd Mould first met at the age of 9 in East Ham market. He was attracted by the various items –

assegais, shields, muskets – for sale and bought a bayonet for a shilling. He became friends with the son at grammar school, even though he was a little older, and they wrote and designed a satirical magazine, *The Troll*, which was an anti-publication to the official school magazine. Mankowitz rewrote several poems by Bret Harte for it and, by his own account, improved them. Mould also recalls a catastrophic venture out of East London by Mankowitz Senior who bought a boat, called *The Lucky Ann*, and attempted, with the family, to circle Eel Pie Island in it. But he got no further than going round in circles in the Thames and being the target of anti-Semitic insults from the riverbank. He retreated back east and kept it on a pond in Wanstead. He was an honourable man and Helen recounts with appreciation his conduct during the war when he stayed in London, as an ARP (Air Raid Precautions) warden, after the family had been bombed out of Edith Road in 1940 and evacuated to Swindon and Llandudno. He did the ARP job for the money (£3 per week), but many people offered their homes to him for as little as £5. He refused. 'I'll be here after the War', he said, 'and I don't want to be the Jew who stole your home.' His daughter recalls that when he died everyone remembered him by something he had given them.

Mankowitz, in the Davis interview, tells some of his best stories about his father. He set up as a general dealer but his only specialism was books, 'which he loved to read more than to sell'. On one occasion he was selling a stock of vintage claret, bought at the auction of the effects of 'some houses burnt down in the country', and he then decided to give his women customers free samples. When the licence inspector accused him of selling alcohol illegally he protested he was giving it away. On another occasion his father came home with a huge supply of army-surplus Dubbin. He assured his son that Dubbin was what made the British Army so great as it preserved boots and enhanced the soldiers' marching speed. Mankowitz took a shoebox full of tins of Dubbin to school and sold them off at a penny each to the football enthusiasts. Mankowitz himself was never a sportsman. He sums up, with great good humour, the moral of these tales: 'How does a Jew live? He sells Dubbin and gives away claret!'

How Mankowitz lived in Swindon varied according to the family with whom he was billeted. His sisters and his mother swiftly relocated to an aunt in Llandudno in Wales. With East Ham market bombed out, their father's stock was transferred to Wales and formed the basic goods for a shop which Barbara, still only 13, opened and managed with the assistance of her mother and sister Helen. Helen, in interview, is full of admiration for her sister's determination and business sense and is convinced that she kept the family going financially with the Llandudno shop. Barbara, along with her brother-in-law David Seligmann, would be the driving force behind the business of Gered (Antiques) Ltd, which opened in the bombed-out Piccadilly Arcade in 1947, started selling Wedgwood in 1951 and expanded into a further, modern design outlet in Regent Street in 1964. Mankowitz and his wife received £117,000 each from the 1972 sale of the shares in the business to Wedgwood.[4]

Barbara also, Helen recalls, scrubbed from top to bottom the last family home, 1 Clavering Road, Wanstead, which their father had bought for £300 (which he borrowed), but which needed a thorough clean-up because it had been inhabited for many years by a drunk. Mankowitz and Sid Mould stayed on in Swindon, and Mould remembers that Mankowitz was first billeted with two spinster ladies who objected to his criticism of their afternoon tea arrangements; then with a young married couple who were mean with food; then with a publican and his wife who nearly starved him to death; and finally with a childless family who treated him like a much-loved son.

Mankowitz, now 15, had grown into a young man, even a dandy, in Swindon, according to his friend. He can still see him, tall and large at fifteen stone, sitting at his ease with a glass of grenadine in front of him outside a café in St Malo where they had gone for a brief holiday. His brightly coloured shirts and open-toe sandals created something of a stir round Swindon. Mould read this as a semi-Rupert Brook persona, a slightly romantic figure who signed his letters 'Lupus' and insisted on 'Wolf' as his first name. Helen says that her brother never really came back home after the age of 15. He was, it is clear, seizing the chance offered him by a catastrophe, the war, to play around with various selves in what seems like a most unpromising environment, a staid, dull Wiltshire town. But Swindon was an ideal laboratory. It had no strategic importance. He had no family ties there. He could mix social milieux with the freedom of the outsider, and he could get back to London whenever he wanted. He was an exotic import from the capital but no more so than the rest of his schoolmates. Forty years later he would weave into his experience of Swindon the fantasies of a deranged kabbalist and the scientific expertise of a 13-year-old evacuee which play significant roles in his novel *Abracadabra!*

Mankowitz's self-confidence, an attribute which everyone who knew him remarked upon, now carried him through school debates at Swindon's Commonweal Secondary School, which hosted East Ham Grammar School during its evacuation; debates at meetings of Swindon's Young Communist Group; and a beating from the Swindon school head for, by accident, straying into the girls' cloakroom. Mould also recalls that he persuaded Mankowitz to join the local Home Guard. They would at least get to hold a rifle. Some of their teachers were members, including the art teacher who had been a sergeant in the First World War. But the two pupils were not good at drills and Mankowitz had trouble with his feet, an irritation that became a distinct disability during his national service. This did not prevent him making frequent cycle visits to friends and family in London, a round journey of some 140 miles which must have slimmed him down.

He also claims, and Mould confirms it, to have attended a postgraduate course at Birkbeck College for the year before he went up to Cambridge. This must have been during the academic year 1941/42 when he duly passed Latin to complete School Certificate requirements for Cambridge entry. He was awarded this certificate as a pupil at the Swindon school but, with only one subject to be coached for, it is probable that he spent most of that year in London, where, with typical chutzpah, he was attending University as if he were already a postgraduate.

* * *

Mankowitz went up to Downing College, Cambridge, in January, 1943 and made it his first priority to find ways of supporting himself financially. His father had paid towards his first term's fees of £90 out of the proceeds of his book sale, and he had been awarded an Exhibition Scholarship worth £40 by Downing in December 1942. Essex eventually awarded him a County Major Scholarship of £120 for three years to run from January 1943 but, since the awards were paid at the end of terms, he needed more immediate income.[5] He soon found himself, in the absence of more senior people who had been called up for war service, lecturing to adult education classes throughout Cambridgeshire and Norfolk. He estimates, in the Davis interview, that teaching and travelling took up about fifty hours per week and that he was paid between thirty-five shillings and three pounds per lecture. This employment was a financial lifeline for him throughout his Cambridge years, and his personal tutor, William Lindsell Cuttle, a classics don, wrote a most supportive reference as early as March 1943 to the Cambridge Appointments Board, which must have helped Mankowitz to obtain posts throughout his academic career.

Cuttle writes that Mankowitz's parents 'are Russians who came to England from Central Europe in years gone by: they are Jews', and that 'he is a very intelligent and sensitive young man, whom I like and expect to do well'. He has pro-Russian sympathies 'which would not please everybody of course', but Cuttle has found him 'very sensible and reasonable about them, and his personal niceness makes him attractive'. He mentions Mankowitz's wish not to be a financial burden on his parents and says that he is waiting for a decision by Essex on his scholarship. Cuttle concludes: 'he is in speech and so on acceptable, and many people would find him an interesting person to meet'.[6] In those tight-lipped times this was high praise and expansive warmth from a Cambridge tutor, but his regard was genuine and he gave Mankowitz steady support during the nightmare of his National Service. Their respect was mutual and they were in correspondence until at least 1952.

A note in his first year to Cuttle from Mankowitz gives a sense of the diplomacy with which both men handled Cambridge residential regulations. Mankowitz apologizes for returning late to College and causing 'you to doubt me'. He has been working and talking late with a friend at Queen's, but will return earlier in the future. He has also 'two essays in preparation for Dr Leavis'.[7] Dr Leavis's own comments on Mankowitz's tutorial performances evince a growing regard for his abilities. His summing-up for the Lent Term of 1943 is caustic: 'Very forthcoming but unshaped as yet. If only there were time, he could be educated to some effect.' By the end of next term he 'has a lively mind' but 'You can't be sure he wouldn't do something silly – exhibitionist – and get a III. Much better than that', and by the end of Michaelmas (Winter) term Mankowitz is 'justifying his presence here and is profiting. He has read enormously, and shown good initiative. Still unformed. Somewhere in II.i.'[8]

He was also, according to Syd Mould's account, enjoying himself enormously in Cambridge. Syd stayed with him on several occasions at Downing. They combated hearties who tried to invade their room, attended a Leavis lecture together with both of them in black gowns, invaded a supervision by a philosophy professor and took part in charades on a lawn organized by 'country Fabian people in open-necked shirts'. Syd also donated a couple of his paintings to Wolf's rooms and created a linocut as the design for the invitation to the Socialist Party college dance. Wolf was for some time active in the local Communist Party branch until he was expelled by the chairman for deviations from the party line. The chairman was Robert Bolt. He was popular with women, presumably because of his self-confidence and his imposing presence, and for a brief period he was engaged to an undergraduate, a county girl called Frieda who came from a middle-class family in Northampton where the father was an organist in the cathedral. She was very Church of England and even enticed Mankowitz into attending a church service. The family was worried he would 'marry out' but the relationship soon died a natural death.

Mankowitz not only found time to write his essays for Leavis but also involved himself in the Cambridge college world of small magazines and political publications. The Bulletin of the Universities Socialist Clubs for 2 June 1943 published a letter jointly signed by him and two others which bemoans the retirement from university politics of one John Butler. The tone of flippant irony is very undergraduate and the critique of King's College as a home of decadent aestheticism typical of a Leavisite. '[T]o deny that he managed to split off a section of potentially active socialists in this University is to deny his very cunctatorial qualities' is a sentence which displays clever young men flexing their classically learned muscles. A far more significant contribution to Cambridge intellectual life is his joint-editorship, with Balachandra Rajan, of an impressive number of *Sheaf*, the Trinity College magazine of critical writings sponsored by the Cambridge Undergraduate Council. Its exact date of publication is uncertain, since the copy in Cambridge University Library is date-stamped 22 June 1945, but the magazine was favourably reviewed in the 15 July 1944 number of *The Times Literary Supplement* (hereafter *TLS*). Assuming a lag of some two months before the review we can estimate a publication date of sometime in May 1944. By then Mankowitz had just embarked on the fiasco which was to be his war service and, if he had a copy of *Sheaf* with him, its measured, analytical prose might have been some solace in the heat and the dust of the Newcastle mines.

Sheaf's topics and interests are very much of its period. It looks back to the 1930s but advocates a new role for criticism in the 1940s.

Articles on Kafka, John Cornford, Rubert Brooke and Stanley Spencer are accompanied by poems and reviews. The editorial designates the critic as one who 'provides, as it were, the abstract spatialization which the creative experience of poetry can mould'. Such literary enabling is not prescriptive – 'He cannot tell you what to do' – but it is a 'placing' action – 'he can, if he is sensible, tell you where you stand'. Such critics are serious, not 'coquettes in a critical fantasia', and pugnacious – 'There is a demand for honest hard-hitting criticism, and we hope progressively to be able to apply it.'[9] The Leavis influence is evident and it is no surprise to find that Rajan's article, 'The Bloomsbury Baedeker', is a satirical review of metropolitan literati.

Mankowitz contributes a review of a literary panto mounted by George Rylands, which he declares an 'unconditionally vulgar literary bastard',[10] and a long poem, 'Ruined Acropolis'. Its narrator, who alternates first-person speaker and second-person addressee, stands in the ruins of classical culture, uncertain and confused as to its relevance to the present age, whose 'fractured dream' has dropped to its elements of 'fire and water and broken stones'. A cleaner future is promised but the speaker figures the man of that future as 'Pitiless man within the deep corruption' whose name and strength are elected and nominated 'above the violence'.

The narrator's angst is undergraduate, but Eliot is the source of the classical/modern problematic, as well as the imagery of water, ruined cities and shattered columns. Auden is the source of fears for the hygienic 'ultimate cleanness' of an unheroic future, and of the flattened, conspiratorial tone of the social observer who hears 'a rumour of a new continent discovered / the story of a clean city around the corner / a thousand whispering voices / debating the construction of a tenement'. But, unlike the personae of Eliot and Auden, Mankowitz's 'Trembling man in the phantom-filled arena'[11] finds neither consolation nor explanation in religion. His 'election' is an echo, a faint one, of Athenian democracy.

* * *

There are three documentary sources for Mankowitz's war service. The first is William Cuttle who describes Mankowitz's war career, with masterly understatement, in a letter to the University Registry as 'somewhat chequered'. He narrates, in the cool prose of dates and places, the gradually developing miasma of a young man who volunteers as a coal miner in Autumn 1943; kicks his heels waiting for call-up for five months; is discharged from the mines near Teeside after two months (1 May 1944 – 28 June 1944) on the medical grounds of migraine and flat feet; does some clerical and teaching work extramurally at Durham University while seeking regrading (c. 1 September 1944 – c. 28 October 1944), and is finally dumped in the General Service Corps section of the Royal Army Service Corps, the transport division of the army, for the rest of his service (until August 1945).[12]

Mankowitz fills in the details of his war service in the course of his Davis interview. He felt himself to be, he says, a member of the 'Spike Milligan Brigade'. He is sent down an old mine in Anfield Plain near Newcastle, where he has to feel his way through 'an extraordinary white fungus [that] had grown up like sheets and veils hanging down'. He injures his foot on the coal-loading truck, is invalided out and gets a job as a lecturer in King's College, Durham. Then he is called up for the Durham Light Infantry, whose reputation for bravery is notorious because they run towards the enemy. He does his best to get himself reassigned and the authorities admit their mistake and send him for infantry training in survival methods. He fails the course three times so the army sends him down south to train as a typist, since he claims to be a writer. The repetitive boredom of the task gives him severe migraines and he's sent to the area consultant doctor in Aldershot. The consultant turns out to be a medical graduate from Downing, who agrees that Mankowitz is unfit for military service and gives him a classification that eventually releases him from the army.

Mankowitz must have seen Cuttle, at this time, as his only lifeline back into the academic world he had struggled so hard to enter. A letter to Cuttle of 26 October 1944, from Newcastle, details his sense of entrapment within army bureaucracy – 'I was merely passed from one department to another' – but there is a poignant glimpse at the end of a young man losing hope but holding on to language: 'I have been virtually alone in making my decisions and now I am presented with a ready-made but I can't help feeling, negative synthesis. I am only too happy to accept your help in this question of safeguarding my future, but can't imagine returning to Cambridge for some time.' There is also, perhaps, some resistance in his signature, 'Wolf Mankowitz', to this letter. His birth forenames, which he uses for all university correspondence, are 'Cyril Woolf'. This is the first occasion on which, in his correspondence with Cuttle, he names himself 'Wolf'. A self-image as ruthless predator might help to offset his feeling of helpless victim at this time, and memories of Dr Leavis inveighing against effete Bloomsbury might have persuaded him to disown 'Woolf'.[13]

Cuttle does not, of course, go into the war-service detail Mankowitz provides in the Davis interview (if indeed he knows about it) in his letter of September 1945. He is making the case for Mankowitz to receive his degree after sitting only Part I of his Finals and despite not being in residence in Cambridge for the statutory nine terms, due to military service. The Senate decided this was permissible under wartime regulations and he returned to Cambridge for the academic year 1945/46 and graduated with a 2.1 in the summer of 1946. He was awarded his MA in 1950.

The third, most recent source for Mankowitz's distinguished military career is the first of two MI5 files[14] on him, held at the National Archives at Kew and recently released into the public domain. University staff and students with known communist or Marxist sympathies were, it appears, routinely informed upon by anonymous informants or the police. The first Kew file, however, begins with reports by one R.O. from Cambridge dated 11 June 1944 and 7 July 1944, noting that a Miss A. Seligmann who has recently completed her studies in Moral Sciences at Newnham College, Cambridge, has been elected as a new committee member for the Cambridge branch of the Communist Party. Her address, a very respectable one, is given as 'Wharton Cottage, S. Ascot, Berks'. Miss Ann Seligmann was to become the wife of Wolf Mankowitz the following month, on 2 August, and was, according to a later police report dated 2 January 1945, employed as a regional care officer under the auspices of the Provisional Council of Mental Health. Her husband was at that time employed in the Educational Unit of the army in Bradford.

The report amplifies Cuttle's account of the couple's movements. It states that Mankowitz came to Newcastle with his wife on 5 August 1944, just after their marriage, and left in November 1944 when Mankowitz was called into the army. The report notes that he was 'supposed to serve as a "Bevin Boy" but was released from that employment to undertake a more intellectual vocation'. This presumably refers to his disastrous experience as a miner but, if Cuttle's account is accurate, this occurred in May and June of the summer of 1944 and would have involved some contact with Newcastle. The report, however, largely confirms the chronology of Mankowitz's war and implies that, for them both, a distinction should be drawn between active Communist Party membership, for which there is no evidence, and an allegiance to Marxism whose theories Mankowitz frequently discusses 'with his friends while in lodgings'.

We may also infer, given Mankowitz's state of health – mental and physical – at this time, that his wife's presence and her expertise in the fields of psychology and mental health afforded him great comfort and reassurance. The marriage had certainly been welcomed by the Mankowitz family. Not only was Ann Jewish, she was also, in Helen's affectionate words, 'gorgeous' and 'very middle-class' and beside her elegance Wolf was 'a peasant'. It was to be a very long-lived marriage and produced four much-loved children: Gered, Jonathan, Daniel and Benjamin.

The first Kew file includes a long communication by one I.H.L Smith, writing from Newcastle on 6 March 1945 to one P.F., which attempts a summary of Mankowitz's war service and includes new information. According to Smith he registered for the army in East Ham on 11 January 1943 and was voluntarily enlisted for the period of embodiment of the Territorial Army in Cambridge on 5 May. He was, however, relegated to reserve on 12 May in order to complete his studies. Nobody realized that he had already volunteered and it would appear that two sets of documents were circulating about his call-up without ever encountering each other. Mankowitz himself, according to Cuttle, had volunteered for the mines and began his service in Newcastle a year later. Smith suggests that, to try and discover his exact whereabouts, Record Offices in Edinburgh or Army Education Corps Records in Whitehall should be approached. With what sounds like a sigh of defeat, Smith concludes that 'In view of the confusion about this man's enlistment I am not certain that it can taken as definite that his Army No. now is 14431488.'

Leavis, as well as Cuttle, was supportive of Mankowitz during this difficult period. His letter of 15 November 1944 to the Personnel Selection Officer for the Army Education Corps is, in its commendation of his student's ability and character, worth reproducing in full:

> Since I examined <u>Mr Wolf Mankowitz</u> for a scholarship at this College, I have had him marked as a man of distinguished ability. He was not, of course, able to complete his course at the

> University, but I am able to testify that he was so advanced in reading and development that before leaving Cambridge he had attained to the level of a good degree. He seems to me peculiarly well qualified for service in the Army Education Corps. He has the teaching vocation and has had experience in adult education. Besides the essential academic qualifications he has a great advantage in his personality, which would conduce very strongly to his success. Further, he has had more experience of the world of personal relations than most university students of his age. I recommend him with the utmost confidence, and shall be happy to answer any inquiries about him.
>
> He has much better actual qualifications than most people with impressive academic endorsements and certificates.[15]

Leavis's next comments on Makowitz sum up his progress for the Michaelmas Term of 1945: 'An intelligent man with a genuinely interesting mind. He tends rather to explore, at the expense of the "good student" virtues: not reprehensibly, but a certain indiscipline may prejudice his chances of a good II.i.' This estimate of an inquiring but somewhat wayward intelligence is repeated in Leavis's summary of work for the Lent Term of 1946: 'Very intelligent and keen. Class list prospects uncertain, because he is so far from conforming himself to the straight and narrow path of examination drill. At worst II 2.' The final tutorial report is for Easter Term 1946: 'Has shown great keenness and energy. Perhaps he has indulged his individual interests too much to make the best impression on the examiners. Does Ist Class work. ?II 1?'

We can all grow and change post-university, often as a result of university, but an astute tutor can also pinpoint traits of character and intellect which will remain dominant for the rest of our lives. Mankowitz may not have emerged 'formed' as Leavis might have wished, but this tutor had spotted a swing between scholarship and personal curiosity which becomes more marked as his post-university career develops. At key moments throughout his career he refers with pride to the rigorous training in textual analysis that he was taught at Cambridge and his own early critical work, principally for the influential journal *Politics and Letters*, shows a distinctly Leavisite approach.

His other tutor, Mr Cuttle, refers again, in a letter to A.L. Maycock of the Cambridge Appointments Board dated 4 April 1946, to Mankowitz's war service but then emphasizes the stability that his marriage 'to a very respectable member of British Jewry' has brought to a very intelligent and sensitive man who 'suffered from nervous headaches and was generally worried over his position'. He says that he is very likeable, has been an active member of the Union and 'writes quite good verse'. He then gives a succinct and penetrating analysis of Mankowitz's origins and his relationship to English culture:

> His boyhood did not give him much of a chance of understanding English ways; he was very poor, and had a struggle; and I think he is still more or less of a foreigner. Perhaps for that very reason he could interpret English literature and life rather well, and I do believe that he has a true perception of us and a true admiration for us. He can certainly lecture and teach, and has a good background for such work by this time. On the whole, I would prefer to reserve judgement on him for a little while, for I can see he will not be an easy man to place.

Cuttle's 'placing' of Mankowitz is analogous to Raymond Williams's connection to the Leavis circle. Williams, with whom Mankowitz would collaborate closely on *Politics and Letters*, describes it as 'real, but a displaced one'.[16] Williams, scholarship student at Cambridge, from a politicized Welsh working-class family, interrogates his and his class's place in English culture throughout his life. But he is British and he knows where he comes from. Mankowitz was more concerned at this stage in his life about where he was going to and that, after a brief interlude in Essex, was back to the metropolis.

He says in interview that at Cambridge he wrote more poetry than anything else and got a poetry award from the Society of Authors in 1946, but he published very little because it didn't bring in money and he was always conscious of his need to be self-supporting. But he did contribute reviews to *Granta*, the university paper, and short fiction to, among other publications, *The Bridge*, edited by Geoffrey Moore from Emmanuel College, and *The Norseman*, a literary and political review with a Norwegian editorial board and a central London address. His *Granta* review of Dylan Thomas's *Deaths and Entrances* and Edith Sitwell's *Song of the Cold* criticizes the former's collection for lacking a 'unity of form and substance: the former is all external, almost idly applied, and the latter falls to pieces at a critical touch'. Sitwell's poetry is pretentious, purveying an 'opaqueness

[that] will probably be assumed to hide profundity, and flashiness to indicate something remarkable happening on the page'. Her work is too inclusive to be serious.

Virginia Woolf is another target for Leavisite disdain in his review, for a later number of *Granta*, of David Daiches's short study of her work. Mankowitz is less impressed than Daiches by her detachment from ordinary life. Her experience is 'severely limited – but in a manner which is only possible for those who occupy a position of complete economic security'. Daiches assumes that Woolf had great intelligence, but Mankowitz finds it limited to a traditional model of the comfortable scholar, 'clearly ... one equipped for recognition in academic circles'. The very different work of Henry Miller, *The Cosmological Eye*, receives even harsher treatment in the same number. He has no 'coherent attitude' to the sexual perversions which both fascinate and disgust him, and contrasts unfavourably with Lawrence's much saner and certain attitude to sex. Miller's impetus is so emotional that he slips too easily into sentimentality and his preoccupations are perhaps those of a 'guilt-stricken inverted puritan'. He knows his situation; what he lacks is 'a balanced valuation'.[17]

His contribution to *The Bridge* is 'A Death by Suicide', a very short piece which could be the imagined thoughts and memories, rendered in the third person, of a bedridden prominent public figure as he awaits death and interment. It could equally be the disordered fantasies of a dying derelict. It is a most accomplished piece of writing which combines precision of realist detail – 'The metal rail of the bed gleamed like blue metal on guns. The guns of the bed groaned for a dying general' – with surreal shifts of scene. A sequence where the dying man envisages his cortège and burial then shifts to memories of a bitterly cold winter when he 'limped through the marketplace to a stall where split frozen cabbages were lying unattended'. He doesn't want to linger in this place among people, each of whom is 'surrounded by his own loneliness, down the lanes from which light is most often hidden'. A contrast of light with dark runs through the piece but this deathbed cliché is animated by the scene-shifts and a narrative tone which remains even and steady through the story's twists and turns. 'A dark wing was falling towards his face ... It became too dark to argue any longer, and the edge of the wing struck the bridge of his nose.'[18] Kafka and Hemingway are influences but the story belongs to Mankowitz.

'The Art of Dying Slowly', his contribution to *The Norseman*, represents an evening scene of domestic peace, with a middle-aged couple, quiet and solicitous for each other, disturbed by the news that an aunt has died. They visited her regularly but they hadn't gone to see her when they were told a couple of days ago that she had taken a turn for the worse and the man reproaches himself for his neglect, but he had a great deal to do. 'His day was well-filled. His wife went often. But to be old. He was sorry about it.' Beneath the man's calm bubbles mania. Everything seems in order but this 'clean pattern' is only maintained by his power to control numerous, daily, personal irritations. He has to focus his attention on higher goals. His notebook is a vital resource. In it is a scrap of paper on which are tabulated 'the names and natures of today's worlds subjugated together with those of tomorrow in the order in which they were to be attacked'.

Dramatizing the madness beneath domestic routine we now see as the province of Ionesco and N.F. Simpson. Exposing the cruelty of family cliché would become a standard procedure in the works of Harold Pinter. Mankowitz's theatre work would go in a different, more populist direction, but he is alert here to an Absurdist view of the world which became increasingly influential in the Royal Court repertoire of the late 1950s. Raymond Williams remarks of Mankowitz in the late 1940s: 'I used to think he could write virtually anything.'[19]

NOTES

1. Helen Legg, interviewed by Daniel Mankowitz, September 2006.
2. Helen Legg says she only ever heard Latvia mentioned as her paternal grandparents' place of origin, and their alien documents confirm this. It may be that Solomon Mankowitz made his way to England by way of Lithuania in a period when Baltic states' boundaries were fluid.
3. Syd Mould, interviewed by Daniel Mankowitz, 26 July 2006.
4. *Wedgwood Review*, September 1964; *Daily Telegraph*, 19 August 1972.
5. Letter from H.C. Whalley-Tooker to Wolf Mankowitz, 18 December 1942, tutorial file DCAT/1/2/1293, Downing College, Cambridge; letter from Essex County Council to Wolf Mankowitz, April 1943 [?], tutorial file, DCAT/1/2/1293, Downing College, Cambridge.
6. Letter from W.L. Cuttle to A.L. Maycock, 25 March 1943, tutorial file, DCAT/1/2/1293, Downing College, Cambridge. All further correspondence cited is from this file.
7. Note, Wolf Mankowitz to W.L. Cuttle, probably 1943.
8. Tutorial file, C.W. Mankowitz, English. All subsequent reports by Leavis are from this file.
9. *Sheaf*, published by the editors at Trinity College Cambridge, sponsored by Cambridge Undergraduate Council, 1944, p.2.
10. Ibid., p.25.
11. Ibid., pp.29–31.
12. Letter from W.L. Cuttle to Registrary [*sic*], 6 September 1945, tutorial file, DCAT1/2/1293

13. Letter from Wolf Mankowitz to W.L. Cuttle, 26 October 1944, tutorial file, DCAT 1/2/1293.
14. Files numbered KV2/3384 and KV2/3385, held at the National Archives, Kew. All subsequent references will be to 'the first Kew file' and 'the second Kew file'.
15. Held in the Mankowitz Family Archive.
16. Raymond Williams, *Politics and Letters: Interviews with New Left Review* (London: New Left Books, 1995), p.76.
17. *Granta*, 8 March 1946, pp.30–1; 5 June, 1946, pp.56, 57.
18. *Bridge*, 1, 1 (April 1946), pp.29–31.
19. See Williams, *Politics and Letters*, p.76.

CHAPTER TWO

The Siege of London (1946–53)

Mankowitz, his wife and his baby son Gered spent most of the winter of 1946 in the remote Essex village of Mistley near Manningtree on the River Stour. This is confirmed by the ever-vigilant informers to the police and MI5. The first Kew file has preserved a report of 29 December by a redacted informer who gives details to Special Branch of the recent residence in a farm labourer's type of cottage at Mistley Heath by Mankowitz and his father. He has spent quite a lot of money on it and it is rumoured he will give lectures in the area for the Communist Party. The informer has met the father, who is a dealer in plate in East Ham, and a typical Jew, 'proud of his son whom he says is a great man'. The informer thought it appeared 'a little odd for a Cambridge University Professor (if such he be) to settle in such a forsaken place in a labourer's cottage'. There is no mention of the wife or child. He adds a footnote that 'Mankowitz recently had a flat in the West End but I have forgotten the address.'

The informant may be referring to the art and antiques gallery that Mankowitz, his sister Barbara and his wife's brother David Seligmann were in the process of setting up at this time. They called it Gered (Antiques) Ltd and it was situated in Piccadilly Arcade. It was to become an important source, not just of income, but also of knowledge and themes for Mankowitz's early commercial fictions. The antiques business, however, was only one of Mankowitz's interests in this exciting period. In a letter of 13 December 1946 to Cuttle he announces receipt of the poetry award from the Society of Authors and adds that 'journalism – for me [is] increasingly dishonoured and disgusting', but he will soon be freelancing as an advertising copywriter and turning out numerous articles for Hugh Cudlipp's *Sunday Pictorial*. Journalism suited him, he says in the Davis interview, because 'everything was new' and he could write in a wide range of styles. He was eager and ready to make his name and fortune both in academic journals and Fleet Street weeklies. He was already developing his own 'balance of culture', a term pregnant with meaning for this study, but one he would use for the first time some ten years later to describe the programming policy of the Royal Court Theatre.[1]

He was as happy, therefore, to contribute critical articles to reputable journals as to submit copy for newspapers. He has an essay on Eliot's 'Gerontion' in a 1947 collection edited by B. Rajan, which Leavis found one of the best contributions. A 1948 review for *Time and Tide* of a new edition of Swift's *Journal to Stella* contrasts its analysis of Swift unfavourably with that of Leavis in an essay of 1934; and in a letter later that year to *Time and Tide* Mankowitz praises the achievement of Eliot in terms barely distinguishable from those of Leavis himself. 'His poetry', Mankowitz writes, 'proceeded from a serious and intelligent concern for the language itself and for the living values embodied in its finest expression.'[2] But his most sustained attempt in this immediate post-war period to continue the life of the mind that had so impressed him at Cambridge was his collaboration, with Raymond Williams and Clifford Collins, on the writing and editing of *Politics and Letters*.

It ran for four numbers (one a double number) from the summer of 1947 to the summer of 1948. Its sister journal, *The Critic*, with the same editorial team, ran for two numbers, in the spring and autumn of 1947. Willams recalls that Collins solicited most of the journals' articles, although it was Mankowitz who persuaded Leavis to contribute to *Politics and Letters* and did the bulk of the editorial work. In the Davis interview, Mankowitz takes the credit for obtaining paper, a rare commodity at that time, at favourable rates. Fred Inglis, in his biography of Williams, describes Mankowitz and Collins as amongst Williams's closest intellectual collaborators, sharing a 'Left-Labourist provenance which was the best political weather of the day', combined with 'the characteristic Leavisite inflection that an independent criticality playing over cultural matters was the guarantee of a moral politics and a necessity of democracy'.

He catches the excitement of a new literary venture by a new post-war generation, describing the editorial office on the third floor of 7 Noel Street in Soho as 'a shabby little room with a plank floor' covered in newspapers, articles, carbons and spare clothes. Williams is kind and judicious, Collins 'intense, fluent, nervous' and Mankowitz 'garrulous, talented, disorganised, irresistibly prodigal and energetic and filled with optimistic schemes for movies, musicals, novels, political movements, chiliastic delirium'. Noel Street has since been renumbered and the present number 7 is diagonally opposite the building that housed *Politics and Letters* which stands at the corner of Noel Street and Berwick Street. As late as mid-2007 the present number 7 was a fire-gutted building, but the name of the shop on the ground floor was still visible. It was a record shop called 'DEAL REAL', two terms whose relationship Mankowitz puzzled over and interrogated throughout his career. Another record shop, up Poland Street, the next street after Berwick Street, was called 'Mr Bongo'.[3] These ambitious young men mixed, according to Inglis, with the worlds of London letters and London journalism, but also with the 'new broadcasting elite of the BBC' and 'the new Marxist historians group'.[4]

Williams's retrospective account of the journals' aims and objectives is more soberly political. But he confirms Inglis when he says that the editors' desire was to launch an 'alliance between Left politics and Leavisite criticism'.[5] The editorial, 'The Reading Public and the Critical Reader', to the autumn 1947 number of *The Critic* finishes by declaring that the journal is 'partisan rather than polemical, direct rather than oblique, puritan rather than catholic', and assigns to its sister journal *Politics and Letters* the responsibility for commentary on the context of art and society. That *The Critic*'s approach to text and society is *Scrutiny*-inspired is evident in the opening sections where the editors announce that 'whilst no one denies that intelligent people still exist, no one suggests that they exist as an *intelligent reading public* with the organic unity which that phrase suggests' (emphasis in original). It follows, therefore, that the 'absence of taste in the general reading public is something which we can assume as proven' and the editors see themselves as continuing the critical values associated with Middleton Murry, Eliot and Leavis.[6]

But the editorial title to the first number of *Politics and Letters* (Summer 1947) is 'For Continuity in Change', a cautious dialectic more typical of Raymond Williams than the dogmatism of Leavis's *Scrutiny*. And it is the unmistakeable voice of Williams that ruminates in this editorial about 'the crucial problem of the synthesis of human and material richness' or insists that 'the structure of society ... be constantly assessed by standards resting on certain immediate qualities of living, qualities which social history scarcely records, but which, 'for continuity', our cultural tradition embodies'.[7] Williams and Mankowitz both read English at Cambridge, but it was Mankowitz who was at Leavis's College, Downing, and who came more directly under his influence. As Williams recalls in the *New Left* interviews, 'all I heard of Leavis myself was at second-hand from Mankowitz and Collins ... They probably gave what he was saying a gloss that was closer to our outlook.'[8]

The editorial to the double number (2–3) of *Politics and Letters* represents such a gloss. The key term, italicized throughout, is 'responsibility', that of the literary critic to the text, that of the writer to society. D.H. Lawrence and William Blake – touchstones, for Leavis, of literary integrity – are cited with approval. But the editorial also calls for the 'integration' of such achievements into society as a whole and, at the end, suggests 'sociology as of prime concern to the critic in his work of integration'. This discipline, it goes on, 'is the means of assessing those trends in society with which literature might ally itself, and through which its educative influence must percolate'.[9] Their swerve towards sociology, however, signals a partial emancipation from the influence of Leavis, who had little confidence in that discipline's capacity for literary analysis.[10]

Mankowitz makes a significant number of contributions to these journals which continue critiques and polemics already noticed elsewhere. In his review of Henry Miller's *Sunday after the War* he criticizes Miller for promoting neurosis as the basis of art. To this infantilism Mankowitz counterpoises 'The mature artist' who 'is an adult, interpreting an adult world – his interest in the infantile is adult also – his comment on the pain an analysis not an obeisance'.[11] He also commends Elias Canetti's *Auto-da-Fe* for resisting symbolic and psychoanalytical representations of the principal characters, and any resemblance between Joyce and Canetti 'begins and ends in their community of literary perception'.[12] In the first number of *Politics and Letters*, he reviews a translation of Sartre's *Les Mouches* and *Huis Clos*. He insists on a clear distinction between artistic and philosophical criteria for critical judgement of *Huis Clos*[13] and senses a disjunction between the esoteric characters on stage and the experiences of a normal viewing public which is 'far less exotic, far less flashy'. Sartre's plays, in his view, have quickly dated. They seem 'academic and quite unrelated to the very next problem one will have to negotiate in one's actual living'.[14]

The double number of *Politics and Letters*, covering winter and spring of 1947–48, contains Mankowitz's most sustained contributions as a fledgling literary critic. His reviews of works by Lawrence, Salvador Dali and Graham Greene, all in some sense 'outsiders' like Miller, Canetti and Sartre, draw them within the compass of Leavisite criteria. Greene's *Nineteen Stories* demonstrate an asymmetry between emotional content and 'beliefs which neither organise nor make adult the emotions they transfix';[15] a review of Dali exhibits in an exhibition on the theme of the Temptation of St Anthony leads to an attack on the 'slick dialogues' of film noir and a Hollywood that 'accepts and propagates the idea that only bad sex is *really* exciting and desirable';[16] film noir is also attacked in Mankowitz's comparative review of Italian, Swiss and English versions of *Lady Chatterley's Lover*, where the Italian version is a 'reverent account of the growth of a relationship' and contrasts with the commercial techniques of the pornographic *The Postman Always Rings Twice*.[17]

His only essay for the journals, a reading of Blake's *Songs of Experience*, is in the same number and, with the claim in the first paragraph that Blake has suffered from the misinterpretations 'of untrained readers', we are on familiar ground. But his own training in close reading produces an astute analysis of how the very forms and rhythms of the interlocked stanzas that make up 'The Clod and The Pebble' revalue love and sexuality through inversion yet, he insists, this remains 'a literary device and it yields to literary analysis'.[18] His interpretation of the famous 'mind-forg'd manacles' in 'London' as 'The Earth is chained as much by its own psychological disposition as by social justice'[19] is persuasive and links back to his earlier analysis of the numbing materiality of earth in 'Earth's Answer'. 'Infant Sorrow' is likewise linked to 'London' when the newly born child gives up its instinctive, fiend-like struggle against the constraints of parents and swaddling-clothes to sulk resentfully on its mother's breast.

This 'birth of a representative citizen of Blake's London' has already been inducted into 'forging its own mental manacles' so that it can look forward to 'a life in which "Love! Sweet Love! (will be) thought a crime"'.[20] The essay concludes, after a brief discussion of 'The Tyger', that speculation as to the identity of 'God' in Blake is fruitless theologizing: 'Man is limited to being man. Blake's most considered conclusion appears to be that Man's most creative occupation is to develop to his fullest within that structural limitation.'[21] The essay pays scrupulous attention to literary context, rhythm, vocabulary, literary devices and thematic variations. It may be Leavisite but it is distinctive and individual and could stand in the company of early work by such distinguished Blake scholars as Northrop Frye and S. Foster Damon.

* * *

The *Politics and Letters* venture was exciting and influential but to be so it had to be situated at the confluence of new tendencies and influences in post-war London. This metropolitan life, however, with its literary coteries and petty feuds, was despised by Leavis and shunned by Williams, who remarks that Mankowitz, 'broke right away from the minority culture positions' and 'took his own material into the most popular forms'.[22] The Mankowitz–Williams alliance was temporary. The former was, in effect, already a professional writer; the latter, for whom the collapse of the journal was a personal crisis, inched his way, during the next ten years, towards the style and politics which would make him a major public intellectual. Mankowitz may have been already maintaining his own 'balance of culture', between academe and the market. The bulk of his fictions and films in the 1950s, however, dramatize two questions that, in the aftermath of 'The People's War', and with the establishment in Eastern Europe of 'People's Democracies', academics such as Williams and his near-contemporary Richard Hoggart were also posing: Who are the people? What is culture?

Williams's long essay 'The Idea of Culture',[23] published in 1953 and a first draft for his highly influential book *Culture and Society 1780–1950* (1958), traces nuanced distinctions between 'culture', 'civilisation' and 'class' in the works of a wide range of artists, critics and political theorists, all of whom feel the pressure of redefinition from the new industrial society which they are seeking to understand. His later essay, 'Culture is Ordinary',[24] locates the author as a Cambridge scholarship boy of Welsh working-class origin, whose 'way of life with its emphases of neighbourhood, mutual obligation, and common betterment, as expressed in the great working-class political and industrial institutions, is in fact the best basis for any future English society'; as for the other definition of culture, the arts and learning, they are 'in a real sense a national inheritance, which is, or should be, available to everyone'.[25]

The enemies of these two cultures in the essay are exemplified by the cinema advertisements for the TV pop music programme 'Six Five Special' and a cartoon version of *Gulliver's Travels* that the narrator notices as he waits for a bus after looking at a precious mediaeval map in the local cathedral. This third culture is one of dehumanized technical efficiency, created by men 'who were or wanted to be writers or scholars' but are now 'advertising men, publicity boys, names in the strip newspapers', men who exploit the 'inexperience of ordinary people', who sit in 'offices with contemporary *décor*, using scraps of linguistics psychology and sociology to influence what [they] think of as the mass-mind'.[26] London, the centre of this 'smart, busy, commercial culture' gave the narrator, he recalls, violent headaches whenever he passed through it.[27]

Richard Hoggart, grammar-school scholarship boy and WEA (Workers' Educational Association) lecturer like Mankowitz and Williams, also contributed an essay on contemporary popular culture to *Conviction*. Its tone is more speculative and persuasive than Williams's. The enemy is still advertising and 'skiffle and teddy-boy clothes',[28] although the positive heritage of 'the way the older and class-based popular art was able to root itself in local, particular and concrete detail' needs to be valued but also integrated into this new, image-based culture of mass communications.[29] This new culture is the way we live now and the way we will live in the future. It offers the possibilities of both a classless culture and a blandly conformist society. Mass media promote hysteria, celebrity and hypocritical morality and thus appeal to 'the "popular philosophy" of democracy in a debased form'.[30]

But these media are also always conscious of audience reaction and thus alert to refigure and re-present what Hoggart perceptively calls 'that abstraction – "the people" '. It, and its culture, may then as well be reshaped by 'the informed minority', whose numbers have grown considerably as a result of recent educational and cultural changes. This is not a class-bound, stratified group: 'most of us at some time, with some part of our experience, belong to this group ... we are all at intervals among the dissident, the concerned, the serious'.[31]

The previous year, 1957, Hoggart had published *The Uses of Literacy*, an analysis of working-class life and its cultural resources, and a founding text, along with Williams's *Culture and Society*, for the discipline of Cultural Studies as developed in academe in the 1970s. Hoggart wrote his book over the four years from 1952 to 1956, precisely the period in which Mankowitz, through a wide variety of forms in fiction and film, was establishing his ethnically inflected versions of 'the people' and their culture. Hoggart intended his book as both a tribute to and an adjustment of Q.D. Leavis's *Fiction and the Reading Public* (1932), which he had found too distanced from and dismissive of the popular fiction material she analysed. Chapter 9 of Hoggart's work, first given as a BBC talk in spring 1955, is entitled 'Unbent Springs: A Note on a Scepticism Without Tension' and ponders scepticism and cynicism as both modes of resistance to overweening authority and as stances of moral vacuity. The then popular phrase 'I'm not buying that' was, for Hoggart, linked to 'the traditional spirit of "I do not conform"', but, on the other hand, 'if you assume most things are a "sell", it is easy to accept every bad charge, hard to accede to a call for praise and admiration'.

Later in the same chapter he dissects the cynicism of the spiv or near-spiv, a figure to be found in all classes, 'a sort of inverted "go-getter", a "casher-in" on disorder'. The spiv is a realist, a figure who is always in the know; in intellectual circles he is the man with a well-informed mind whose 'acute intellectual curiosity operates from a non-attached base'.[32] We shall see to what extent such attitudes and figures are critically represented in Mankowitz's fictions of the 1950s, but it has seemed pertinent to situate his products for London's smart commercial market in relation to debates launched at the same time about redefinitions of 'culture' and 'the people' by colleagues and contemporaries who would go on to distinguished careers in academe.

Clause Four of the then Labour Party Constitution, dating from 1918, committed the party to effecting, for the working class, 'the common ownership of the means of production, distribution and exchange'. Mankowitz, Williams and Hoggart would all have considered themselves left-wing writers, with Mankowitz and Williams more Marxist-influenced than Hoggart. Williams and Hoggart concentrated their analyses, in common with many other left-wing intellectuals, on the production, distribution and (a new post-war concern) consumption of cultural goods and ideas in capitalist society. Mankowitz's major fictions, by contrast, foreground the issue and the moment of exchange. His characters are not, like Williams, repelled by a busy commercial culture. They are fascinated, even consumed by it. Hoggart's cynical worker may say 'I'm not buying that', but Mankowitz's dealer will riposte 'Make me an offer.'

His dealers are a version of Hoggart's spiv – 'tricksters', in fact – whose mythological archetype is the Greek god Hermes, patron of thieves, merchants and messengers and master of 'the magic formulae which bind'.[33] They thrive in the disordered economy of austerity Britain, where increased demand for goods and services bulks up against State control of supply and prices through rationing and nationalization. The dealer is the hinge over, in Marx's terms, the 'cleavage between the utility of things in so far as they directly satisfy wants, and their utility in so far as they are suitable for exchange', with the result that '[t]heir use-value parts company with their exchange value'.[34]

Charlie, the narrator of Mankowitz's first extended prose fiction, *Make Me an Offer* (1952), is an antiques dealer specializing in Wedgwood, the eighteenth-century pioneer of mass-produced ceramics. His particular obsession since childhood has been the Portland Vase in the British Museum. The vase, according to some experts, is a funerary urn of the Roman Emperor Alexander Severus and his mother, dating from the third century AD, which has arrived at the British Museum by way of private owners such as William Hamilton and the Duke and Duchess of Portland. The vase is unique, but the Wedgwood copies are not, although they are of varying quality. One copy, however, has almost the status of the original. It is in green glass, not the blue to black of the original, and was apparently stolen from the Drage collection in 1886. Charlie thinks he has discovered, at the end of the novel, the green Portland in the lodge of the near-senile groundsman of the great house, whose contents are being auctioned off to a motley crew of East End Jewish and Gentile dealers and rapacious American collectors.

His granddaughter, a beautiful redhead, also lives there and has earlier upset the calculations of the invasive dealers by bidding up the prices of the house's contents, a rearguard action to preserve some trace of the house's residual use-value, but hopelessly compromised by the exchange-lottery of the auction. The tone and register of Charlie's language change, however, from that of the knowing, wisecracking dealer to one of poetic awe when he describes his first sight of the green Portland:

> The white cameo was laid upon a silk-smooth jasper of green which had never existed before. It was the translucent green of deep sea-water, a green with more green in it than any other colour, but with every other colour there too. And there wasn't a doubt in the world that it was an early copy – nothing later than 1795 could have that precision and clarity, that quality of sheer genius which spoke to you clear from the other side of the room ... [yet] First Portlands don't exist, and if they do, they aren't green, but this did and it was the greenest green in the world.[35]

Charlie sees beauty but he has to price it and so negotiates the sale of the vase with the girl for £80, money obtained that day by way of various complicated deals. But beauty still haunts exchange-value and a second passage of extended literary figuration follows shortly after, where only the 'full beauty of [the girl's] hair' could bring out that Portland green, greener even than the jungle 'which looked after the tiger, [but] sometimes let the bird of paradise, the flash of light under the trees, take a quick flight round the festering mangrove swamps'.[36]

Something of the wonderment of Charlie as child in the British Museum attaches here to his vision of the fused beauty of the girl and the vase. When he first meets her, before the auction, she accuses him of only caring about the 'value' of the house. Charlie is stung into giving her a complex lecture on aesthetics. Most people, he claims, want a beautiful object because of its rarity. They want something no one else has got and they couldn't care less about its beauty. He sees himself as 'only responsible for the rarity and beauty of the thing I sell', not for the reasons why people buy it. And it emerges that the girl is eager for the house to fetch the highest price because her grandfather will get some share of the proceeds. He points out the contradiction: 'Here you are, telling me all about beauty, when what really worries you is what price it's going to fetch', and reflects that his acquaintance with the girl will give him entry to the lodge where he thinks he sees a vase on the mantelpiece.[37]

Charlie, we could say, is of the dealers' world but not wholly in it. The first-person narrative allows for introspection, and therefore distancing from and within a realist fictional world. He has a stable domestic life but he keeps irregular hours due to the nature of his work. Many of his reflections on that work come to him in early morning. In Chapter 3 he awakes from a nightmare in which he imagines his father has sold the lease on his shop and set him up in the jewellery business. This leads him to narrate his father's career as a salesman, his own schoolboy business in stamp-selling, and the nature of dealing itself: 'It's a funny game, this dealing. Nothing's worth anything until you sell it, and then it's worth whatever you can get for it.'[38] The last scene in the book is of him at two o'clock in the morning gazing at a green Portland Vase on his kitchen table as he gazed at its original in the British Museum.

But the very existence of this vase has been questioned throughout the book, so maybe introspection transports Charlie into a childhood world of obsessive dream. A dream-world of children, after all, is how he first figures forth the world of dealing after the auction: 'The dealer was the ring-master in a dream circus – he flicked his catalogue and presto, another routine.' He then switches into the world of classical myth: 'As for him, the dealer, the Autolycus of the auction-rooms, he never owned a thing in his life, and he knew it.'[39] We (and Charlie) may be familiar with Shakespeare's tattered, cunning salesman in *The Winter's Tale*, but Norman O. Brown points out that Homer, in *The Odyssey*, has an Autolycus, one of the Argonauts, upon whom Hermes bestows the gift of 'stealthiness and skill at the oath', an oath being understood as 'a magic formula that binds parties to a given action'.[40] Its secular version in *Make Me an Offer*, as we shall see, is the 'knock-out', a price-protection ring organized by the dealers.

Charlie's fellow-dealers know nothing of high cultural matters. The only print they read is catalogues. When he first visits the great house he sees it with their eyes. The gates are worth £120 and the Wedgwood plaques that line the frieze of the huge central room are all fakes. When he returns a second time, a 'repeat' that parallels the sub-theme throughout the novel of the complex relationship between an 'original' and a 'copy',[41] he sees the house through the eyes of an eighteenth-century landscape painter: 'The stone toned into the colours of the fields, and the house sat there as if it had grown up with the hill ... Four corinthian [*sic*] columns formed the central entrance. The wings swept round on each side to form a crescent.'[42] But this time he is with Abe Sparta, his landlord, a 'big, broad, curving old man with a heavy moustache and down-turned eyes tucked away among grizzled eyebrows' who spoke 'a rich cockney flavoured with Yiddish phrases and gestures'.[43] He has retired from dealing but can never resist a little business. His gaze down on this ancient space of elite values is the gaze of pure exchange. 'It's a beautiful house', he agrees with Charlie. 'It would be nice to have the breaking of it.'[44]

The rhythm of economical realist description and the tone of deflated idealism are Charlie's register when he talks about his people and the culture they all share. Armstrong, the Gentile dealer who brings along two American buyers, Mr Mindel and Mr Sweeting, has 'eyes like oil, dark and dead' and 'a hand like a dead fish-ball'.[45] Wendl, another demolition man with a long-standing and incomprehensible feud with Sparta, replies to Charlie's interest in the Wedgwood room: '"Wedgwood you can have", he repeated, like God giving the sea to the fishes.'[46] Charlie, in one of his early morning analyses of the ethics of dealing, concludes: 'We don't have to be in love with the customer. We just have to take him upstairs. Anything after that is a cultural question.'[47] When he reflects on the post-war invasion of the antiques market by Americans, with their 'good hard dollars' and their lack of discrimination, he sees his profession disappearing. 'To hell with it', he concludes, 'it's only another deal.'[48]

Charlie's ambivalence about price and value is therefore expressed as much by his ability to assume a variety of cultural voices as by the movement of the plot. He alludes to, even mimics, other writers. The last quote above is a prime example. Critics detected the influence of *New Yorker* story-writers on *Make Me an Offer*, but the flat, abrupt descriptions and disillusioned dialogue of Hemingway are a more potent source. *Fiesta* (1927) is a novel which enacts at every level the unstable equilibrium between price and value. Bill Gorton, a successful American writer, is walking along the Boulevard St Michel with Jake Barnes, a journalist and the novel's narrator. They stop in front of a taxidermist's. He tries to persuade Jake to buy a stuffed dog. 'Mean everything in the world to you after you bought it', he says. 'Simple exchange of values. You give them money. They give you a stuffed dog.'[49]

But no exchange is simple for Jake, in love with Lady Brett Ashley, but impotent through a war-wound. They can exchange words but nothing more. Alone at night, and next door to Brett and her current lover, he holds his suffering at bay with the same Americanism Charlie uses: 'To hell with women anyway. To hell with you, Brett Ashley', and inspects the theory of exchange-value only to conclude that, although it 'seemed like a fine philosophy', in five years' time 'it would seem just as silly as all the other fine philosophies I've had'.[50] Charlie echoes this clear-eyed stoicism during one of his early morning reveries: 'leave auctioneers and people who like to deal with them, leave auctioneers and knock-out men and profits and losses alone. It's a philosophy. You can have a different philosophy if you like but you can't alter this one.'[51]

Charlie next enters, by auction-invitation, the dilapidated great house along with his people and their culture. He is only distanced from them by his greater guile at his trade. Charlie, Wendl, Sparta, Armstrong and the Americans are a new, alien people from below and abroad who price and strip the great house of its goods and transform its values from use to exchange. Mankowitz is historically accurate in locating such a sale in the early 1950s. Peter Mandler, in *The Fall and Rise of the Stately Home*, calls the period from 1950 to 1955 'the peak period of demolition [of country houses] in the twentieth century', with 204 such houses destroyed: 'This represented a greater loss than had been incurred between the wars.'[52]

Mankowitz's novel, therefore, could be said to dramatize a high point of the replacement of aristocratic with democratic values by 'the people'. This moment, however, was short-lived. The Historic Buildings and Ancient Monuments Act of 1953 granted, for the first time, public monies to private ownership by way of the Historic Buildings Councils for England, Wales and Scotland, and empowered the National Trust to act as an agent for the Councils.[53] Lord Montagu of Beaulieu opened his house, grounds and small-scale Motor Museum to the public at Easter in 1952 and the Duke of Bedford opened Woburn Abbey at Easter in 1955. Both were following the example of the Marquess of Bath who had opened Longleat at Easter in 1949.[54] From now on 'the people' would be 'the public', paying in ever-increasing numbers to access a 'culture' which was a hybrid of high art and popular spectacle.[55] Stately homes would construct the people as consumers, whereas the free British Museum had impelled the young, working-class Charlie into scholarship.

But Mankowitz's 'people' is fractured, and by its own culture. The dealers agree to work the knock-out system for the bidding, whereby one of the group buys, then they all reassemble and auction it again between themselves and 'whoever gets it puts the extra money into the kitty and it's split seven ways' so that the buyer can make a profit and everyone else gets their expenses back.[56] But Charlie, with the stealth of Autolycus, has renegotiated his 'oath' with each separate dealer, and with the auctioneer. The result, after complex trafficking, is a ninety-pound profit for him, eighty pounds of which, as we have seen, he pays for the green Portland copy, which was not up for sale, and may not even exist. He also, most importantly, retains the goodwill of his fellow-dealers. Sparta is his landlord, Wendl knows his father, Armstrong is a local dealer. They are bound to meet again, at another auction, or in the East End or the West End of London. There is constant two-way traffic across the capital, as later Mankowitz fictions such as the TV series 'East End, West End' and the musical *Expresso Bongo* (both 1958) make clear.

Make Me an Offer was published by André Deutsch on 28 July 1952 and was a market success, selling 17,000 copies within weeks of publication.[57] Reviews in both Britain and the United States were favourable. For C.P. Snow (*Sunday Times*) it was 'edged with both poetry and intelligence'; the *Evening News* reviewer placed it 'in the tradition of European (and American) Jewish folk-lore'; and J.D. Scott of the *New Statesman* found Mankowitz's narrative 'provides the same kind of entertainment as a three-card trickster'.[58] C.R. in the *Spectator* admired its 'cynical-sentimental comic idiom' and related it to the 'shrewdly humorous humanity of the Brooklyn School of *New Yorker* writing'.[59] The *TLS* reviewer also detected a *New Yorker* influence, but praised the work in its own right as one which 'describes the underworld of the antique-dealer's business with wit, charm and the passion of one who, however he may satirize the vultures of his trade, adores it. Mr Mankowitz reveals a genuine comic talent; he writes concisely and with agreeable lyrical undertones'.[60] The *New Yorker* itself suggested that the novel had 'no claim to elegance, but is a briskly entertaining comedy of the antique world in which the worlds of art and low life make contact', while the *San Francisco Chronicle* called it a 'Swiftian satire ... a beautifully done little yarn'.[61]

Mankowitz tries to estimate the value of this, his first novella, and his forthcoming books on the Portland Vase and on Wedgwood, in one of his last letters to Cuttle. It is a letter which announces, right at the start of a successful professional career, a conflict about the value of his work which is enacted, and remains unresolved, to the end of his life. He thanks Cuttle for encouraging him to send copies of his books for Downing College library and encloses a copy of *Make Me an Offer*. This has 'the dubious merit of being a best-seller', but they both know that 'this is no criterion of quality'. He promises to send Cuttle copies of his forthcoming monograph on the Portland Vase and the survey of Wedgwood. Neither of these has any particular literary merit but the monograph is the only definitive work on the subject. He is haunted, and suspects he will be haunted for at least the next ten years, by 'the Downing critical training which makes it very difficult for a writer to satisfy himself'. He finishes by thanking his old tutor for his interest and repeats that 'it is with the greatest possible pleasure that I will send you whatever books, of whatever doubtful merit, may appear with my name subscribed'.[62]

An hour-long TV version of *Make Me an Offer* swiftly followed the novella. It was broadcast by the BBC at prime time, 8.15–9.15 pm, on 17 December 1952. It was produced by Caryl Doncaster, an old Cambridge friend with a growing reputation as a documentary film-maker, and the script was Mankowitz's own adaptation from his novel. Its structure is different from both the novel and the feature film two years later. It opens and closes with an encounter between Charlie and a Lord Mountfitchett in Charlie's antique shop on the Fulham Road. The aristocrat bought the Drage collection from Charlie a year ago, but now he finds him staring lovingly at the green Wedgwood Portland on his desk. Mountfitchett wants the vase, and suspects Charlie has abstracted it for his own use from the Drage collection. 'So that's how you got it', says Mountfitchett in the last scene, but he still wants to buy it. Charlie insists it is for his own contemplation; the aristocratic buyer insists he wants it, and the last shot is of Charlie saying 'Make me an offer', with a wink at the camera.[63]

The bulk of the TV film is therefore an extended flashback of the novel's events and characters: the auction, the 'knock-out', the deal for the vase with the redhead and her aged grandfather, Armstrong and the Americans, Wendl and Sparta. What this version, however, insists on is the representation of dealers, auctioneers, buyers and collectors as a community with its own laws and practices, a people with its own culture. The cast of characters is much larger than in the novel. Mankowitz has added a lord, a pair of camp collectors (Anthony and Ferdie), a German dealer (Smeltz), a Swedish sailor, a brace of local dealers, Fred Bread who is Charlie's assistant, and a couple of bemused sightseers. They understand nothing and are terrified when they get caught up in the bidding. They are English but outsiders. Foreigners, gays, lords, even naive redheads, are insiders and all are united in the pursuit of the best price for the best exchange.

The domestic influence on Charlie has been reduced to the intermittent voice of his wife on the phone reminding him to get their pram moved from the hall. His shop is his centre of value. Smeltz considers London dealers 'wild like beasts in the jungle',[64] and if we add together his and other names like Mountfitchett, Bread, Floggett the auctioneer and a country house called Dogwood, we have been invited into an aptronymic world of ruling passions and insatiable commerce first satirized by such as Pope and Hogarth. As with the mature work of these eighteenth-century artists, pastoral harmony is cut open by metropolitan greed. Charlie has his moment of aesthetic appreciation of the great house as he and Fred stare through its gates: 'There isn't a dealer in fine things who isn't a gentleman and a beauty lover.' Fred sighs and agrees as he dates it as Queen Anne, but his sigh is ironic, as is perhaps Charlie's appreciation, when Fred adds: 'It's going to be a wonderful break-up.'[65]

Two later scenes on the balcony of the great house deny the pastoral idyll that neoclassical convention demands from this elevated vantage point. In the first Charlie has brought Armstrong and the Americans out onto the balcony to discuss a deal for the Wedgwood room. The set-direction reads: 'CHARLIE looks unconcernedly over grounds.' Armstrong asks him: 'Well, what do you think?' 'Very nice grounds', says Charlie. 'A bit overgrown, but very pretty.' 'The room', insists Armstrong, 'I mean the room', which not only dismisses the landed estate as privileged source of economic and moral values, but also prefigures the obsessively claustrophobic interiors of such later 1950s New Wave dramatists as Beckett, Osborne, N.F. Simpson, Pinter and Wesker.[66]

The second scene takes place immediately after Charlie has 'bought' the Wedgwood room. He leads his group out of the room onto the terrace and up to the balcony where he insists they do the 'knock-out' and settle up. Armstrong wants to do the deal back in town, but Charlie wants his money now. They might as well be in town for all their interest in the country scenery. The only views that interest them are each other's faces and each other's cash.[67]

Press reviews were very positive. Peter Black of the *Daily Mail* reflected that '[t]here was always a good tale to be told about the antique business, which has rag-and-bone men at one end of it and Hollywood film stars and pool promoters at the other'. *Make Me an Offer* was such a tale with its outrageous old rogues and young shysters 'each with his own point of honour and secret sense of beauty'. The *Evening Standard* praised 'a hybrid programme of play and documentary', and Ken Gordon of the *Weekly Sporting Review* found Sydney Tafler and Harry Fowler excellent in the roles of Charlie and Fred, while 'Arnold Marle and David Kossoff as the feuding Sparta and Wendl, the rival dealers, were gems.' The *New Statesman* found the production 'that rare sight, distinctive contemporary writing wittily bringing the screen to life' and commended 'Mr Mankowitz's Chandleresque view of the English antique business'.[68]

The *Jewish Chronicle* dissented from this consensus. The reviewer noted that nearly all the characters were Jews, that their morality was dog eat dog, 'which would have been revolting were [it] not so funny' and that many honest Jews might well take offence at the play. Mankowitz wrote a letter to the editor in defence of his script, in which he apologized for any offence, reaffirmed his Jewishness and determined to 'write with honesty of the things I know'. How Mankowitz negotiated the relationship between his Jewishness and his profession as a writer will be considered in more detail later, but his stance here is reaffirmed in a range of speeches and interviews at this time of newly accorded fame, and most notably stated in a *Jewish Chronicle* report of a speech at a literary luncheon in December 1953: 'A writer who, like himself, was a Jew, a Londoner and an Englishman, should reflect in his works all those elements of the community within which he lived ... it was absurd that Anglo-Jewish writers must necessarily concentrate on Jewish characters or Jewish subjects.'[69]

NOTES

1. Quoted in a report by *The Stage*, 21 June 1956, of an address to the Arts Club Theatre on 18 June.
2. *Time and Tide*, 27 March 1948; 16 October 1948.
3. My thanks to Peter Collins of Westminster Council Archives for this renumbering information.
4. Fred Inglis, *Raymond Williams* (London: Routledge, 1995), pp.130–1.
5. Raymond Williams, *Politics and Letters: Interviews with New Left Review* (London: New Left Books, 1995), p.76.
6. *Critic*, 1, 2 (Autumn 1947), pp.6, 5.
7. *Politics and Letters*, 1 (Summer 1947), pp.3–4.
8. Williams, *Politics and Letters*, p.67.
9. Editorial, 'Culture and Crisis' *Politics and Letters*, 2–3 (Winter/Spring 1947), p.8.
10. See F.R. Leavis, 'Sociology and Literature', in F.R. Leavis, *The Common Pursuit* (Harmondsworth: Peregrine Books, 1962), pp.195–203.
11. *Critic*, 1, 1 (Spring 1947), p.56.
12. *Critic*, 1, 2 (Autumn 1947), pp.63–5.
13. The locus classicus of Leavis's defence of literary criticism as a discipline distinct from philosophy is 'Literary Criticism and Philosophy', in Leavis, *Common Pursuit*, pp.211–22.
14. *Politics and Letters*, 1 (Summer 1947), pp.68–70.
15. *Politics and Letters*, 2–3 (Winter/Spring 1947), pp.121–2.
16. Ibid., p.106.
17. Ibid., pp.104–5.
18. Ibid. p.19.
19. Ibid., p.21.
20. Ibid., p.22.
21. Ibid., p.23.
22. Williams, *Politics and Letters*, pp.76–7.
23. Raymond Williams, 'The Idea of Culture', *Essays in Criticism*, 3, 3 (July 1953), pp.239–66.
24. Raymond Williams, 'Culture is Ordinary', in N. Mackenzie (ed.), *Conviction*, (London: MacGibbon & Kee, 1959), pp.74–92. (First published 1958.)
25. Ibid., p.76.
26. Ibid., p.78.
27. Ibid., p.81.
28. Ibid., p.132.
29. Ibid., p.129.
30. Ibid., p.126.
31. Ibid., pp.135 and 134.
32. Richard Hoggart, *The Uses of Literacy* (London: Chatto & Windus, 1960), pp.226, 232, 236, 238. (First published 1957.)
33. Norman O. Brown, *Hermes the Thief* (New York: Vintage Books, 1969), p.14. Brown explicates with exemplary historical scholarship the interconnections between these attributes.
34. Karl Marx, *Capital*, Vol. 1, introduced by G.D.H. Cole, Everyman's Library series (London: J.M. Dent, 1962), p.65.
35. W. Mankowitz, *Make Me an Offer and A Kid for Two Farthings* (London: Readers Union, 1955), p.80. All subsequent citations are from this edition of these texts.
36. Ibid., p.85.
37. Ibid., pp.69–71.

38. Ibid., p.25.
39. Ibid., p.79.
40. Brown, *Hermes the Thief*, pp.8, 12.
41. Mankowitz, in his admittedly historical work *The Portland Vase and the Wedgwood Copies* (London: André Deutsch, 1952) notes that numerous copies of the vase, pre- and post-Wedgwood, had been made, in a wide variety of materials, from 'moulds which were made from moulds which themselves had been taken from mould-copies', p.17.
42. Mankowitz, *Make Me an Offer*, pp.55–6.
43. Ibid., p.15.
44. Ibid., p.55.
45. Ibid., p.49.
46. Ibid., p.48.
47. Ibid., p.27.
48. Ibid., p.33.
49. E. Hemingway, 'Fiesta (The Sun Also Rises)', in E. Hemingway, *The Essential Hemingway* (London: Arrow Books, 2004), p.58.
50. Ibid., p.119.
51. Mankowitz, *Make Me an Offer*, p.27.
52. Peter Mandler, *The Fall and Rise of the Stately Home* (New Haven, CT: Yale University Press, 1997), p.326.
53. Ibid., p.347.
54. Ibid., pp.373–4.
55. Mandler notes that 'Bedford and Montagu had become characters in the popular press and on television by the early 1960s, including their double-act, singing Noel Coward's "The Stately Homes of England" on BBC's *Tonight* programme', in ibid., p.375.
56. Mankowitz, *Make Me an Offer*, pp.26–7.
57. Dennis Barker, Wolf Mankowitz obituary, *Guardian*, 23 May 1998.
58. *Sunday Times*, 10 August 1952; *Evening News*, 2 August 1952; *New Statesman*, 22 August 1952.
59. *Spectator*, 19 September 1952, p.376.
60. *TLS*, 8 August, 1952, p.513.
61. Both reviews are cited in the 'Wolf Mankowitz' entry in Bernard Oldsay (ed.), *Dictionary of Literary Biography, 15 (Part 2): British Novelists 1930–1959* (Detroit, MI: Gale Research Co., 1983).
62. Letter from Wolf Mankowitz to William Lindsell Cuttle, 21 October 1952, DCAT1/2/1293, Downing College archive, Cambridge.
63. Final Dialogue Script (Unchecked) of 1952 TV 'Make Me an Offer!', p.66, Mankowitz Family Archive. I have been unable to trace a copy of the TV film itself.
64. Ibid., p.8.
65. Ibid., p.28.
66. Ibid., p.42.
67. Ibid., p.56.
68. *Daily Mail*, 18 December 1952; *Evening Standard*, 18 December 1952; *Weekly Sporting Review*, 20 December 1952; *New Statesman*, 24 January 1953.
69. *Jewish Chronicle*, 26 December 1952; 9 January 1953; 11 December 1953.

CHAPTER THREE

Into Film and into Theatre (1953–55)

Make Me An Offer! was released on 9 December 1954. It was directed by Cyril Frankel for the Group 3 film company and distributed by British Lion. W.P. Lipscomb wrote the screenplay and produced the movie and Mankowitz is credited with additional dialogue. The novel's sequence of events and its characters are broadly maintained. Young Charlie has his epiphanic moment in front of the Portland Vase in the British Museum; adult Charlie makes his two visits to the decayed country house; the London dealers operate their 'knock-out' to secure the Wedgwood room; Charlie obtains the Wedgwood copy of the Portland from the red-haired girl; and scenes of domesticity with wife and children are juxtaposed, and sometimes interwoven, with scenes of dealing.

There are, however, important rewrites of character and dialogue. The most significant is that of the red-haired girl and her aged charge, and her exchanges with Charlie. The film, unlike the novel, shows her meeting Charlie on his first visit to the mansion. Charlie follows her and her dog round to the cottage adjoining the mansion, and Nicky's (she is named in the film) first words to him are: 'You're a dealer, aren't you?' She then tries to bargain Charlie up from ten shillings to two pounds for a statuette. This sets the tone for their subsequent relationship. In the novel the anonymous girl is naïve and good-hearted, anxious only to get the best price for the house and its contents so that her grandfather, a retired groundsman, can have some share of the profits. In the film she is the 'poor relation' who wants to be rich. When Charlie finds the green Wedgwood Portland in the attic she demands £100 for it to buy a fur coat. When, towards the end of the film, he comes to make the deal, she tells him the price has gone up to £150. Charlie is outraged: 'That's a mean thing for a nice girl to say, isn't it?' 'I don't want to be nice', she replies, 'I want to be rich.' The price she can get for the things she has access to equals the value she puts on herself. She threatens to smash the vase if Charlie won't pay her price. Charlie, in an uncanny foreshadowing of the scene in *Look Back in Anger* when Jimmy Porter threatens to lay out his wife's friend Helena,[1] threatens her. 'I'm no gentleman, I hit back', he says and raises his hand to her. 'You do?' she replies. 'I do', he confirms. 'Oh', she says, and they go together into the sitting room to consult the infirm old man in his chair.

He cannot speak, like his counterpart in the novel, but he is no groundsman. He is Sir John Nightingale, submerged in debts which even the sale of mansion and contents will not meet, and, according to Nicky, 'He owned the whole estate once. He was very wicked.' His wickedness turns out to be the theft, by some means, of the Wedgwood Portland from a fellow-collector, Lord Drager. When Charlie accuses him, Sir John nudges him and laughs. Charlie and Nicky are kneeling at either side of Sir John, battling for the vase across him. Charlie wins when he says that Lord Drager is dead and has no heir. Charlie wants to 'inherit' the vase, not to sell it but 'to keep and to enjoy'.

There follows a series of silent close-ups, of the vase, Sir John, Charlie, Sir John, Charlie, Sir John, who nods agreement. Nicky is left beating her fists in exasperation on a cupboard. This is an unusually long sequence of silent close-ups. It underlines not only the dramatic nature of this exchange, but also a cultural shift. 'The people' have been invited in to renew 'heritage'. The gentry, Nicky as much as Sir John, are a decayed and corrupt class. The film proposes that Charlie, the East End Jewish dealer, has inherited the finer feelings for beauty and non-utility to which the gentry formerly laid claim. But he is still a dealer.

Sir John's nudge and laugh also allude to another, older relationship in English culture, the collusion between elites and the workers to squeeze out the middle classes. It has a long history: Lady Chatterley and Mellors, the Bucks and Bruisers of the Regency, the uninhibited obscenities of Lord Rochester's Restoration poetry and life at court. William Empson, in his 1953 review of an edition of Rochester's poetry, elucidates the implications of this cross-class alliance. 'The reason', he says, 'why [Rochester] could talk in this absolutely plain-man way was that he was a great lord and a favourite of the king ... only in real high life could a man learn to talk so that anyone could understand him at once.' The enemy of both is the professional classes who talk in a more affected manner. He concludes that there are probably other instances where a 'frightfully superior young lord has had the effect of publicising a democratic way of speaking'.[2] A ghost of this relationship haunts the stuttering declarations of Lord Ralph Mayhew's love for his lugubrious estate worker Ted in 'The Fast Show'.[3] At least, unlike Sir John, he can speak.

In her analysis of the film output of Group 3, Sue Harper underlines the importance of landscape as 'the fulcrum of all desires; it stimulates and slakes them, and heals all divisions', but points out that 'this kind of ruralism was thoroughly *passé* in the 1950s'.[4] In this respect, *Make Me An Offer!* could be said to be one of the more forward-looking of Group 3's films. The bulk of its action takes place in interiors, domestic or business. Most external shots are the cityscape of a lively East London market. The great house and its owner are decayed. The one extended shot of the grounds has two workmen, unable to lever up a sundial for display in the auction room, concluding 'He'll [the auctioneer] have to sell it where it is.' They exit and Sparta next appears, kicking a statue on the ground, and observing that the great house will 'break up fine'. But perhaps Frankel, Lipscomb and Mankowitz are alert to the revivification of the country house, already in progress, as we have seen above, through an injection of government funding and a fee-paying public. Cockney dealers and American collectors are then its vulgar forerunners.

The film's other significant rewrite is of the relationship between Charlie and Bella. In the novel she is the patient wife, bringing up two children in a rented flat and coping with a husband with erratic working hours and income. Her main concern is to get permission from their landlord, Abe Sparta, to park her pram in his tool-shed. The pram is a running motif in the film, but this Bella is far less acquiescent. She wants money for a fur coat, criticizes her husband's clumsiness around the house and is losing patience with the antique trade. She stalks off to bed on one occasion with the declaration: 'If you're so keen on antiques you can sleep with them and like it.' Bella is no virago. There is genuine love and affection between the couple. An earlier quarrel, about a fur coat for her, ends with the witty amity of Bella saying that Charlie just wants a row to make himself feel good, and Charlie wishing she could 'nag like any decent woman'.

But Nicky also wants a fur coat and she wants it immediately. She is the aspirational poor relation and, in 1950s terms, a man-eater. If Bella is a forerunner of Alison in *Look Back in Anger*, then Nicky is her actress friend Helena. When Charlie gives Nicky £100 for the vase she kisses him, although shortly before she has tried to brain him with a statuette. Charlie backs off and there is no suggestion of an affair, but his relations with the redhead were strictly professional in the novel. He buys Bella her fur coat too, but by the end it seems that only the vase, standing in the dark of the sitting room, can give him peace.

Reviews of the film were mixed. The critic for *The Times* welcomed a lead character who 'does seem, although somewhat unconventionally, to put in some time at his job', but the film as a whole was 'a slight, jumbled sort of comedy which leads the audience through the mysteries of the auction room and the dealers' rings on too slack a rein'. Peter Finch's Charlie convinced with his 'rugged honesty [and] guileless air of good nature'. For C.A. Lejeune of the *Observer*, however, Finch's style in this 'friendly British comedy' was paradoxical: 'with wind-blown hair, loose tie, jacket slung casually over shoulder and open-air look, [he] gives the man a most unpleasing substance'. Fred Majdalany, of the *Daily Mail*, was enthused by a tale of 'those extraordinary men called Dealers and the double-, triple-, and even quadruple-crossing of one another they go in for, while remaining the best of friends'. He also noted that the original novel had introduced a fresh field for comedy – the antique trade.[5]

Group 3, as Sue Harper and Vincent Porter conclusively demonstrate,[6] was not a success as a State-sponsored film company for unconventional productions, but to have his first novel turned into a publicly distributed film within two-and-a-half years of publication represented a success for Mankowitz. As he remarked in a long interview for *John Bull* in 1959, when he had become a very prominent figure in London's literary world: 'It [*Make Me an Offer*] was published in several countries. I made a television play out of it. I sold it for filming. They gave me fifteen hundred pounds for it. For me it was a lot of money at that time. I was very happy to sell it.'[7]

In the Davis interview, Mankowitz recalls the genesis of both *Make Me an Offer* and his next extended piece of prose fiction, *A Kid For Two Farthings*. The former had been written in about ten days to fulfil the conditions of a part-bursary he had been awarded by the Society of Authors in late 1946, whereby Hodder & Stoughton would expect a novel from him at the end of three years. They rejected *Make Me an Offer* because it was too short, but Miron Grindea, the editor of the international fiction magazine *Adam*,[8] recommended that he submit it to a new Jewish Hungarian publisher, André Deutsch. Its commercial success has been noted above and Deutsch, who had also published *The Portland Vase and the Wedgwood Copies* in November 1952, were happy to publish *A Kid for Two Farthings* in 1953.

The theme of this new novella was prompted by a Cambridge friend of Mankowitz, John Metcalf, who had quickly achieved prominence in the new post-war complex of public relations/advertising/journalism, and had afforded an entrée into that world for Mankowitz himself.[9] Mankowitz recalls that, over tea in Fortnum & Mason's, Metcalf suggested he write an East End story. Mankowitz demurred but Metcalf insisted: 'Why don't you write something about childhood, with some element of the fantastic?' Mankowitz became interested and said, 'What about this kid who finds a unicorn?' Metcalf was taken aback, but Mankowitz was intrigued by their idea and, along with extensive journalism for (among others) Hugh Cudlipp at the *Sunday Pictorial* and Charles Wintour at the *Evening Standard*, as well as attending to his third interest in Gered (Antiques) Ltd in Piccadilly Arcade, he wrote *A Kid for Two Farthings* in a couple of weeks and it was published by Deutsch on 14 September 1953.

Although the title embodies the notion of exchange, it quotes from a song at the Jewish Festival of Passover which reminds its listeners that all equivalences, all links in the chain of man and nature, will be superseded by death. The death in the tale is the death of a certain moment of childhood innocence and fantasy for the main protagonist, Joe, aged 6. He buys in the market, with the help of his landlord Mr Kandinsky, a kid goat with deformed hind legs and the stub of a horn in the middle of his forehead. He is convinced it is a baby unicorn which will make all their wishes come true, and his landlord encourages him in this fantasy. The boy is lonely because his mother works all day at the nearby milliner's and his father is away on business in South Africa. He calls the kid Africana and tends it throughout a cold, wet spring, but when it dies he is heartbroken because that seems to signal the death of his father. Mr Kandinsky consoles him by saying that the kid (whom he has smuggled off so that it can die with care in The People's Dispensary) has gone back to Africa and left him a gold sovereign. In any case, 'Unicorns can't grow in Fashion Street, but boys have to.' His mother tells him it's time he started school, but he hangs onto the remnants of his dream: 'For a little while he missed Africana but soon he thought of something. In the end, it brought him safely to Africa.'[10]

Fashion Street is off the Whitechapel High Street end of Commercial Road. Arnold Wesker, in the first volume of his autobiography, says the street was anything but fashionable, and traces the evolution of its name from the seventeenth-century Fossan Street. His early childhood was spent at number 43 and he notes that, in the first draft of *Chicken Soup with Barley*, Act I was set in an attic tenement flat modelled on Fashion Street.[11] Mankowitz, as we have seen, also spent two early years there, at number 45. The street's name was as much a misnomer for him as for Wesker and, as he also remarks in the Davis interview, it was far from fashionable with its dilapidated tenement buildings and shared taps and privies. From this unpromising material Mankowitz fashioned a tale which not only embodied his delight in the 'fantastic' tradition in Yiddish folk tales, particularly those of Sholem Aleichem,[12] but was also a matter of social observation. Bernard Kops, in interview, criticized *Kid* for its 'inauthenticity about time and place' and the inability of 'the English actors in the piece to understand the emotional wave-length' of that kind of East End Jewish community.[13] Kops's critique can justifiably be applied to the film of the novel which is, as we shall see, a strange mix of styles and modes, but Mankowitz has said of the novel proper that it is set in the Jewish East End of the 1920s and 1930s.

It is therefore better read as a fictional counterpart to the first section of Richard Hoggart's *Uses of Literacy*, where a kind of literary anthropology traces and analyses significance in the multiple signs of everyday life – 'the kind of life I had known as a boy'[14] – in working-class Leeds between the wars. Hoggart's observer, using the historic present for immediacy, notes: 'Life centres on the groups of known streets, on their complex and active group life', then later switches point of view to that of an 11-year-old boy travelling his urban patch to buy his comics, then

> pass[ing] a shop where they never grumble at being asked to sell pennyworths of sweets, here a pal's father smoking in the doorway in his shirtsleeves, after the last shift before the weekend; here a broken-down wooden fence out of which large spiders can be teased; here the off-licence with its bell clanging as someone comes out with a small jug of vinegar.[15]

Joe's patch in Mankowitz's novella is Fashion Street, Club Row Animal Market and the Whitechapel Road. His people are working-class Jewish, their culture is Yiddish-English and what politics they have are left-wing unionist. Their high point of entertainment is the wrestling match between Shmule, Kandinsky's assistant in his trouser-pressing shop, and the Python Macklin at the boarded-over baths on the Whitechapel Road. Joe is too young to read comics but, on one occasion, when shadowing a meths-drinking tramp whom he calls 'the cannibal king', since he is convinced he wants to abduct and eat Africana, he spots a shop window full of lurid magazine covers with 'rockets going to Mars, the red planet of mystery, and boxers beating one another bloody, and cowboys shooting and gangsters shooting and Huns shooting'. He finds the pictures exciting but 'not very real because you never saw things like that in Fashion Street'.[16]

The overall point of view here is that of an omniscient third-person narrator but 'you' begins to move us into direct speech and the mind of the child. Mankowitz makes frequent use of this 'free indirect speech', where there is a blur between what a character is saying or thinking and what the narrator is telling, elsewhere in the novel. At the start of Chapter 2, the narrator tells us that 'Joe had his own way of walking through the market', but the next sentence is spoken by both Joe and the narrator: 'It made it much larger if you started in the middle where the herring women fished salted herrings out of the barrels with red hands, dipped them in water and cleaned and sliced them thinly with long thin knives.'[17] A subplot of the tale is the inability of Shmule to provide an engagement ring for his fiancée, Sonia, a butcher's daughter with muscles to match Shmule's, who works in a local blouse factory. The other girls twit her about the ring but 'she couldn't tell Schmule all that. The only thing to do was to keep at him, because, give credit, a girl engaged is, after all entitled to a ring. Say what you like, right is right.'[18]

But as well as this narrative technique, developed by such modernists as James Joyce and D.H. Lawrence out of Jane Austen, Mankowitz also deploys the technique of detailed description to reveal the everyday life of an underclass. Joe takes his unicorn-goat for a walk up a very realist Fashion Street, past a derelict shirt factory and a group of tramps, to introduce him to the local tradespeople: Mrs Abramowitz who runs a fancy button shop and always pinches his cheek; the tobacconist with the twisted mouth; and Mavis the greengrocer who always saves the best leftover greens for the goat and doesn't charge him for them. Shmule's wrestling match with The Python is the climax of this realist mode, indeed the climax of the book. Its elision of technical detail into exciting action and crowd portrayal puts it in the tradition of such American naturalist writers as Frank Norris and James T. Farrell. It is prefaced by a long third-person passage in which precisely orchestrated and impartially valued details of dress, work, posture and entertainment render a people and its culture with a clarity that forestalls any blur of nostalgia:

> In the Whitechapel Road it was all bright lights and crowds of people, smart as paint, taking a Sunday night stroll after working the week as machinists and under-pressers and cabinet-makers.
>
> They queued at the Roxy for the second house, two big pictures, while an acrobat turned somersaults in the road for pennies, and sang *Any old iron*, jangling a string of real medals. They crowded into restaurants for lemon tea, and swelled out of the public houses waving bottles, their arms around each other's necks, their children waiting at the doors with glasses of lemonade clasped to their narrow chests. They walked slowly along, bright ties and high-heeled patent leather shoes, eating chips out of the newspaper, careful not to let the vinegar spill onto their new clothes. Arm in arm they walked, in trilby hats, brims down, girl-friends with bright lips and dark eyes and loud laughter, mothers and fathers arguing together, calling to children licking toffee apples and taking no notice, old men talking quietly raising their eyebrows, knowing the truth of things.[19]

Julian Symons, in his review for the *Manchester Evening News*, highlighted this description, along with the 'splendid piece of humorous reporting' which is the wrestling match, as evidence for Mankowitz's 'original powers as a descriptive artist'. The *TLS* also noted the originality of the writer but found it cohabited with a 'second-hand commercial sentiment' which could endanger the full development of an abundant talent. *Tribune* accurately placed the tale's setting in the 1930s but wondered what this 'very good writer of an unusual species' would do for subject matter when his vein of memory ran out. Alexander Baron of the *Jewish Chronicle* both praised Mankowitz's presentation of Jewish characters as fallible and virtuous human beings like any other, and criticized him for being over-conscious of the 'sales-value of the exotic and the picturesque. The stock Jewish-isms creep in.'

The *Observer* disliked 'this arch story of the little boy who bought a kid' by an otherwise interesting writer, while George Scott, reviewing for *Truth*, considered the story 'a charming, sentimental picture of a Jewish world though the eyes of a Jewish child'.[20] With whatever reservations, all critics agreed that Mankowitz was an important writer with new observations to make on the culture of 'his' people. Radio producers also agreed. There was a reading of the book in five weekly instalments by David Kossoff for 'Home for the Day' (BBC Light Programme) from 22 November 1953, an interview on 'Woman's Hour' on the same day, and a review on 'The Critics' (BBC Home Service, 27 September 1953).

The film version of *Kid* was given its first public showing as a London Trade Show to a packed house at the Rialto on 20 April 1955. Extensive coverage in the specialist, popular and quality press of the film's shooting in Petticoat Lane and Shepperton Studios from July 1954 had ensured such widespread interest. It received a royal premiere on 28 April and its West End premiere at the Plaza on 13 May. The book-trade press reported that André Deutsch had reprinted 10,000 copies of the novel with a new three-colour jacket showing the child star of the film, Jonathan Ashmore, with his unicorn in his arms to coincide with the premiere; that show-cards and stills of the film would be made available to booksellers; and that copies of the revamped novel would be available in cinema foyers when the film went on general release in July. The *Evening Standard* would run a serialized version of the screenplay from 16 May.[21] *British Toys* reported in June that a 'Kiddicorn', a model of the unicorn in the film, was on sale to the general public. In the event, *Kid* did not go on general release until 15 August, perhaps to capitalize on its success at the Cannes Film Festival where it won second prize.

That the film should be considered a viable merchandizing vehicle, as well as of significance in its own right, indicates that Mankowitz had made a noteworthy advance in his screenwriting career. He was now in the distinguished company of Sir Carol Reed, who directed and produced, and Alexander Korda, executive producer and founder of London Film Productions. His director of photography was Ted Scaife, a cameraman with long experience at Gainsborough Sound Department and Technicolor Ltd. The music, as variegated as the film's acting styles and cinematic allusions, was composed and conducted by Benjamin Frankel, whose expertise covered the gamut from wartime propaganda to comedy and horror films.

Reed, for his first film in colour, assembled a very varied cast of unknowns (Jonathan Ashmore as Joe), established Jewish character actors (David Kossoff as Kandinsky, Irene Handel as Mrs Abrahamowitz, Sidney Tafler as 'Madam' Rita and Sidney James as a new character, Iceberg), established and upcoming female leads (Celia

Johnson as Joe's mother Joanna, Diana Dors as Sonia) and non-professionals (Joe Robinson as Sonia's fiancé, renamed as Sam Heppner), and Primo Carnera as Python Macklin. Reed also recruited a local character, Meier Leibovitch, to play Reb Mendel Gramophone, a minor figure in the novel, but here elevated to the role of a sombre harbinger of maturity and death whose melancholy music counterpoints the youthful fantasy of Joe and the optimistic traders of Fashion Street.

The variety of actors is matched by the film's medley of styles and modes. Reed/Mankowitz retain the novel's central storyline of the child's fantasy about a unicorn that can make all the working-class community's dreams come true, but they develop the Sam/Sonia/Python relationship such that, about two-thirds of the way through the film, their tale of the golden couple threatened by the dark snake is intertwined with Joe's passage from innocence to experience. Since all four characters are Gentiles they seem to have been parachuted from some mythic world, a combination of the biblical Eden and Hollywood epics, into a Jewish world of business and exchange.

The cut-glass accents of Jonathan Ashmore and Celia Johnson, the trained enunciation of Diana Dors and the massive physiques of Joe Robinson and Primo Carnera reinforce this sense of two separate worlds. They are linked throughout, however, by David Kossoff as Kandinsky, who plays the role of a man thirty years older with assured verisimilitude and effects the reintegration of the golden couple into the community by offering Sam a partnership in his business in exchange for a second-hand trouser-press, bought with Sam's prize money from his defeat of Python Macklin. Sonia had wanted an engagement ring for four years. Sam's engagement with The Python in the wrestling-ring has produced a far more durable partnership. Sonia lusted after a 'bathroom ... all set out with a pink w.c. and black marble wall-paper'; Kandinsky suggests: 'Furniture you can get on the hire-purchasing system. But a future – where are you hire-purchasing that?' Mercantile values, updated to the 1950s, will underpin the couple's relationship, but the last shot shows Reb Mendel trundling his gramophone-cart up a darkening street and playing the melancholy Passover music that undercuts all earthly transactions.

There are other, fleeting 1950s references, as when Mimi, a co-worker with Sonia in the local milliner's, observes that platinum-blonde Sonia is like Marilyn Monroe in a rash, or when another colleague, Dora, announces that none of the debs are showing cleavage that year. The most extended and significant sequence begins, however, with intercuts between jivers dancing to big-band music on Fashion Street at night, and domestic rituals between Joe, his mother and Kandinsky in his shop overlooking the street. Python has invited Sonia out and promised her a good time. Sonia gives him an ironic 'Sure'. The next scene, a bravura combination of the skills of Scaife and Frankel, is an overhead shot of whirling skirts and tee-shirted brawn driven on by wailing trumpets and trombones from the jukebox in the 'Lots Of Fun Arcade'.

This is big-band music, but it is not the anodyne music of Geraldo or Ted Heath, the backing bands for the tale of four factory girls (among them Diana Dors) enjoying a Saturday night out in Charles Crichton's *Dance Hall* of 1950. This music is a prelude to the insistent beat of rock 'n' roll, which is just on the horizon of British working-class culture with Bill Haley's 'Shake, Rattle and Roll' staying in the Top Ten for the first eight weeks of 1955. By the end of 1955, 'Rock Around The Clock' would be at number one and *Blackboard Jungle*, the film which made that music a hit, would be drawing audiences all over Britain.

Mankowitz and Reed give Fashion Street two faces. The first is the daytime thoroughfare of cheerful crowds and roguish dealers; the second is a dark canyon out of which suddenly erupt the sex and violence of dancing in the street and Python's pursuit of Sonia and the kid. 'Dancing in the Street' is the introductory title to Charlie Gillett's *The Sound of the City*, an authoritative history of rock 'n' roll'.[22] *A Kid for Two Farthings* may be the first British film to take jive and beat music onto the street. Meanwhile Joe, the other kid, looks out on the scene from his bedroom window and is tucked up in bed after a goodnight kiss from his mother, but can still hear the music outside. It insists on its presence; it persists for the rest of the film; it announces another, future world.

At the same time the film looks back. A shot of the top half of a telegraph pole gradually wreathed in train-smoke refers us back to *Brief Encounter*. But it clears to close-up on Sonia describing her dream bathroom with the pink wc – a woman of consumption, not austerity. A blonde in pencil skirt and high heels walking down a dark city street raises film noir expectations, but this film is in colour and in England, so the fight between Sam and Python over Sonia, transfixed as a modern pietà against a darkened shop window as she cradles the kid in her arms, halts as a policeman steps from an alley and gazes at them.

Peter William Evans, in his comprehensive study of Carol Reed's films, praises what he calls the film's 'hybridity' which 'balances fantasy with reality' and thus undermines any 'celebration of the East End ethnic and classless idyll'.[23] This is a shrewd analysis, but this 'balance of culture' is more precarious than Evans allows. It teeters back and forth, between Jewish and American popular cultures, austerity and consumption, a folk tale for city-dwellers. The film is a 'liminal' movie, quoting from the past, but on the threshold of a future intuited only in outline.

Charlotte Brunsdon notes how the opening sequence of the flight of a pigeon establishes a filmic proximity between West and East End. This is a London, she suggests, 'caught between the prosaic and fantastic worlds of the pigeon and the unicorn' and an East End 'on the cusp of modernity'. She also notes the establishment of St Paul's, which cannot in fact be seen from Petticoat Lane, as a midway point between the two zones of the city, a reminder of the national unity engendered by the war: a unity, however, which is interrogated not only by the post-war hybridity of Petticoat Lane but also by what she later calls 'the very materiality' of the colourful dresses and fabrics in Madame Rita's.[24] Pauline Kael suggests that Reed 'can't quite solve the problem of *how* to tell the Mankowitz story',[25] but neither can Mankowitz, who wrote a screenplay that deliberately juxtaposed incipient rock 'n' roll with a Jewish lament at Passover. His narrower focus on the new popular music business in the stage musical and film scripts of *Expresso Bongo* (1958 and 1959, respectively) will produce more coherent narratives.

The film was an immense popular success. *Today's Cinema* reported that within three days of its London premiere it had 'smashed the all-time records held by [Reed's] previous box-office winner *The Third Man*'.[26] For the *Daily Express* it was 'a splendid human picture in which director Reed smartly pulls in the slack caused to his reputation by two previous pictures', while Fred Majdalany of the *Daily Mail* saluted 'a kindly monument to little people whose only wealth is courage, hope and laughter'. The *Daily Sketch*'s Harold Conway applauded a 'masterpiece – plucking beauty from garbage heaps and magic from the faith of simple, penniless folk' and the *Jewish Chronicle*, although regretting the transformation of Joanna and Joe from Jew to Christian, still considered the film 'a beautifully acted serio-comedy of East End life'. The *Manchester Guardian*'s reviewer had a mixed response, admiring Reed's humorous reticence which forestalled Jewish sentimentality, but regretting he had not tackled a more demanding theme. For the *Observer*'s C.A. Lejeune, it was when Reed moved away from the film's central theme that it became 'a puzzling and unsure affair' as well as being 'extremely noisy, with a music-track that seems hell-bent to keep on going, whatever competition may be affected', but the *New Statesman*'s reviewer thought it was the film's combination of disparate elements, including 'the glamour of street dancing and bombed sites by the railway at night' that would guarantee its success.

The specialist film journals were more critical. Derek Hill's critique in *Films and Filming* of the film's structure and registers was scathing. Its 'shilly-shallying between something akin to near realism and a half-hearted artificiality' is the film's undoing, and he cannot understand why Joe Robinson and Diana Dors have been 'allowed to deliver dialogue in the Jewish idiom in near-Kensington accents'. Catherine de la Roche, who had written a sympathetic review of Carol Reed's career and the shooting of *Kid* for the December number of *Films and Filming*, was disappointed, in her *Sight and Sound* review, by the final product where the 'episodic structure imposes limitations on the actors who have to present sketches rather than rounded portraits' and 'an East End background fantasticated and prettified', including dancing in the streets, elides the novel's clear distinction between fantasy and realism. The review in *AJA Quarterly* sums up this contemporary approach: 'The dark back alleys, neon-lit cafes with jitterbugging in the streets, a lover's lane with a steam train going by ... this is neither the real East End nor the intensely Jewish one portrayed in Mankowitz's book.'[27]

Robert F. Moss's retrospective, academic analysis of the film endorses the criticisms of the more 'elite' reviewers. Although he cites it as an example of Reed's concern for 'the ideals of cultural pluralism', its plot 'usually suggests more will than imagination, more creative intentions than actual accomplishment' and the structure displays 'insufficient ingenuity in the balance between the magical and the realistic developments'. His conclusion, that '*Kid* is certainly the low point in Reed's long string of flawlessly acted films', is as damning as Derek Hill's.[28] Matthew Reisz, editor of the *Jewish Quarterly*, provides a critical postscript on the occasion of the film's showing at the National Film Theatre in September 2006 as part of their comprehensive Carol Reed season. Reisz also finds the Kensington accents intolerable, the soulful Kandinsky 'the ultimate Jewish cliché' and the film full of 'lively, but obvious, local colour'. But he does think that recent movies portraying English-Jewish life present stories 'set among respectable, joyless, narrow-minded suburban Jews', the obverse of the vibrant vulgarity of the East End. '*A Kid for Two Farthings* has many faults', he concludes, 'but at least it has a bit of energy.'[29]

The critical reaction, then, divides along popular and elite lines about a film set in London's East End, a heavily over-coded space for representations of 'the people' and their 'culture' ever since the late nineteenth century. Henry Mayhew, in his 1851 report on the characters and occupations of the London poor, observes that the 'inferior [Jewish] jewellers ... are also at the East-end, about Whitechapel, Bevismarks and Houndsditch', a purely geographical location for trade.[30] But the East End as, in Peter Ackroyd's words, 'the ultimate threat and the ultimate mystery', a zone which is the city's 'heart of darkness', the repository of all the repressed desires of the civilized gentry of the West End, is not invented until the 1880s.[31] Jack the Ripper now haunts its alleyways, Dorian Gray searches for new sensations in its opium dens, George Gissing finds there a nether world, and Jack London entitles his East End explorations *The People of the Abyss*.[32] These people are a medley of Christian missionaries, communist revolutionaries, Jews, Huguenots, Chinese and every variety of working-class British.

By the mid-1950s, then, 'the East End' is as much a space for multiple readings, of a people and its culture, as it is a mapped area of the city. At the same time as *Kid* was being scripted and shot, Michael Young and Peter Willmott were doing the fieldwork for their now classic study of a working-class community in Bethnal Green which was published as *Family and Kinship in East London* in 1957. They found a stable community of reciprocal support on a neighbourhood basis, similar to that recollected by Richard Hoggart in *The Uses of Literacy*. 'Bethnal Greeners are not lonely people', they concluded: 'whenever they go for a walk in the street, for a drink in the pub, or for a row on the lake in Victoria Park, they know the faces in the crowd.'[33]

The sociologists did not, however, spot the faces of a very different version of family and kinship in East London, those of the Kray brothers, whose mother had, from the late 1940s, established their home in Vallance Road, just off Bethnal Green Road, as 'the true centre of their world, the hideout of their Cockney clan'. By the mid-1950s they had a local reputation for violence and extortion and John Pearson notes that the Epsom spring meeting of 1955 'was a historic one for gangland and for the twins' when they launched a bid for the leadership of East London's criminal underworld'.[34] *Kid* may be structurally disjointed, but it was scripted by an East Ender who knew its Janus face and presented here yet another wrestling over its soul between the forces of light and the forces of darkness.

Darkness, if with little light, is the motif of *The Bespoke Overcoat*, Mankowitz's other cinema success of 1955. By the time this thirty-seven-minute film, produced and directed by Jack Clayton for the Woolf brothers' Romulus and Remus production companies, had its London premiere at the Curzon cinema on 25 November it had gained the first prize for an entertainment short at the Venice Film Festival that August, as well as an award at the Edinburgh Film Festival in the same month. It would go on to win a British Film Academy award in 1956 and a 1957 Hollywood Oscar, the first for a British film, in the Best Two-Reel Short Subject category.

Critical acclaim was unanimous. The *Glasgow Herald*'s reaction to the Edinburgh showing was representative. The story, adapted from Gogol's *The Overcoat* and set in London's East End, was 'warm, humorous and infinitely pathetic' as well as being 'magnificently acted by Alfie Bass as the elderly Jew whose downtrodden life is about to be crowned by the ownership of the coat, and almost as good is David Kossoff playing the tailor'. The *New Statesman*'s critic, at the London opening, praised the 'art with which emotion of the most palpable kind has been refined into dialogue as bare, repetitive and touching as that which relates how the old fellow got the sack', and notes, as do other critics, Clayton's successful technique of dissolving between realism and fantasy without notice: 'We never lose track of the real existence of this odd pair, though one may be dead and the other drunk.' *Tribune*'s Richard Findlater, after comparing the film favourably with Olivier's *Richard III*, pinpoints what he calls its '*cinematic* virtues' – how Mankowitz and Clayton have released film from its inherited conventions of the theatrical picture-frame, and created a film which is 'completely self-contained and self-subsistent'. He concludes that it would have been rapturously received in France or Italy.

It ran, in fact, in tandem with Fellini's *La Strada* for a year at the Curzon, another example of a close Mankowitz relationship with the avant-garde in this period. *Sight and Sound*'s James Morgan called it a 'short story film of quality' and the backgrounds of warehouse, meagre rooms and a single melancholy street 'almost an abstraction of poverty'. The February number of *Films and Filming* gave a page to Jack Clayton, where he recalled his admiration for the film's original stage play of 1953, gave details of the shooting time – a week for interiors at Marylebone Studios, three days on location in the East End – and reflected on the financial wizardry necessary for 'a feature in miniature' which, to recoup its money, 'has to scale down its cost from 1/3 to something like 1/30 of the average full-length feature budget – still maintaining the same high quality, and, probably, using artists of a similar calibre'.[35]

Lighting cameraman Walter Suschitzsky recalls in interview the light-hearted behaviour of crew and cast on and off the set, in contrast to the sombre film they were creating. 'We all had great fun during the shooting', he says, and describes the actors as continuing in role and in costume at the bus stop outside the tiny studio where the interiors were shot. The death scene was shot in a very small room upstairs with an old-fashioned dolly. Furniture had to be moved around constantly to avoid it and the technicians had to climb over its arm from one side to another to get the right angle-shots. Jack Clayton was 'very pleasant to work with' and all the shots were composed under his direction.[36]

It was indeed an interior world that Mankowitz and Clayton, building on Alec Clunes's 1953 stage-set of darkness broken by three constantly moving areas of light, devised for their film version. The lonely, bachelor clerk in Gogol's original story moves between his office and his lodgings in St Petersburg with hardly any contact with other human beings. He is forced into human intercourse when he comes into work one day in a new bespoke overcoat which has exhausted all his savings and his colleagues throw a party to celebrate the event. The clerk is confused by the event and dazed by the space of the city when he wanders back home. Two thugs rob him of his new coat on a 'vast square, a terrible void, on the far side of which the buildings were barely visible'. He gets no help from the authorities, particularly a 'certain *important personage*' (italics in the original),[37] dies and comes back to haunt the city, tearing coats from the backs of people at random. He only disappears when he has seized the coat of the important personage as he is being driven to an assignation with his mistress.

Mankowitz and Clayton narrow Gogol's tale down to four characters

– Morry the tailor, Fender his friend and long-time employee in the warehouse of Ranting, Ranting himself, and a fat man who wheels Fender's coffin to the Jewish cemetery at the start of the film – and three interiors: Morry's room, Fender's room and Ranting's warehouse. The interiors are all dark, relieved only by the light of candles, the ghostly paleness of Fender, and the smudged whitewash of the walls.

The scene where Fender tells Morry he has been sacked by Ranting is prefaced by a medium shot through Morry's eyes from the top of his basement stairs. Fender is slumped forward behind a table with his head in hands. He is framed by two objects on the table, a teapot on the left and a flickering candle on the right, then by the top-bars of Morry's bedstead in the left-hand corner of the room and the dim outline of an overcoat hanging on the dirty wall to the right. It is a held shot of utter degradation and poverty.[38] This could be one of Jack London's people of the abyss or, as Bernard Kops remarked in interview: 'If you saw it today you might be talking about the lower depths.'[39]

On the other hand, this chiaroscuro and the film's frequent dissolves serve to blur the boundaries between realism and fantasy so that we are never sure if Fender, as Neil Sinyard puts it, is 'a real ghost ... a product of his [Fender's] imagination [or] his guilty conscience'.[40] He feels guilty because he could not finish Fender's overcoat in time to prevent him dying from pneumonia. He could not finish the coat because Fender was sacked by Ranting and couldn't give Morry his final payment. Exchange is thus vitiated by friendship and Morry offers to make the coat anyway, but Fender is after his due from Ranting, a sheepskin coat in exchange for forty-three years of devoted service. They enter the warehouse at night, after a drunken dance outside – the only occasion in the film when their bodies are released from their bowed toil of tailor and clerk. Fender selects his coat and fades away 'down there', where there is central heating and their old friend Lennie is doing a roaring trade in herrings. Morry, back in his basement, lights a candle and recites the Hebrew prayer for the dead as the undertaker trundles an empty wheelbarrow past the basement window.

Neil Sinyard considers that, with this first film, Jack Clayton staked out emotional territory such as the humanity and poignancy of friendship, as well as showing 'a predilection for stories of haunting beyond the grave', which he would mine in more detail in his later works.[41] It may, therefore, have been artistic, as well as budgetary, considerations which led Clayton and Mankowitz to cut four 'modernizing' scenes from the original stage play of 1953 and its television version of 1954.[42] They are scenes 6, 9, 12 and 14. They represent Ranting's gradual transformation of his archaic warehouse practices by means of modern technology and modern living.

In Scene 6 he is recounting to an unseen audience his admiration for new office technology he has seen at an exhibition: 'a dictation machine, a suspended filing system, a place special for telephone directories, and a permutation for working out football pools so they should win'. With such technology he won't have to worry over his old clerk's mistakes.[43] Scene 9 has Ranting as a straphanger on the underground Central Line, extolling the quality of his new 'America style' coat and quick to assure us it isn't his own merchandise. Scenes 12 and 14 feature a new clerk, Fender's replacement. He has his head in his hands at the end of Scene 12, exhausted like Fender at the pace of Ranting's stocktaking, but by Scene 14 he is upright and virile, informing Ranting that he doesn't gamble or box because he's developing his muscles to compete as Mr Universe. His is the 'body beautiful', he tells Ranting – the body, it is implied, of the new order, not the hunched and dying bodies of the old regime.[44]

Mankowitz's skilful counterpoint of old to new in the stage version went unnoticed by the critics. They concentrated, positively and negatively, on the Jewishness of his first play, and on the accomplished performances of the principal actors, David Kossoff and Alfie Bass. The *Manchester Evening News* considered Alfie Bass's playing of Fender 'a fragment with wistful humour creeping out now and then from the mounting shadows of the inevitable tragedy'. But the play's idiom and location were specific: 'It's as London as Aldgate pump, it's as alien as herring sandwiches, yet not a nuance was lost on the audience.' The *Stage* linked it to the avant-garde by calling it a 'bold, neat expressionistic piece', but *Tatler*, while praising the acting, considered the play a 'piece which seemed to glitter with all the qualities which Semitic salesmanship can offer'. For *The Times* it was 'an odd little fantasy', and for Paul Holt of the *Daily Herald* the play didn't have any point: 'It stops without any end. It is a sad whisper and not a shout of anger at the unhappiness of unlucky men.'

Richard Findlater begins his championship of Mankowitz here with his far-ranging review for *Tribune*. He sees 'theatrical persons not animated photographs' on stage, Jews who have 'a common idiom, with a rhythm of its own, rooted in a common society', and a 'wry, self-mocking, pessimistic humour which saves it from mere whimsy'. The play's form is fluid, 'using the electrician to create atmosphere and punctuate the story, but above all liberating the actor from the stuffy conventions of the naturalist, fourth-wall play, with asides and soliloquies galore'. He compares *The Bespoke Overcoat* with its companion play in the programme, Shaw's *Arms and the Man*, as the quick with the dead: 'This kind of staging was already dying when Shaw used it for his own ends, and now the corruption has spread to the characters.'[45]

Findlater's analysis could have been written by Kenneth Tynan, who was at this time developing his reputation for vituperative iconoclasm with his theatre reviews for the *Evening Standard*. He remarks of a revival of E. Temple Thurston's *The Wandering Jew* in June 1953: 'Have we really progressed so far? In 1920 the play survived 390 performances; today not a line of it but rings flat and false.'[46] Young critics were desperately searching at this time for signs of new life in post-war British theatre. For Findlater, Mankowitz's one-act play was a promising shoot.

Critics, as well as praising actors and narrative, were also impressed by the technical inventiveness of the play's TV production on 17 February 1954.[47] Producer Eric Fawcett retained the three pools of light in surrounding darkness from the stage production, but added a close-up address to the audience by David Kossoff's Morry, 'at times almost leaning into the room as though with his arms on a window-sill'. The *Glasgow Herald*'s critic devoted a long section to Fawcett's production as a production for *television*, an issue of great interest in the early 1950s when the medium had not yet settled its specific conventions. The review is worth quoting at some length:

> The dispensing with sets, the dependence on isolated objects, we already know, but there was in 'The Bespoke Overcoat' a positive use of the screen itself. When Morry, the tailor, tried in inebriated ineffectiveness to raise the sash-window of the warehouse, it was our screen, the single window in thousands of homes, that he pushed against and failed, as indeed as the huge-hearted but unlucky little tailor he had to fail, to lift. He was actually and symbolically struggling with the insuperable, and we in our position were part of the effort. Turning to go, at another point, Morry went *out* on the right hand side of the screen, a leaving more subtle and final than any disappearance through a door

> because in a sense it was our room he left. He ogled his darling bottle of whisky, then swung it confidently, large and alone on the screen before our eyes, that we might almost share its bouquet.

The reviewer for the *TLS* also stressed the particular intimacy between audience and viewers that this production created. With a minimal set and clear light/darkness contrasts, the narrative moved backwards and forwards in time so that 'a moment of darkness can be a bridge in space and time'. Without realistic surroundings, 'the characters abandon all pretence that the audience has caught them unawares. They are there to communicate with us, whether through direct confidences, or by talking with each other in our hearing.' The TV audience participates in the fiction with 'trusting complicity'.[48]

The producer, in fact, has understood that this new medium is what the literary critic and media-analyst Marshall McLuhan called a 'cool' medium, one that invites its audience to participate in and 'complete' the action and the actors: 'The TV actor does not have to project either his voice or himself.'[49] Although the main content of *The Bespoke Overcoat* could be said to be an archaic world of Jewish poverty and clannish bonding, its productions for the three media of stage, film and television were attuned to new modes of representation in post-war Britain.

NOTES

1. John Osborne, *Look Back in Anger*, Act II, Scene I (London: Faber, 1979), p.57. (First published 1957.)
2. William Empson, 'Rochester', in J. Haffenden (ed.), *Argufying, Essays on Literature and Culture, William Empson* (London: Chatto & Windus, 1987), p.275.
3. BBC, 1994–2000.
4. S. Harper and V. Porter, *British Cinema of the 1950s: The Decline of Deference* (Oxford: Oxford University Press, 2003), p.188.
5. *The Times*, 13 December 1954; *Observer*, 12 December 1954; *Daily Mail*, 10 December 1954.
6. Harper and Porter, *British Cinema of the 1950s*, pp.185–7.
7. Wolf Mankowitz, interviewed by Lionel Davidson, *John Bull*, 6 June 1959, pp.17–19.
8. In 1950, *Adam* published a long short story by Mankowitz, 'The Inspector', a brilliant depiction of the calmly alienated mental world of a Russian totalitarian functionary. Kafka, Camus and Arthur Koestler are clear influences. Reprinted in W. Mankowitz, *The Penguin Wolf Mankowitz* (Harmondsworth: Penguin, 1967), pp.217–49.
9. A glimpse of this relationship can be seen in the six successive articles on contemporary television and radio which Mankowitz wrote for the *Spectator* between 31 September and 5 November 1954, immediately followed by six more by Metcalf between 12 November and 17 December 1954.
10. W. Mankowitz, *Make Me an Offer and A Kid for Two Farthings* (London: Readers Union, 1955), pp.189–90.

11. A. Wesker, *As Much as I Dare* (London: Century, 1994), pp.18, 19.
12. Mankowitz's first co-production with Oscar Lewenstein was *The World of Sholem Aleichem* (Embassy Theatre, 11 January 1955), and his introduction to I. Howe and E. Greenberg (eds), *A Treasury of Yiddish Stories* (London: Deutsch, 1955), applauds these writers' 'authenticity ... their robust, vulgar, poetic Yiddish ... a great and sweet language for men to write in'.
13. Bernard Kops, interviewed by the author, 24 November 2003.
14. Richard Hoggart, *An Imagined Life: Life and Times 1959–91* (London: Chatto & Windus, 1992), p.5.
15. Richard Hoggart, *The Uses of Literacy* (London: Chatto & Windus, 1960), pp.46–7. (First published in 1957.)
16. Mankowitz, *Make Me an Offer and A Kid for Two Farthings*, p.139.
17. Ibid., p.103.
18. Ibid., p.114.
19. Ibid., p.170.
20. *Manchester Evening News*, 17 September 1953; *TLS*, 18 September 1953; *Tribune*, 25 September 1953; *Jewish Chronicle*, 25 September 1953; *Observer*, 11 October 1953; *Truth*, 25 September 1953.
21. *Bookseller*, 15 May 1955; *National Newsagent, Bookseller, Stationer*, 14 May 1955; *Smith's Trade News*, 14 May 1955.
22. Charlie Gillett, *The Sound of the City* (London: Sphere Books, 1971).
23. Peter William Evans, *Carol Reed* (Manchester: Manchester University Press, 2005), pp.130, 132, 133.
24. Charlotte Brunsdon, *London in Cinema: The Cinematic City since 1945* (London: BFI Publications, 2007), pp.173–76.
25. Pauline Kael, *Kiss Kiss Bang Bang* (Boston, MA and Toronto: Little, Brown & Co., 1968), p.291.
26. *Today's Cinema*, 19 May 1955.
27. *Daily Express*, 11 May 1955; *Daily Mail*, 13 May 1955; *Daily Sketch*, 11 May 1955; *Jewish Chronicle*, 13 May 1955; *Manchester Guardian*, 14 May 1955; *Observer*, 15 May 1955; *New Statesman*, 21 May 1955; *Films and Filming*, August 1955; *Films and Filming*, December 1954; *Sight and Sound*, July 1955; *AJA Quarterly*, June 1955.
28. Robert F. Moss, *The Films of Carol Reed* (Basingstoke: Macmillan, 1987), pp.209–13.
29. Matthew Reisz, 'Eastenders – but not as we know it', *Guardian*, 16 September 2006.
30. Henry Mayhew, *Mayhew's London*, introduced by Peter Quennell (London: Spring Books, n.d., probably 1956), p.278.
31. Peter Ackroyd, *London: The Biography* (London: Vintage Books, 2001), pp.679, 675.
32. O. Wilde, *The Picture of Dorian Gray* (1891); George Gissing, *The Nether World* (1889); Jack London, *The People of the Abyss* (1903).
33. Michael Young and Peter Willmott, *Family and Kinship in East London* (London: Routledge & Kegan Paul, 1957), pp.167, 92.
34. John Pearson, *The Profession of Violence* (London: Panther Books, 1973), pp.26, 84.
35. *Glasgow Herald*, 21 August 1955; *New Statesman*, 10 December 1955; *Tribune*, 30 December 1955; *Sight and Sound*, January 1956; *Films and Filming*, February 1956.
36. Walter Suschitzsky, interviewed by the author, 24 August 2007.
37. Nicolai Gogol, *Plays and Petersburg Tales*, edited and translated by Christopher English, World's Classics Series (Oxford: Oxford University Press, 1995), pp.133, 135.
38. Release Script of *The Bespoke Overcoat*, BFI Scripts, no. 10377, shot 71, BFI [British Film Institute] National Archive, Berkhamsted.
39. Bernard Kops, interview with the author, 24 November 2003.
40. Neil Sinyard, *Jack Clayton* (Manchester: Manchester University Press, 2000), p.32.
41. Ibid., p.35.
42. Arts Theatre, 25 June 1953 to 19 July 1953, for thirty performances; BBC TV, 8.15 pm, 17 February 1954. These scenes were also cut from David Kossoff's recording of the play on a Pye Golden Guinea LP (no date), where he plays the parts of both Morry and Fender. No. ILP0113574, British Library Sound Archive, London.
43. Wolf Mankowitz, *The Plays*, preface by Anthony Dunn (London: Oberon Books, 2006), p.132.

44. Ibid., pp.135, 138, 140–1.
45. *Manchester Evening News*, 30 June 1953; *Stage*, 2 July 1953; *Tatler*, 8 July 1953; *The Times*, 26 June 1953; *Daily Herald*, 26 May 1953; *Tribune*, 10 July 1953.
46. Cited in Dominic Shellard, *Kenneth Tynan: A Life* (New Haven, CT, and London: Yale University Press, 2003), p.71.
47. In the absence of any existing script or copy of the TV film, I am reliant on critics for information about this production.
48. *Evening Standard*, 18 February 1954; *Glasgow Herald*, 20 February 1954; *TLS*, 26 February 1954.
49. See Chapter 31, 'Television: The Timid Giant', in Marshall McLuhan, *Understanding Media* (London: Sphere Books, 1967), pp.329–60. (First published 1964.)

CHAPTER FOUR

Author and Impresario (1954–55)

The Bespoke Overcoat received its second professional production as part of a double bill which opened at the Embassy Theatre in Swiss Cottage on 13 January 1954 and ran for about three weeks. David Kossoff and Alfie Bass reprised their roles as Morry and Fender, but Kossoff also played the role of Nathan, the grocer, in the lead-play, *The Boychick*, Mankowitz's first attempt at a two-actor. *Bespoke* was praised as before, but *The Boychick* was felt by the *Financial Times* to be 'more a promising preliminary sketch than a satisfactory, finished work'. The *Liverpool Daily Post* acknowledged Mankowitz's ability to 'create an occasional Oriental glow in character and atmosphere' but criticized him for 'think[ing] in flashes which makes his themes seem thin and episodic'. Bernard Levin, for *Truth*, admired Mankowitz for creating Jewish characters and situations without self-consciousness. 'He is concerned neither to defend nor to apologize, still less to preach.' He is simply trying to write a play whose Jews 'are neither saints nor devils, but human beings'. But his greater praise was reserved for *Bespoke*, which he called a masterpiece.

The *New Statesman*'s review gave an accurate resume of *The Boychick*'s central encounter, between Sergius 'a bankrupt actor-manager ... in his decaying theatre awaiting the return from America of his only son, dreaming of a fortune and a restored theatre and prosperity all round' and the son, Alex (stage name Blue), 'who turns out to have been nothing more than a small-time music-hall turn without his father's talent but very much with his capacity for easy self-deception'. The review went on to summarize the critical consensus about the play's structure: 'There are a variety of moods well caught, but the material never begins to form itself into any satisfying shape.'[1]

In retrospect *The Boychick* rewards more detailed critical analysis. The play's central conceit, of a theatre as a 'home' and the theatre as a 'place' of illusions, draws on a long Western tradition from Aristotle to Pirandello and Brecht of dramatic representation as 'the fiction of the *presence* of a world known to be hypothetical'.[2] But it also appropriates that tradition, unselfconsciously, for a play of Jewish characters, for whom 'home', 'place' and 'identity' are emotively charged terms in post-war Europe, characters who speak a Jewish idiom, and are pursuing a dream of reviving Yiddish theatre.[3] At the same time, 'home' in drama and the novel usually denotes the domestic realist mode; in *The Boychick*, Nathan the henpecked grocer, his wife Bella, and Blue's long-suffering girlfriend Sadie act out that convention.

'Place', however, is far more indeterminate, a site for symbolist or expressionist theatre. Sergius, his beloved wife now dead, eats and sleeps in his theatre which has four years left to run on its lease. In Act II, Scene I, Sergius persuades Blue that they can go into joint production and revivify the theatre. As the lights come on and the curtain rises and falls, it is as if his home is being refurbished. By the start of the second scene of Act II, 'The stage is crowded with improbable properties, and a large costume trunk'[4] and the home has its new furniture. But from the moment in Act I, Scene I when Sergius reads out Alex's letter from America, his home was always likely to be no more than a place. Alex finds himself 'between places, neither in the last place, nor in the next place. In fact in no place at all. But sometimes there is no place to be in like no place. And that's where I am.'[5]

At the start of Act II, Sergius is serving his son coffee and rolls in their stage-bedroom, but father and son soon swerve from mundane domesticity to existentialist reflection, a version of what Cheyette, with reference to Pinter, calls 'assimilationist modernism':[6]

SERGIUS:	You want all your life to come to a certain place but when you come there you don't want to look in case it should be a different place after all.
BLUE (Alex):	The place is different. But it's the same place.
SERGIUS:	So. Tell me about the world. Did you ever come to Hollywood?
BLUE:	I came everywhere. It's the same place, if you got no money to bring out the difference – and that costs money.
SERGIUS:	Ach – the picture papers and the films killed it. Now, before you get to a place you have seen it a hundred times already ... That's why you might as well stay where you are. Where you are is the only place you can know ...

BLUE: Did you have to close down the place?
SERGIUS: Four years now, closed down.[7]

Sergius wants to reopen his place and put on the old Yiddish melodramas, but Blue is fresh from his career as a magician and tale-teller in American vaudeville and he knows that a modern audience wants 'girls, songs, jokes, movement, colour ... Automatic machines – iced drinks, hot coffee, hamburgers.' Sergius is astounded and confused but Blue presses on and asks him if he wants 'Strindberg with Tchekov with Shakespeare with Ibsen', and Sergius replies with pride: 'That's all I want. That's all I want, all the time.' Blue then accuses him of cultural snobbery, since his repertoire was only ever tear-jerkers and melodramas, but Sergius answers him with a commitment to artistic value which unites and fuses very different theatrical traditions:

> We played the other things, the tear-jerkers, the melodramas, the load of crap. But we played it as if it was Ibsen with Shakespeare. The Tchekov in us played it. The Shakespeare in the heart came into the tired out words and gave them new life. We did what we could do. We knew what was good and remembered it.[8]

And where better for these doublings – of elite and popular art, of Jewish folk-theatre and Western classical theatre, of, perhaps, Mankowitz himself as Leavisite and populist – to take place than in a theatre, the quintessential site of masking and shape-shifting? The joint productions of father and son cannot succeed any more than can the joint production of a milliner's shop as proposed by Sadie to Blue. Father and son dream the dreams of different generations, and the economics are impossible since, at the end, Nathan finds himself having to sell the stage-props to pay the interest on the loan to purchase them, which has been raised by pawning the theatre lease to a neighbourhood bookie.

Blue is a gambler, not an investor, an actor, a storyteller, another of Mankowitz's tricksters. Production is not his forte. He flourishes best with exchange, of his charm for Sadie's love, of his soul for the American Dream. The horse which fails to deliver the winnings which could finance the new theatre is called End Product, and he defines himself to Sadie at the end, when they are discussing marriage, as a man who has to be 'a big deal, the biggest deal ... So I let the horses work it out for me. If they win I am just a big deal. If they lose I am just me.'[9]

We have already noted a verbal parallel between an exchange in the film version of *Make Me An Offer!* and one in *Look Back in Anger. The*

Boychick, in theme and metaphor, could be said to 'prefigure' *The Entertainer*, Osborne's next play, which he began researching in late 1956 by observing variety acts, often dreadful, in the remaining music halls of London. The play opened on 10 April 1957 at the Royal Court, with Laurence Olivier in the lead, and ran for thirty-six performances. In his note to the published text, Osborne laments the death of the music hall which was 'truly a folk-art' whose conventions and mystique 'cut[s] right across the restrictions of the so-called naturalistic stage'.[10] Osborne, like Mankowitz, links cultural to technical questions, so that the intergenerational quarrels of the Rice family are framed as dramatic 'turns' with all the sentimentality and ham-fisted timing that Osborne had observed in the music halls. The stage direction reads: 'The scenes and interludes must, in fact, be lit as if they were simply turns on the bill. Furniture and props are as basic as they would be for a short sketch.'[11]

Osborne's play has a far wider scope than Mankowitz's, with three generations of the Rice family on stage, a son killed in Suez, a daughter demonstrating in Trafalgar Square, and the play itself as a metaphor for the decline of an imperial power into incompetence and self-delusion. But it is at least plausible to read *The Entertainer* as an English continuation of *The Boychick*, had Sergius and Blue reopened their theatre. The stage directions to *The Entertainer* go on to propose: 'Music. The latest, the loudest, the worst', and Blue's dream of 'girls, songs, jokes' could be said to be fulfilled by a gauzed front-cloth in Osborne's play on which are painted 'enormous naked young ladies, waving brightly coloured fans, and kicking out gaily. Written across it in large letters are the words: ROCK'N ROLL NEW'D LOOK'.[12] The play is punctuated by hackneyed jokes and bitter songs; Billy Rice maintains his dignity as a famed music-hall performer, a fine figure of a man in his seventies, while his son Archie – inept, furtive, self-loathing, a drinker and a tax-evader – could be a married Blue, twenty years on.

The first picture we are given of Blue in *The Boychick* is when Sadie describes a trade-card of him from New York 'dancing in a top hat and evening clothes with a cane'.[13] Twenty years on, his Fred Astaire poise would have degenerated into Archie's dance-shuffle, but he would have kept his bow tie and his cane, and maybe substituted a bowler for his top hat, as in Olivier's famous performance. Such 'prefiguring' is an instance, one of many, where Mankowitz lights upon a character, a theme, a structure, even phraseology[14] which other writers will develop more fully and consistently as part of the New Wave writing in fiction and theatre in the later 1950s. Such anticipations, however, are also a tribute to Mankowitz's extraordinary ability to fuse elite learning with new forms of popular culture in a far wider variety of media – fiction, film, theatre, television, journalism – than any of his contemporaries.

Lynne Stephenson (then Reid Banks), who worked as a secretary for Mankowitz in this period and would begin a successful career as a novelist with *The L-Shaped Room* (1960), remembers a man who was full of energy, engaged in many different projects, from overseeing her write-up of art crimes for the *Evening Standard* to overenthusiastic participation in rehearsals for *The Bespoke Overcoat/Boychick* double bill. When he roared at Miriam Karlin from the stalls she fled backstage. Lynne found her there weeping with rage. 'They're all so fuckin' *stchoopic* darling', she sobbed. But it all came right on the night'. He was great fun to work with in his office above Gered (Antiques) Ltd in Piccadilly Arcade, although he got a bit tetchy when he sensed that her own writing career was beginning to challenge his. Phone calls began coming into the office for her after the success of her first BBC TV play, 'It Never Rains', as their Play of the Week for Easter, 1954. This was a big breakthrough for her but he got fed up with the phone calls not being for him and finally said 'Look, you're on your way and I don't need you any more, so thanks, goodbye and *mazal tov*.'[15]

Mankowitz's own, second Russian-based play for television in 1954 was 'The Baby', a BBC broadcast of fifteen minutes on 7 July, another production by Eric Fawcett. Mankowitz transposed Chekhov's brief story 'A Transgression' from a holiday resort to an urban block of flats, and Chekhov's main protagonist, a middle-ranking bureaucrat called Miguev, becomes an unnamed ironmonger. Miguev's porter, Yermolay, is a boiler-man in Mankowitz's version, but he, by whatever name, turns out to be the real father of the illegitimate baby that the main protagonist finds outside his house and thinks is his. Miguev's childless wife, Anna Fillipovna, is as much constructed by him, by way of the fearful internal dialogues Miguev imagines with her when he tells her about the child, as is the ironmonger's wife by her husband. But Anna makes a brief appearance at the end of Chekhov's story, whereas the wife is always offstage in Mankowitz's.

Both stories are shrewd essays in a respectable man's struggle between social status and human affection. But Mankowitz's hero is a businessman, so his father-feelings for the baby and his imagined discussions with the orphanage are interspersed with reflections on his origins, details of his business stock – 'We stock seventy-eight brands of paint' – and mistrust of his chess partner. He is a self-made man who has risen from being 'the boy who takes the six-inch nails that get into the four-inch box, out, and naturally puts them in the six-inch nail box' to the owner of the business. But now he seems to have made a child and he doesn't know what to do with it. Does he own it, or will it become like his business which, he concludes, 'owns me'?[16]

Mankowitz's hero has, in effect, a sustained monologue to camera, and the critic for *The Times* praised David Kossoff's ability to 'sustain the cunning poise of the piece' which was a 'kind of long confession'. The *Glasgow Herald* critic admired Larry Adler's music as 'the final nick in the key by means of which the screen became an open door, and we passers-by able to look right into The Man's experience, knowing his innocent pride and extent of his momentary joy'. This critic also mentions the clarity of the tele-recording, a new technology for the time, which Peter Black's review for the *Scottish Daily Mail* clarified as an electronic photograph on a 700–800-line system, borrowed from Norman Collins's ITV Company, and a marked improvement on the prevalent 405-line system.[17] Critics therefore noted new modes of acting and production of the play in this threshold period of television development.

A year later, on 9 August 1955, the BBC showed an hour-long double bill of Mankowitz plays, *It Should Happen to a Dog* and *The Girl*. The first, which had had a reading with the same cast at the ICA (Institute of Contemporary Arts) on 31 October 1954, had Alfie Bass as Jonah and David Kossoff in the four roles of Man, Sailor, King and Angel. It portrayed Jonah as a travelling salesman for 'Braces For The Trousers; Fair Lady Fancy Buttons; Hold Tight Hairgrips' who is a most unwilling traveller in the belly of the whale and a grumbling prophet of the destruction of Nineveh. From the title, and from various speech inversions in the text – 'It cranks me such a beautiful tree should die like that, apart from now I am in the sun again and can catch a sun stroke any time' – we know that this a Yiddish view from below of the high, heroic myths of the Hebrew Old Testament. God is a joker in this version of Jonah and the whale. Jonah delivers his prophecy to the King of Nineveh; it turns out to be wrong and he is a laughing-stock. The Angel is also fed up – 'it's no joke following you or any other prophet I happen to get assigned to around the whole time' – and agrees with Jonah that theirs is a dog's life.

The language of Mankowitz's humour may be Yiddish but its technique, to deflate the heroic with the humdrum everyday, is also very English. 'The Goon Show' had been puncturing Britain's imperial pretensions since 1951, Tony Hancock began his career as intellectual punchbag for Sid James in the first episode of 'Hancock's Half Hour' on 2 November 1954, and when Jonah picks up a copy of the *Tarshish Gazette* in Nineveh and reads that Mrs Zinkin has been presented with her third daughter – 'That's bad'[18] – he foreshadows the Sermon on the Mount scene in *The Life of Brian*, which takes place on a Saturday afternoon, about tea-time somewhere in Galilee.

It Should Happen to a Dog was produced and directed by Tony Richardson, who, together with George Devine, had been hunting for a theatre in which to put on new drama since 1953,[19] and who would direct the new play, John Osborne's *Look Back in Anger*, which opened on 8 April in the following year, 1956, and which would guarantee the fame of the new theatre they had leased, the Royal Court. Mankowitz, as previously noted, would also have a close association with the Royal Court until 1960 by way of his co-production company with Oscar Lewenstein. The second play, *The Girl*, produced by Patricia Foy, imagined the fantasy reactions to a pin-up girl, played by Diana Decker, of three boxers in an East End gym. Alfie Bass saw himself as a spaceman, David Kossoff as a great lover and Harry H. Corbett as a jungle Romeo. The script moved between prose and song for the boxers' visions.

Reviewers noted the experimental nature of the two productions, with Maurice Wiggin of the *Sunday Times* recording only a partial success in this retelling of Jonah's story in a modern setting and the interpretation of 'the amorous daydreams of three boxers in a context of universal mythology', but he reflected that 'it will be a sad day when nobody dare experiment any more. Not even with public money.' The *Daily Mail* reviewer found the writing 'blazed with humour, sympathy and vitality', but the *Daily Express*, the *Daily Sketch* and the *Daily Mirror* reported a significant volume of angry calls to the BBC about the plays' irreligiosity or incomprehensibility. Fergus Cashin of the *Daily Mirror* summed up the reaction of many of the popular press's reviewers: 'I found Jonah as played by Alfie Bass touching and sincere. His prayers ... were unorthodox maybe but not offensive. As for the second play, "The Girl", I just don't pretend to understand what it was all about.'[20]

With *A Kid for Two Farthings*, Mankowitz and Reed, earlier in the year, had challenged existing conventions of film narrative with their ethnically grounded fusion of fantasy and realism. With these two plays for television, Mankowitz and his producers can be seen trying to construct new conventions for a new medium with the same mix. Philip

Hope-Wallace, for the *Listener*, was alert to this as he commended the productions of what he called Mankowitz's 'playlets or charades' which Richardson and Foyle had 'handled with a welcome attempt to make something of those visual excitements possible, now and again, on television'. He added that these innovations were a good start although 'a long way from what Orson Welles can do with a cinema screen',[21] a directorial comparison which had a particular resonance for Mankowitz's career as producer at this time.

The first Lewenstein/Mankowitz co-production, *The World of Sholem Aleichem*, which opened at the Embassy Theatre in Swiss Cottage on 11 January 1955, dramatized three stories by the Yiddish writers Sholem Aleichem and I.L. Peretz. They were adapted for the stage by Arnold Perl, directed by Sam Wanamaker and starred Alfie Bass, Miriam Karlin, Meier Tzelniker and David Kossoff. Reviews concentrated on the minimalist props and abrupt lighting shifts. The *Stage* noted the effect in the first story, 'A Tale of Chelm', adapted from Aleichem's 'The Enchanted Tailor', of 'the spotlight choosing various areas of the stage for its many episodes and the actors largely miming [their roles]'. By the third play, 'The High School', the reviewer had tired somewhat of 'the constant black-outs and brief scenes', but praised the actors, particularly David Kossoff as Mendele, 'an itinerant bookseller of rich humour and human feeling who acts as a kind of narrator and commentator'.

T.C. Worsley of the *New Statesman* also highlighted a theatrical method which 'virtually disposes with scenery and the action moves with the rapidity of a film'. Harold Hobson's notice for the *Sunday Times* was brief and general – 'a series of sketches of innocence and simplicity in which Mr Alfie Bass is particularly pleasing' – but significant in that a major London critic should review a compilation of Yiddish stories in a suburban theatre.[22] A bare and episodic narrative, materialized through the spotlighting of discrete narrative segments, would become staple techniques in New Wave theatre and cinema. With this production, and with the television and stage productions of *The Bespoke Overcoat*, we can detect their earlier genesis.

If *Sholem Aleichem* kept alive for contemporary audiences the lost world of the Yiddish shtetl, the next Lewenstein/Mankowitz co-production, Orson Welles's *Moby Dick –Rehearsed*, which ran for 27 performances from 19 June 1955 at the Duke of York's Theatre, also confirmed Mankowitz's association with the theatrical avant-garde and his personal affinity with Welles himself. Welles's adaptation of

Melville's prose epic is an exercise in meta-theatre in which a group of late-nineteenth-century actors rehearses this version of the hunt for the White Whale, slipping in and out of their roles as Young Actor and Ishmael, Serious Actor and Starbuck, Young Actress and Pip, miming the pursuit and harpooning of Moby Dick, and using minimal props of ropes and platforms. Welles played the Actor-Manager, Father Mapple and Ahab and created a script which mixed prose with blank-verse renditions of Melville's prose.

The venture was as overreaching as its hero's mad quest for vengeance. The critic for *The Times* watched a first half which left the audience dizzy at the interval with the illusionist skill which conjured a typhoon out of 'a dense tangle of ropes with here and there a spar', but the fight with the whale in second half failed pathetically and Welles as Ahab had 'an impressive voice and an impressive face, but neither the voice nor the face is particularly expressive'. Brian Inglis for the *Spectator* admired the rehearsal conceit and read it as a metaphor for the impossibility of representing Melville's novel in a proper play, but Welles diminished Melville's Ahab, a man 'cut away from the stake, his limbs wasted though not consumed by the fire', to 'a corn-fed Middle-West senator up for a filibuster'. T.C. Worsley for the *New Statesman* found the voyage and the hunt pure theatre, 'all embodied out of the imagination alone', but the play 'sinks finally beneath a spate of words that never come alive in the theatre as the make-believe does'.

J.C. Trewen for the *Illustrated London News* also praised the imaginative economy of the stage-props: 'A twist-and-twine of ropes has fallen from the flies; lamps sway overhead. And there, with voices and off-stage noises suitably orchestrated, is as fierce a hurricane as we could wish.' But by the end his enthusiasm had deflated into the faint praise of the well bred: 'rather tedious experiment ... a curiosity ... a fantastic thing to attempt anyway; no doubt we should be glad of fantasy, however devised'.[23]

Mankowitz was very proud of the *Moby Dick* production, its technical bravura, its actors (who included a young Joan Plowright, Patrick McGoohan and Kenneth Williams) and its near-sell-out audience.[24] He and Lewenstein raised £6,000 from American backers Henry Margolis and Martin Gabel, who had worked with Welles on his Mercury Theatre production of *Danton's Death* in 1938 and had been impressed by Welles's extreme economy of means to produce the richest theatrical effects. But Mankowitz had already put his business skills at Welles's disposal earlier in 1955. He had met him in Paris and found him 'cutting some footage of *Don Quixote* with scissors'. Mankowitz realized Welles was 'incapable of accountancy', but he also recognized in him 'an artist and a bohemian, and this is reflected in his attitude to money. I sympathize, I have a similar attitude myself.'[25] He sold the novelization rights of Welles's film *Mr Arkadin* (title in England: *Confidential Report*) to a French newspaper which ran the novel serially before the film opened in Paris in March. In London, Mankowitz negotiated with BBC TV for a series entitled 'The Orson Welles Sketchbook' to finance him during the period of preparation for the production of *Moby Dick*. It was a success and he was offered a second series.[26]

Mankowitz therefore cut successful deals for Welles, which is a kind of magic, while identifying with Welles's insouciance about money because Welles was a great artist. His artistry was that of the trickster, with which Mankowitz also identified himself early on in the Davis interview when he said that nearly all his books had been about the trickster archetype, that he himself had been a great trickster, and that Welles 'was like a character I might have written if I'd had the talent, but Orson wrote himself because he did have the talent'.

In the Peter Bogdanovich interviews, Welles concedes that he was a magician, a professional magician who had played Las Vegas twice and had always performed for money 'except for the *Wonder Show* which was done for the army'. *The Mercury Wonder Show*, put on free for the troops in Las Vegas in 1943, starred, among others, Jo Cotton and Marlene Dietrich, and featured acts such as 'The Miraculous Chicken Farm', Rita Hayworth as 'The Girl With The X-Ray Eyes', 'Princess Nephrotite' and 'Grand Finale – VOODOO!' Welles recalled with glee that the only paying seats, the Sucker section, were for Hollywood celebrities, whom the performers demeaned and humiliated in front of the servicemen every evening, breaking eggs over their heads and giving them blocks of ice to hold.

Simon Callow, in the second volume of his biography of Welles, sums up the intentions and effects of the *Wonder Show* as 'a classic example of [Welles's] determination to unsettle expectation, an unrelenting bombardment of the audience with an absolute indifference to polish or decorum'.[27] But Welles's Mercury Company had already played its greatest trick on the American public, its 1938 dramatization of H G. Wells's novella, *The War of the Worlds*, which convinced nearly two million Americans that Martians had indeed landed in the United States. Welles could muse with justification in interview that he was 'the highest paid magician in the world, come to think of it. Certainly the best.'[28]

Mercury was the Latin equivalent to the Greek god Hermes, and Yuri Slezkine's historicization, in *The Jewish Century*, of this god's mythical attributes so subtly traced by Norman O. Brown, reveals a more profound, even representative affinity between an Orson Welles and a Wolf Mankowitz. Slezkine argues that, until the twentieth century, Mercurian groups such as Jews, Armenians, Parsees in India, Chinese in Southeast Asia and Lebanese in Latin America and the Caribbean, were tolerated by the natives of their host-country, the Apollonians, because the Mercurians as 'professional cultivators of people ... use words, concepts, money, emotions and other intangibles as tools of their trade (whatever the particular trade may be)'. The alien Mercurians located value in dealing and exchange, whereas the native Apollonians located value in the physical strength of warriors in battle or peasants working the land.

With the growth of trade and scientific knowledge, however, these 'service nomads', as Slezkine calls them, became indispensable to both prince and peasant. They were literate, multilingual, mobile, mentally agile and curious. They developed from clerks into professionals: 'Businessmen, diplomats, doctors, and psychotherapists are literate peddlers, heralds, healers and fortune-tellers.' Magic and material reality seemed to the Apollonians to be intermingled in Mercurian practices, yet Mercurians were indispensable bridges over the boundaries between tribes, kingdoms or states. Slezkine reminds us that 'Hermes's name derives from the Greek word for "stone heap", and his early cult was primarily associated with boundary markers.'[29]

Modernity, in Slezkine's analysis, required just the skills that these displaced Lebanese, Chinese, Parsees and, above all, Jews had been cultivating for centuries. It was about 'everyone becoming a service nomad: mobile, clever, articulate, occupationally flexible, and good at being a stranger', and 'everyone' included native Apollonians. They would have to be adroit and supple, particularly in the new American mass-entertainment industries where a strong Jewish presence existed from their start.

Welles was just such a figure, of mid-Western business origin, but a cosmopolitan modernist in his film and theatre practice. His career after *Citizen Kane* was that of a stranger everywhere, a saga of aborted projects, films patched together from segments shot in different countries, roles in work of wildly varying quality, haphazard financial deals. What

Thorstein Veblen, quoted in Slezkine, forecast of the modern Jew in an essay of 1919 could as well be applied to Welles, the Wandering Gentile: 'He becomes a disturber of the intellectual peace, but only at the cost of becoming an intellectual wayfaring man, a wanderer in the intellectual no-man's-land, seeking another place to rest, further along the road, somewhere over the horizon.'[30] Welles in interview expressed his great admiration for Yiddish theatre as the only international theatre in history. 'Movies', he said, 'are the second.'[31]

Mankowitz, too, combined Mercury with Apollo. He cut the deals for Welles, dramatized his Yiddish-Jewish inheritance throughout his career,[32] found 'home' in England, Ireland, New Mexico and Europe, jumped from genre to genre in his writing and scripted films of very varying quality. At the same time he gave as much weight to his cockney Britishness as to his Jewishness. In a 1958 interview for the *Jewish Chronicle* he summed up his position: 'to me London at four o'clock in the morning with a wet pavement is a natural environment. On the other hand I feel a tremendous association with the community of Israel, because I find it to be the most intelligent I've ever travelled through.'[33] He was an antiques businessman but acknowledged that his sister was the entrepreneurial brains behind the Wedgwood shops and when, in the Davis interview, he was categorized as a rabid capitalist, he insisted that he 'never lived on capital' but off the proceeds of his work and that he was 'opposed to any kind of investment' until his ill-health forced him into a private pension scheme.

He made use of Yiddish material at all stages in his career, but his critical allegiance was also to the international avant-garde where the work of those service nomads Joyce and the Surrealists enacted, for him, the supreme achievement of the artist as trickster. F.R. Leavis was an anxious influence over Mankowitz's work throughout his career because Leavis combined the Apollonianism of Cambridge with the Mercurian dedication to scriptural exegesis. But Leavis was both an outsider within Cambridge and a heroic fighter for his discipline. The attributes of Slezkine's typology shift back and forth and recombine. If Welles was a Wandering Gentile, then Leavis was a rabbi-warrior.

In the same month and year (April 1955) that *A Kid for Two Farthings* received its first London showing at the London Trade Show, Dutton's of New York published another short novel by Mankowitz, *Laugh Till You Cry*. The calm tone and classical formality of the sentences with which Ronald Rantz, salesman for the Rantz Joke Company, whose trade-motto is 'Laugh Till You Cry', tells his story of shipwreck, encounter with natives and reassessment of self and society constitute a mode of writing which is a hybrid of Robinson Crusoe's journal and an anthropological field report. Like Crusoe he salvages tools and food from the wreck; unlike Crusoe his most valuable salvage is a box of novelty items such as itching powder and firecrackers. Rantz is a salesman, not a sailor, and he regards his island as a potential market, rather than – like Defoe's hero – as a theatre for providential reconstruction. Like an anthropologist he observes and itemizes the culture and economy of the Ditt, the indigenous tribe of the island; unlike an anthropologist, Rantz takes a mistress from the Ditt and, through the 'magic' of his novelty items and manipulation of the Ditt's peculiar 'gift' system, becomes leader of the tribe, and undergoes the same revaluation of his ethics as they do.

The Ditt's is a subsistence not a trading economy. Value is established, not by the price agreed for the exchange of commodities, but by the amount of sacred objects offered as gifts. The high priest determines each season what those objects will be and has his acolytes accumulate a store of them before each gift contest. He who offers the greater amount in these frequent contests between leading members of the tribe 'purchases' his opponent, who has to leave the tribe in disgrace. Rantz, keenly observant of this economy for his own safety, since the chief will try and purchase him, concludes that 'the Ditt valued life as the greatest of man's assets. It was capital of the greatest worth ... It was not that they loved life, but to destroy purchasing power, your own or someone-else's was to them the lowest action of the criminal degenerate.'

Rantz is appalled and fascinated by the social consequences of what the Ditt call their 'purchase-magic'. The birth of a child is marked by grief and mourning since the parents know that the child will eventually overtop them in purchasing power. Women are virgin until marriage and men work so as to increase their purchase-magic by wealth and honour. For both sexes, 'embraces are assets too valuable to be thrown away without the assurance of a profitable return'.[34] Rantz, who has assigned to the gift system of the Ditt something of the 'fetishism'[35] that Marx assigns to the world of commodities, concludes his observations of the tribe with a very eighteenth-century European reflection: 'The malevolent ethics of the Ditt made me sad for that far-away life where sanity rules under the benign banner of humanity's most highly evolved ethical system.'[36]

During the rest of the tale, Mankowitz has Rantz experience a range of idylls. Crusoe owned a thriving plantation in Brazil when he was wrecked on his island. He worked with patience and ingenuity to reproduce his plantation on the island. Rantz, however, is a salesman without an exchange economy, so he has to manufacture his visions of the good life from utopian bric-a-brac. He has an enjoyable sex life with his mistress, Kuala, but he cools towards the dark-skinned, exotic maiden when he finds that her savage mind cannot appreciate his many projects and schemes for the improvement of his estate. Through a series of strategic alliances and betrayals he has now become the wealthiest of the Ditt so, a typical nouveau riche, he has his subjects build him 'a magnificent landscape garden in the English style'. But his subjects have no conception of the eighteenth-century gentleman, so he purchases the rest of the Ditt, who troop off into exile, Kuala included.

He is now alone and tests the Romantic idyll of man in a state of nature. Nature proves an inexorable invader of civilization. She overwhelms his garden, creeps nearer and nearer to his house and threatens his very life when he lies immobile for three days with a leg injury. When he finds that his two remaining books have been eaten away by a yellow fungus he anathematizes this dispassionate destroyer in a superb passage of Leavisite contempt:

> 'You make no critical distinctions', I cried, 'you are entirely lacking in discrimination. You are senseless, monotonous, mechanical, thoroughly promiscuous in your attachments, entirely capricious in your affiliations. You have defeated me and the time has come for me to leave you. I welcome my defeat and my exile.'
> An animal screamed in answer, a long note of bestial idiocy.[37]

Rantz now explores the island and encounters, on the far side, the exiled Ditt. They have renounced their gift economy and live out the third idyll of the tale, a society without chiefs or priests or alienated labour. Private property has been abolished and all contribute their specific skills to the common good. The Ditt live the communist idyll envisaged by Marx: 'From each according to his ability, to each according to his needs.'[38] Rantz contributes his joke-novelties, which are now used for communal entertainment. His uncle is prepared to ship him a regular supply, their cost being offset against the allowance his uncle has made him as compensation for the sale of his shares in the company since he had been presumed dead. The island becomes known in the area as Laughing Island and the islanders 'still carefully cultivate nothing which is of the least use to civilisation, and thus we hope to continue a way of life most satisfactory to us'.[39]

Laugh Till You Cry, as an English exercise in that quintessentially French mode of narration, the *conte philosophique*, is yet another example of Mankowitz's versatility in narrative forms. But he wears his learning lightly and allows for a satirical reading of the hero's travails in the space created between the neoclassical control of Rantz's narrative voice and his fatuous occupation. He is another of Mankowitz's tricksters, but framed, on this occasion, by subtle and extensive allusions to Robinson Crusoe, Lemuel Gulliver and Candide. American reviewers noted the literary references but were divided as to the power of Mankowitz's satire. The *New York Times* felt that it had 'neither the conviction nor the consistency which true satire demands' since pure satire is too black and white for 'the author's ... realistic acceptance of life as contradictory and various'. *Time* magazine considered Mankowitz 'too soft a man for satire and [he] lets his shrewd observations on the human condition melt into sugary fantasy'.

But Edme Seton's full-length review for the *New York Herald Tribune*, plus reproductions of two of Heather Standring's illustrations to the book, admired the fact that 'Wolf Mankowitz draws no arbitrary line between questions of morality and downright foolery' and concluded that 'his sophisticated originality is applied to a moral theme with great originality. It is a wonderfully provocative book.'

John Goodspeed's review for the *Baltimore Evening Sun* found a source for Mankowitz's portrayal of the Ditt in Ruth Benedict's anthropological description of the Kwakiutal Indians of Alaska in her *Patterns of Culture* (1934). Her description of the Kwakiutal chiefs' prestige contests, where the victim shamed his rival either 'by presenting him with more property than he could return with the required interest' or 'by destroying property', certainly approximate to Rantz's descriptions of the Ditt's practices. But Benedict's account has no stylistic allusions to Defoe or to Voltaire.[40] John Goodspeed was dissatisfied with the communist idyll – 'some sort of vague social transformation' – but acknowledged the story as 'typically stylish and entertaining'.[41]

Most of the critics found the communist Utopia passive and unconvincing, but it is worth noting that both Rantz the outsider and the native Ditt find their way to truth and happiness by way of 'exile', as emotive a term for a Jewish salesman as was 'home' for Sergius and Blue in *The Boychick*. And the transplantation and alienation that all the island's inhabitants have to undergo can as well be read as an existentialist programme for the birth of an authentic self. In 1957 Albert Camus published a collection of short stories entitled *Exile and the*

Kingdom, an apt philosophical subtitle to Mankowitz's *Laugh Till You Cry*.

Majollika and Company, published by André Deutsch in September 1955, had no pretensions to philosophy, but as a collection of stories for children it added to Mankowitz's range of fictional modes. Majollika the Golliwog and his friend Gerald the Glow-Worm have exciting adventures. They are captured by Horridhawk and kept prisoner in his nest until rescued by their friends the squirrels. They explore an underground cave and meet a Diplodocus dressed in a stained pink bib and a pair of old galoshes who is delighted to welcome his first visitors in millennia.

But the fixed centre of this fantasy world is a shop, run by Majollika and Mrs Tessie who sell nuts and acorns to the squirrels. Their shop, in one tale, is ransacked by a large, ill-tempered squirrel called Pegleg Squints. He is arrested by the constables 'all dressed in the same kind of bright red pantaloon trousers and carrying strings threaded with conkers which they used as truncheons'.[42] Mrs Tessie wasn't there because she had gone to the market where the bees were selling their honey, the frogs their watercress and the sparrows their straw. Another tale features a magic act for the Mole Brethren at the Beech Tree Hotel. Uncle Borlack takes buttons and farthings out of everyone's pockets and Majollika is entranced until the trick of his wide-sleeved coat is revealed. Speaking animals are a staple of children's fiction, but emphases on commerce and magic are typically Mankowitz inflections of this familiar mode.

Mankowitz definitively 'arrived' on the cultural scene in 1955. He had scripted two films of his own works that had won international awards, was joint partner in a distinguished production company for New Wave theatre, maintained a presence as a television scriptwriter, and published two very accomplished works of prose fiction in completely different modes, dystopian satire and children's stories. But he was also consolidating his presence as a public 'personality', someone equally at home in the worlds of serious book publishing, women's magazines, daily journalism and television entertainment. In the month before the theatre production of *The Bespoke Overcoat*, the readers of the *Evening Standard* knew Mankowitz as 'Mr Fat', competing to lose weight with 'Miss Slim' (actress Yvonne Marsh), who was trying to gain weight. For three weeks from 19 May their daily food intake was detailed and scrutinized by a nutritionist and they did, for what it was worth, lose and gain weight. In August 1953, *Men's Wear*[43] asked him, along with Gilbert Harding (whose TV column for *Picture Post* he took over for some months from March 1954) and Kenneth Tynan, to comment on current men's fashions. The May 1953 number of *Modern Woman* featured him advising on Victorian Wedgwood and, in January 1954, *Woman* magazine gave him a brief notice for his expertise in Wedgwood china.

Mankowitz, with a young family of his own, child-centred fictions and an expertise in food and ceramics, was always considered attractive to female audiences, and contributed several humorous features to 'Woman's Hour' in the early 1950s on the joys and exasperations of his growing family. The *Brighton Evening Argus* for 15 August 1953 reported Mankowitz as a member of the judging panel for a holiday beauty contest, jointly sponsored by Brighton Corporation and Butlin's holiday camps, and shown by BBC TV; and the *Illustrated* for 26 September of the same year had a full-page overhead shot of the studio layout for a popular TV panel game, 'Guess My Story', with Mankowitz as one of the panellists. All the technical staff, such as Studio Manager and Boom Operator, are clearly marked by their titles, as well as the panellists. Television was a new medium and the aim of the photo was to demystify the medium's operations and its stars for its new audience.

Mankowitz also expanded his interest in ceramics into other areas of interior decoration. Documents in the Mankowitz Family Archive show proposals and audited accounts for a firm called Basketweave Ltd from November 1954 to November 1957. It is a partnership between Mankowitz, his old Cambridge colleague John Metcalf and Terence Conran. The address of the company varies between Piccadilly Arcade and Conran's showroom in Belgravia, but Conran is clearly the principal figure in the partnership. The accounts show only a very a small profit on a slender turnover. Conran would open his first Habitat shop in 1964 but by then he was already a veteran of British domestic design and retail. If only by this association, Mankowitz was aware that there was an impending change in British middle-class taste where Wedgwood would cohabit with duvets and Cone Chairs.

By 1955 Mankowitz was a kind of media star who operated, with his TV and film-scripts, on both sides of the camera. He was becoming the impresario of himself. Two lengthy profiles, by Charles S. Spencer for the June 1954 number of *Menorah* and by Herbert Howarth for the March 1955 edition of the South African magazine *Jewish Affairs*, attempt to summarize Mankowitz's personal and artistic impact on

English and Jewish culture and predict his future direction. Both emphasize his bulk and his presence. For Spencer he is 'one of those heavy, loose-limbed bear-like men ... whose constant activity discloses a nervous energy which, in his writing, has been carefully controlled and stylised'. Howarth finds a man who at 30 has 'the weight, physically and personally speaking, of a Grand Old Man. A combination of youth and solidity goes all the way through him.'[44]

Spencer then reviews his career to date, calling his 'literary combination of Yiddish and English ... astonishingly successful' and emphasizing that Mankowitz has 'always aimed at reaching the widest possible public'. He discerns that Mankowitz is caught between being a Jew and being a writer, between being a man with 'an easy public manner and a superficial jocularity', and a man who is 'probably basically reserved and certainly, as one can see from his writings, a sensitive person'. Spencer concludes that Mankowitz has reached an important turning point in his literary career and would need to progress to 'a new development in both style and subject-matter'.[45]

Howarth gives more emphasis to what he sees as the peaceful coexistence of opposites in Mankowitz: 'He is a dealer. He is a writer. The two activities merge and make each other ... for business, he explains, entails "negotiation", and so does the passing of the written word to the unknown reader.' But he also detects in Mankowitz's work a move beyond the worlds of Zangwill and Golding, where joy issued from grief and small domestic pleasures, to a world where comedy could fuse with pleasure, a pleasure that derives from perceiving a rich world of objects and devising, in business and in art, the most enterprising ways of possessing them. Howarth finishes by cautioning Mankowitz against too many happy endings. This 'poet of victories' should also be able to represent the 'stumbles, hesitations and drownings that are the more common lot'. Howarth must have forgotten *The Bespoke Overcoat*.[46]

NOTES

1. *Financial Times*, 14 January 1954; *Liverpool Daily Post*, 16 January 1954; *Truth*, 22 January 1954; *New Statesman*, 27 January 1954.
2. Keir Elam, *The Semiotics of Theatre and Drama*, New Accents series (London and New York: Methuen, 1980), p.113.
3. See Bryan Cheyette's authoritative survey of this issue in his editorial introduction to *Contemporary Jewish Writing in Britain and Ireland: An Anthology* (London: Peter Halban, 1998), pp.xiii–lxxi.

4. Script of Wolf Mankowitz's *The Boychick*, Act II, Scene II, p.24, Mankowitz Family Archive. All subsequent citations are from this manuscript.
5. Ibid., Act I, Scene I, p.5.
6. Cheyette, *Contemporary Jewish Writing*, Introduction, p.xxxii.
7. Mankowitz, *Boychick*, Act II, Scene I, p.2.
8. Ibid., Act II, Scene I, pp.3, 4, 5.
9. Ibid., Act II, Scene II, p.39.
10. John Osborne, *Plays 2* (London: Faber & Faber, 1998), p.3.
11. Ibid., pp.7–8.
12. Ibid., p.8.
13. Mankowitz, *Boychick*, Act I, Scene I, p.14.
14. Compare Mankowitz, *Boychick*, Act II, Scene I, p.14: 'SERGIUS (to NATHAN): He understands horses like a father. NATHAN: It's a gift.' with Harold Pinter, *The Homecoming* (London: Methuen, 1966; first produced 1965), Act I, p.10: 'MAX: By the look deep down in her [the filly's] eye I could tell whether she was a stayer or not. It was a gift. I had a gift.'
15. Lynn Stephenson, interviewed by the author via email, 10 July 2009.
16. Wolf Mankowitz, *Five One-Act Plays* (London and New York: Evans, 1964), pp.32, 31. (First published 1956.)
17. *The Times*, 8 July 1954; *Glasgow Herald*, 10 July 1954; *Scottish Daily Mail*, 8 July 1954.
18. W. Mankowitz, *Wolf Mankowitz: The Plays*, preface by Anthony Dunn (London: Oberon Books, 2006), pp.149, 157, 158, 155.
19. Richard Findlater (ed.), *At The Royal Court* (Ambergate: Amber Lane Press, 1981), p.12.
20. *Sunday Times*, 14 August 1955; *Daily Mail*, 10 August 1955; *Daily Express*, 10 August 1955; *Daily Sketch*, 10 August 1955; *Daily Mirror*, 10 August 1955.
21. *Listener*, 18 August 1955.
22. *Stage*, 13 January 1955; *New Statesman*, 22 January 1955; *Sunday Times*, 16 January 1955
23. *The Times*, 17 June 1955; *Spectator*, 24 June 1955; *New Statesman*, 25 June 1955; *Illustrated London News*, 2 July 1955.
24. Wolf Mankowitz, interviewed by Gerald Davis, summer 1997 (referred to in the text as 'the Davis interview').
25. Ibid.
26. Barbara Leaming, *Orson Welles: A Biography* (New York: Viking, 1985), pp.392–6; and O. Welles and P. Bogdanovich, *This is Orson Welles*, paperback edn (Cambridge, MA: Da Capo Press, 1998), pp.416–17.
27. Simon Callow, *Hello Americans* (London: J. Cape, 2006), vol. 2 of his Welles biography, p.195.
28. Welles and Bogdanovich, *This is Orson Welles*, pp.177–80.
29. Yuri Slezkine, *The Jewish Century*, paperback edn (Princeton, NJ, and Oxford: Princeton University Press, 2006), pp.28, 8, 29, 9.
30. Ibid., pp.30, 59.
31. Welles and Bogdanovich, *This is Orson Welles*, pp.274–5.
32. *Almonds and Raisins*, released in 1984, late in Mankowitz's career, is a documentary history of Yiddish cinema, scripted by Mankowitz and narrated by Orson Welles.
33. *Jewish Chronicle*, 19 December 1958.
34. Wolf Mankowitz, *Laugh Till You Cry*, in W. Mankowitz, *The Penguin Wolf Mankowitz* (Harmondsworth: Penguin, 1967), pp.18, 28, 29.
35. Karl Marx, from *Capital Vol. I*, in T.B.Bottomore and M. Rubel (eds), *Karl Marx: Selected Writings in Sociology and Social Philosophy* (Harmondsworth: Pelican, 1963), p.183.
36. Mankowitz, *Laugh Till You Cry*, p.30.
37. Ibid., pp.54, 62.
38. Karl Marx, from *Critique of the Gotha Programme*, in Bottomore and Rubel (eds), *Karl Marx: Selected Writings in Sociology and Philosophy*, p.263.
39. Mankowitz, *Laugh Till You Cry*, p.70.
40. Ruth Benedict, *Patterns of Culture* (London: Routledge, 1935), p.193.
41. *New York Times*, 17 April 1955; *Time*, 18 April 1955; *New York Herald Tribune*, 24 April 1955; *Baltimore Evening Sun*, 18 April 1955.
42. Wolf Mankowitz, *Majollika and Company* (London: André Deutsch, 1955), p.41.
43. *Men's Wear*, 22 August 1953.

44. 'Wolf Mankowitz', *Menorah*, June 1954, p.21; 'Wolf Mankowitz: In the Zangwill Tradition', *Jewish Affairs*, March 1955, p.37.
45. *Menorah*, June 1954, pp.24, 25, 26.
46. *Jewish Affairs*, March 1955, pp.37, 40.

CHAPTER FIVE

The Anni Mirabiles (1956–59)

In the January 1956 number of *Harper's Bazaar*, amid full-length photos of tall, haughty women in huge brimmed hats with tiny waists and Y-line skirts, and adverts for Rinso, Mansion Polish and Versatile Separates, there is a full-page, black-and-white photo of Wolf Mankowitz. The photographer has posed him half-turning to camera, as if for a cigarette-pause from the typewriter on the metal trestle table in front of him which backs up against a wall covered in old playbills. The rays from the single light above have been distorted back onto the wall by a masking apparatus of two oblong strips of perforated metal, so it must be the photographer's flash that has caught the hints of exhaustion and apprehension in Mankowitz's clear, large eyes and meaty, hunched shoulders. This figure of formidable bulk and presence, his cigarette held delicately between the first two fingers of his left hand and a slight bitterness around his full-lipped mouth, needs only braces holding up his sleeves to be a hard-bitten journalist or private eye in a 1940s film noir.

But the brief profile, written by Jane Stockwood as part of a series called 'Above the Crowd', which accompanies the photo, emphasizes his roles as fashion model and impresario. He is, apparently, 'in a tangerine shirt in his office above a china shop', that is his office at Gered (Antiques) Ltd at the top of Piccadilly Arcade, and about to put on, with Oscar Lewenstein, Brecht and Weill's *Threepenny Opera*. This production, Stockwood assures her readers, will not be like the prettified version in Paris two years ago, with its beggars 'in pink and blue bowlers and a ripple of harps slipped into the score', but much nearer to the old Pabst film.[1] Stockwood has effected a fine balance here between the cultures of women's fashion and Weimar Marxism.

For Desmond Shaw-Taylor of the *New Statesman*, the production, which opened at the Royal Court on 9 February 1956, was more music-hall London than decadent Weimar. Director Sam Wanamaker, unable to inspire the company with 'cabaret nonchalance', had fallen back on a 'happy-go-lucky semi-improvised style' which left the audience 'at the end of any old pier or tagging along with the ENSA'. He did praise the song 'Mack the Knife', which became a hit in its own right. The critic for *The Times*, however, damned the music – 'Weill's music is not sweet but rank' – but praised the casting and production and was relieved that Wanamaker had not tried to reproduce the 'unrelieved sordidness of Berlin in the twenties'. Anthony Hartley of the *Spectator* lauded the enterprise of the production, the first performance in the West End of any play by Brecht, and had only some minor quibbles about Marc Blitzstein's translation, also used for the New York production, and the redistribution of some of the songs.[2]

Mankowitz complained about his financial loss on this production, but his co-producer Oscar Lewenstein, with a background in the Communist Party and the Unity Theatres of Glasgow and London, was very keen to produce it. He bought back the rights from the Royal Court, agreed to give it a small percentage of any profits and, after raising production money from the wife of a West End impresario, formed Peachum Productions Ltd as its production vehicle. It ran for 167 performances at its various venues. Its premiere at the Royal Court, just before the English Stage Company was formed, should now be considered the first marker for the company's subsequent long engagement with the theory and practice of Brechtian theatre. This production also, with a Jewish director and translator, when taken together with Neville Blond's astute financial and political skills as chairman of the ESC Council and Lois Sieff's (of Marks & Spencer) tireless championing of the company, signalled a determined Jewish commitment from the start, which has gone unrecognized in histories of the Royal Court, to an enterprise which would revolutionize British post-war theatre.

The Threepenny Opera transferred from the Royal Court to the Aldwych Theatre on 21 March, where it ran for nearly three months. The *Daily Mail*'s social columnist reported a party on the Aldwych stage, on 16 May, which seems now to have anticipated the stagecraft, not of Brecht, but of Samuel Beckett: 'Champagne was drunk out of – you'd never guess – dustbins. But then "The Threepenny Opera" company were toasting the success of their joint backer WOLF MANKOWITZ's new novel, "My Old Man's a Dustman"',[3] which will be given detailed consideration at a later stage.

Mankowitz also had a relationship with the Royal Court as writer and critic in this period. John Osborne records, with the bilious brilliance that characterizes his two-volume autobiography, that 'the writer Wolf Mankowitz ... laughed loudly, and alone' at the first performance of

Look Back in Anger, while Oscar [Lewenstein] 'glanced around him like a managing clerk anticipating a disastrous verdict from the jury foreman'. With the success of *Look Back*, Osborne and his wife Mary Ure were keeping company with Marilyn Monroe, the Burtons, Emlyn Williams and Cecil Beaton, the theatrical elite. At a party in Beaton's garden, Osborne recalls a series of instructions from Wolf Mankowitz on 'how to write plays, the genius of F.R. Leavis, good butchering, and how to impregnate a girl and outwit the Inland Revenue'.[4] The list is as eclectic as the selection of plays by his production company with Lewenstein, but it shows Mankowitz playing the role of theatre-mentor to an only slightly younger generation (he was five years older than Osborne), as well as pinpointing two areas of considerable importance throughout his career, F.R. Leavis and the Inland Revenue.

At the end of the decade, the *Evening Standard*'s 'In London Tonight' columnist compares the gentler and more reasoned debates of Arnold Wesker, Lindsay Anderson and John Mortimer at the Sunday Night discussions at the Royal Court with the 'old warhorses ... Colin Wilson, Wolf Mankowitz and Elaine Dundy' of a few years earlier.[5] The Royal Court offered itself in those years as a venue for discussion of such topics such as censorship and the relationship of theatre to the New Left, and hosted a League of Dramatists' debate 'The Trouble with the Theatre', as well as initiating after-play discussions on Monday night performances beginning with *Look Back in Anger*.[6]

Kenneth Tynan chaired one debate of particular interest, reproduced in full in the June–July 1957 number of *Encore*[7] on 18 November 1956. The main participants were Arthur Miller, Colin Wilson and Wolf Mankowitz. Miller played the courteous American abroad. He teased at differences between American and British theatre traditions and found a greater presence in American theatre of 'the people' and their vernacular. 'I sense that British theatre is hermetically sealed against the way society moves', he suggested early on, but he later praised *Look Back in Anger* as the only modern play he had seen in British theatre, combining intellect and passion, yet it 'seems to have no reflection elsewhere in the theatre'.

There is an antagonism between Wilson and Mankowitz throughout the debate. Wilson presents himself as a naïf, ignorant of theatre conventions, impatient of discussions about the use of the vernacular in theatre – 'Wilson: The language that was good enough for Shaw and me is good enough for anybody ... Mankowitz: It's not bloody good enough for me, mate' – and suggesting himself as the hero of any modern play he might write. In his statements and interjections, Mankowitz attempts an amalgam of different discourses and approaches. When he calls for 'some kind of constructive, forward-looking planning in the theatre' which may lead to 'some kind of consecutive group work', he is arguing against the random entrepreneurialism of the current West End. But when the discussion moves to the role of the intellectual in the theatre, he seems to adopt the persona of the hard-headed businessman: 'the theatre is concerned with the production of commodity, and ... unless this commodity is produced in such a way as to ensure its adequate sale, it doesn't exist anyway'.

He has earlier stated that he lost a lot of money on the *Threepenny Opera* production, but his later praise of Brecht – 'the Berliner Ensemble which has made a tremendous contribution to the European tradition, a great section of which is Communist ... the breaking down of so many of the naturalistic conventions' – shows an alertness to the importance of the Ensemble's London visit that summer. When Miller suggests that talk of a play as a commodity is somewhat abstract, Mankowitz cuts in with 'Nothing more concrete than money', an observation that either the Marxist Brecht or a capitalist West End producer could have made.

Wilson's contempt for the vernacular goads Mankowitz into an impassioned defence of what he has earlier called 'certain fundamental things people have always known about from their guts and their stomachs [which] you can use the people's language, the people's vernacular to write about'. Mankowitz later underlines this commitment to a populist vitality when he declares: 'the most vital poetry, the most exciting verse, the most exciting plays, the most exciting novels have always in all countries been drawn from the language that is spoken by the people who are vitally concerned and vitally involved in their living experiences'.

Dan Rebellato has traced the extent to which such terms as 'life' and 'vital', central to the discourse constructed by F.R. Leavis of an organic literary culture, were adopted by a new generation of post-war critics and writers such as Raymond Williams and Richard Hoggart, who were finding their own passage from tradition to modernity. In particular he produces convincing evidence to show that these terms were 'distributed equally through the works of the New Left and the New Wave'.[8] Mankowitz exemplifies Rebellato's thesis by the discourse of organic vitalism with which he defends the vernacular in this debate at the Royal Court, the home of New Wave theatre.

Tynan's last question to all the participants is 'About what contemporary English hero would you like to write a play?' Ben Levy suggests John Wilkes, a democratic if not a left-wing politician. Colin Wilson gets a laugh with 'since all plays are essentially about oneself, I guess me'. Miller deliberates on a play about a man who is conscious of a certain stasis or pause in the evolution of English society and feels himself surrounded by 'an absence of will, perhaps, or a confusion of aims'. Mankowitz, who precedes Miller, has the most precisely formulated figure. He is 'the veteran Cockney, old, out-moded, old-fashioned, an infantryman who sweats, and stinks, and is stewed to the eyebrows, and has no place at all, and who is not wanted, can contribute nothing, yet embodies – for me – much more fundamental qualities than the outsiders, the insiders and the backsiders'. This contribution was greeted with laughter and applause.

Mankowitz's fourth short novel, *My Old Man's a Dustman*, has as its central character just such a stinking infantryman. It went on sale on 18 May 1956 in Britain (and in September in the US, with the title *Old Soldiers Never Die*), its title taken from a First World War song: 'My old man's a dustman/He fought in the battle of Mons', which the skiffle player Lonnie Donegan updated to a dustman with gorblimey trousers and a council flat for his number one hit in 1960. Mankowitz, however, locates his two principal characters, Old Cock and Arp, minders and scavengers of a municipal rubbish dump, in an indeterminate zone between the local council, represented by the officious Mr Bates, and Rambam's shop on the Roman Road, exchange centre for the two men's pickings from the dump.

Arp, who is dumb from trauma during the London bombing raids, is meticulous in his selection and preparation of objects for sale from the dump. His task, as the narrator voices it for him, is 'simply to tidy up the world which was all these dumps of rubbish'.[9] Old Cock supplies enough language for both of them. His eulogies, tirades and philosophical excursions make him a cross between Shakespeare's Ancient Pistol and Laurence Sterne's Uncle Toby. But Mankowitz is concerned here to extol this 'foul-mouthed commoner' who has respect for 'neither man nor permanent official, but merely cringed before the frown of authority, fiddled his way round the rules [and] flogged whatever came to hand'.[10] Old Cock is another trickster, but he is the trickster as orator, not as merchant. The rubbish dump he guards yields few items for exchange. It is, in Marx's terms, a site of 'so-called primitive accumulation',[11] a mound of potential not actual value. What does accumulate, drawing on a medley of literary sources, is Old Cock's language, an actual existing plenitude of human value.

He has, for example, his version of a Hamlet soliloquy which he unloads onto the silent Arp after a humiliating encounter with his sworn enemy, Mr Bates:

> What is a man, Arp? Ask yourself the simple question, what keeps him alive? Forget for the moment boasts of bedizened piss-proud fools who call him god, lord of creation, or plain king of the animal world. Forget he is a masterpiece of the mastermind and all that crap. Look him bold in his damned face and see the thought working there of who can I catch and cook and eat, who can I suck dry as a fly, who can I stab for a fountain of blood, who flog, who flay, who drive to suicide, who push to murder, who make quite useless, who curse redundant. For Bates hates me ... but then I am a wrecked old cock, and you are what you silently are, and he is a fellow who believes in stepping-stones to the future, screw you, Jack, I'm all right, competition is the soul of success, success is the spur, it's just unfortunate if the spur happens in this case to be up our arse.[12]

This cultured demotic is deployed to even more powerful effect when the narrator takes us inside the 'battered brainbox' of Old Cock as he inveighs against all bureaucrats while making his way to his union headquarters for advice on his redundancy notice. He will defend

> the right of an Englishman true-born and free to get his beer and baccy, his java, bread and scrape, plum-and-apple, cut off the joint and choice of two veg, his kip, his oats, his noggin and his nooky, good things sent in plenty from heaven above but niggled into pigeon-holes by charity charlies with scrag-end notions of that arithmetical dead loss and bad debt Man ...[13]

Old Cock, however, has his more tender moments. Like Falstaff he can play the lover as well as the conman. He desires the meat pies and meaty thighs of the widowed Emily Goffin who works in the council catering department. At the end, while the old soldier armours himself up in helmet and breastplate and prepares to mount an old dray horse and charge the council officials who have come to repossess their rubbish dump and Nissen huts, he eulogizes Emily in a parody of Don Quixote's praise of Dulcinea:

> I shall seek her by the tram to the far south of the river, through all of Bermondsey I shall seek, Arp, to tell her, Emily, do not look at the dirty shell of this old crab-louse before you. Do not be put off by vain thoughts of why don't he wash his neck and all that fancy poufferey. Have no fear for the future but give me your

> little hand in mine and we will fare together, looking not to left or right, but straight ahead, your bits and pieces safe in the grip of one who ... has lived as he will die a true-blue soldier and gentleman of the other ranks and, dear lady, your personal knight of the – flaming piss-holes![14]

It is not only their Nissen huts that the council has come to repossess. When Old Cock employs Arp (illegally), he shows him to his Nissen hut 'back of Ancient Rome'. They are guarding not only the rubbish dump, but also an abandoned film lot which the council owns and, in the course of the narrative, tries to sell to an American producer, Mr Claygate Corst of 100 Percent American Films Incorporated. Mankowiz, through extended authorial voice, enjoys satirical tilts at leading ladies, hackneyed storylines and film-industry finances. Roda Randolf is 'a talentless sex-machine built by poet-dreamers like Corst out of a hash-slinging scrubber and lay-about'.[15] Corst debates whether to star her as a gypsy with flashing eyes and panting breasts, or as the prize for gladiators in Ancient Rome, or as Calamity Jane Randolf in the Wild West Badlands.

Corst himself is a 'virtual bankrupt trading on a distribution contract provided by the husband of an ex-wife', but with council backing he can get credit to employ workmen to rebuild the set, pay his actors and finance publicity and distribution. The sardonic narrator sums up Corst as 'a producer in production',[16] a two-edged phrase which means both a producer who is producing and a producer of production, someone who can only produce the concept of a film, but not the thing itself. No film is, of course, produced on the council's site because Corst's credit runs out and he ambles out of the text with his head still full of grandiose schemes to mount 'a new burlesque production upon the very next convenient rubbish heap'.[17]

Production is always a precarious site for creativity in Mankowitz's work, but there is a particular asperity to the narrator's representation of the film industry. It may be that Mankowitz, by now heavily involved in screenwriting for major companies, is here playing out again his ambivalent relationship to both elite and popular culture. But Old Cock, the 'foul-mouthed commoner', is the hero of the tale. He represents, therefore, an alternative version of the culture of the people. The novella suggests that film purveys images of beauty and adventure to its audience,[18] but that these images are as flimsy as the sets that sustain them and have, perhaps, less value than the rubbish next to them. Orality has more truth. The indiscriminate mix of cultural registers in Old Cock's rhetorical tirades signals an inventive, oppositional working-class speech, an object of analysis, as we have seen, of the work of Richard Hoggart and Raymond Williams in this period. Old Cock may be bellowing to the dumb but, as his interior monologues reveal, Arp is fully receptive to his language.

Nature, too, blooms once the phantasmagoria of film has been blown away. The last chapter opens with a superb description of the mutual dependency and organic growth of the earth and its vegetables in the allotments that skirt the rubbish dump:

> Even into late spring on the allotments the thick dirty brussel sprout stalks wait rotting to be chopped up and dug in to feed future lettuces whose last yellow dried leaves (mixed with old dried blood) bring on the new green autumn tomatoes which, though they never ripen in the quickly fading summer, at least make chutney to mature through the winter ...[19]

This narrative voice, shorn of its habitual irony, celebrates, with cumulative descriptive precision, the plenitude of nature from below just as it has endorsed Old Cock's plenitude of speech from below. Old Cock and Arp may resemble Beckett's Vladimir and Lucky in *Waiting for Godot*, and the dustman theme might seem to prefigure the two parents in ashcans in *Endgame*, first produced in its French version at the Royal Court in April 1957. But no Beckett landscape is as fecund as this and no Beckett character as profligate with language as Old Cock. His virility may be waning but he is ready for one last stand.

Most critics read 'Old Cock' as 'old cockney' and their debate was about the authenticity of Mankowitz's idiom. The *Spectator*'s review was a cod parody of Old Cock's speeches and *The Times* concluded: 'Mr Mankowitz, like a music-hall comedian sweating under the grease-paint, tries almost too hard to be on jolly and familiar terms with his own creation.' But for Norman Shrapnel in the *Manchester Guardian*, this 'well-organised piece of comic writing ... full of highly impolite language' was 'vulgar in the best sense of the word' and the *TLS* interpreted Old Cock as a 'bit of human wreckage [who] is made the voice for some brilliant indirect comments on our civilisation'.

The distinguished novelist Elizabeth Bowen had a full-page overview in the *Tatler* of Mankowitz's career and considered this 'rich, racy, flavorous, decidedly bawdy epic of the rubbish dump' to be his most achieved fiction to date. She noted the Don Quixote allusions but also paralleled Mankowitz's rendition of London cockney with James Joyce's rendition of Dublin Irish in *Ulysses*, as two highly conscious literary re-creations of everyday speech. The most enthusiastic endorsement of the novella was by John Metcalf. In his book review column for the *Sunday Times* he argued that Old Cock spoke a living language in a living world, not the stage cockney of a Noel Coward; that Old Cock's profanities were an integral part of his world; and that Mankowitz's experiences as a screenwriter had taught him to focus on 'single scenes, throwing them into clear memorable shape as the central structural principle of his narrating'.[20]

Metcalf also contributed a long review of Mankowitz's work to date in the October 1956 number of the American *Atlantic Monthly*, the prestigious journal of arts and politics founded in 1857 by a group of Boston intellectuals including Ralph Waldo Emerson and James Russell Lowell. Metcalf's article brackets Mankowitz along with Kingsley Amis and John Wain in the headline, as all three depict the struggle of the individual to survive in a petty and corrupt society. Mankowitz distinguishes himself, in *Dustman*, by creating a cockney speech which is not only accurate but has a 'gutsy lilt, a bony beauty' to it, and this distinctive inflection Metcalf traces to Mankowitz's Russian-Jewish background. He has 'retained strong affinities to the folk background of the little Russian villages from which his family came' and this foreignness enables him to discern, in ways that a native English writer might not, the 'fragile friendships that grow in the back streets of even the biggest cities'. Metcalf sums up Mankowitz, however, as very much an artist of his time, contributing to all media, old and new, but remaining a 'gleaming, irreverent talent ... squarely committed on the side of the individual'.[21]

That talent had also been engaged in contributing in the same period to the screenplay of *Trapeze*, shot in colour and Cinemascope on location in the Cirque d'Hiver and the Billancourt studios in Paris and released in the US on 30 May 1956 and in the UK a month later on 28 June. Carol Reed directed Burt Lancaster as Mike Ribble, an ageing, crippled trapeze artist who trains up his protégé Tino Orsini (Tony Curtis) to achieve the triple somersault, the Everest of an artiste's ambition. Their homosocial bonding is continuously interrupted by Lola (Gina Lollobrigida), an ambitious trapeze artist herself, who transfers her affections back and forth between the two men. The trapeze sequences, under the cinematographic direction of Robert Krasker, who won an Oscar for his lighting and shooting of Reed's *The Third Man*, enact superbly the perilous beauty of these age-old skills. The film was enormously popular and showed an eight-million-dollar profit on a budget of four million dollars. Robert F. Moss cites a range of unfavourable reviews on both sides of the Atlantic, but concedes that this 'expertly manufactured entertainment' is difficult to fault if accepted on its own terms: 'Reed and his screenwriters steer the plot through its tangles, its rising and falling action, its complications, with unfailing attention to plausibility.'[22]

Peter William Evans, in his later study, proposes a lengthy analysis of *Trapeze* as one of Reed's most powerful films. In the exotic and erotic setting of a Parisian circus, the two male leads, he argues, hunt out each other as father and son with an undertone, so familiar from the western and war-movie genres, of sexual attraction. Lola splits apart this bonding and creates a 'triple' that is as dangerous as the triple somersault. Her costumes, which outline the female hourglass figure of the 1950s femme fatale, counterpoint those of the males: 'their vests, cut to a décolleté, revealing sufficiently their pectorals and sculpted shoulders to gratify the desires of all sexual orientations'. The plot has Ribble finally accept Lola's love which affords him an escape from the narcissistic isolation he embraces in the second half of the film. It is a happy ending, but a happy ending to satisfy the studio and the public. *Trapeze* remains, for Evans, an important mediation of an essentially Anglo-American problematic: 'the period's [late 1940s] growing uncertainty about dominant modes of masculinity'.[23]

In the light of this modern re-evaluation of a mass entertainment movie, Mankowitz's contribution to its screenplay is worth some attention. The story, like the plot of the film, is a tangled one. The *Daily Film Renter* noted he was working on the script in August 1955 and in the same month Art Buchwald filed a humorous account of Reed and Mankowitz warding off fleas in the Cirque d'Hiver for the *New York Herald Tribune*. *Sight and Sound* ran a page of pre-release stills from the film in January 1956 with the screenplay attributed to Mankowitz.[24] He would have been engaged by a storyline that, as in *A Kid for Two Farthings*, dramatized the tensions and ambiguities of a surrogate father–son relationship, and the circus setting united his interests in fantasy and popular culture. Sid James even makes frequent appearances, as a snake-man polishing a python, another oblique reference to *A Kid for Two Farthings*.

We would expect Mankowitz to take full credit for another collaboration with Carol Reed on this, Reed's first Hollywood movie. But none of the various drafts of the script[25] is attributed to Mankowitz. The earliest, from May 1955, where the heroine is called Sarah, is signed by one J. Webb. The Dialogue Sheets of 10 January 1956 are, in effect, the final version of the screenplay. Sid James's role has far greater prominence than before, and Sarah has become Lola, and her contractual battles with the circus owner are given extended treatment, a typical Mankowitz emphasis.

Mankowitz gave his own explanation for his non-accreditation on two occasions in the Davis interview. He insisted that he was so involved in the film that he virtually lived in the Cirque d'Hiver for weeks on end. Watching Reed at work, he said, was an education in film directing. He also noted that Reed was immensely impressed by Lollabrigida's star quality. 'Looking into her face', he recalled Reed saying, 'is like looking into the headlights of an oncoming Rolls Royce.' Later in the interview he returned to *Trapeze* and explained that, on the prompting of Ben Hecht, one of the film's co-producers, he sold his credit to James Webb for $15,000. Webb had been elected president of the Screenwriters' Union for 1957, but did not have the requisite qualifying credit from 1956. So Mankowitz sold him his. The interviewer was surprised but Mankowitz was quite unconcerned and said he sold credits on several other occasions. Once more it is the act of exchange that gives value to the commodity.

Mankowitz as author, however, continued his journalistic and theatrical productivity. 'The ABC of Show Business', an alphabetical series of short, satirical sketches, ran, with some breaks, in the *Evening Standard*, from 19 March to 1 June 1956 and was later published in book-form. Its predominant tone is that of the sardonic, knowing insider. Under the letter 'A' is '**ARNOLD, Tom**, a short, kindly-looking man with a quiet voice and a smile which makes you feel he knows exactly where you slipped up in costing your show.' **LEG SHOWS** 'feature **LEGS**, usually moving up and down more or less in unison', and **TELEVISION** 'pipes show business into the home like warm water from an atomic pile'. **VAUGHAN, Frankie** is 'one of the many pop singers whose discs sell millions to teen-agers who have more money and yearnings than they can properly handle. The great disc boom is a more interesting study of the public than it is of the singing stars it benefits'; but **ZELNICKER, Meier** is 'among the great Jewish comedians of the century and is one of the few players from the East End's Yiddish theatre who has been able to translate the ebullience and warmth of his native language into English'.[26]

The book was the basis for a BBC TV show, 'A–Z', the first series of which, compèred by Alan Melville, ran with some breaks from 12 October 1956 to 30 August 1957. It was billed as 'based on *The ABC of Show Business* by Wolf Mankowitz', but was more a showcase for existing variety and television performers than a satirical look at show business itself. Mankowitz had under the letter 'W' a sideswipe at such phrases as **'WE'LL CALL YOU'**, **'WARM HOUSES'**, **'WOW'**, **'WASHOUT'**, and a second half dedicated to an affectionate but not uncritical portrait of **WELLES, Orson.**[27] The guests for the television version (16 August 1957) were Norman Wisdom, Godfrey Winn, Sam Wanamaker, Bert Weedon and Elsie and Doris Waters, cosy celebrities from popular culture, with Sam Wanamaker as the obligatory representative from high culture.

That the BBC was keen to retain Mankowitz's format is clear from Mankowitz's letter to Cecil McGivern (2 July 1958) where he threatens to sell the property to commercial television unless the BBC finalizes an interest in it, and McGivern's note on the letter to the then Controller of Programmes, Television: 'I do not want this idea lost to ITA.'[28] There was a second BBC series the next year but Mankowitz had to threaten legal action in order to get his name restored to the credits. The show was by then dominated by Alan Melville, who, according to Philip Purser's *News Chronicle* report, had still further softened Mankowitz's original conception of a 'tough, sardonic programme that really took show business apart' into a show of 'wit, sophistication and elegance'.[29]

The Mighty Hunter, another Mankowitz updated 'version' of an Old Testament story, ran from 25 July to 11 August 1956 at the New Lindsey Theatre. It is a slight but clever play in which Mankowitz elides the character of Nimrod, whom Genesis calls 'a mighty hunter before the Lord', into the adjacent Genesis story of the Tower of Babel. Babel, which probably derives from the Akkadian *babilu* meaning 'gate of God', was a city in the territory of Nimrod, whose rule greatly extended the Babylonian Empire. The Babel of the Tower, however, puns on the place name since *babel* in Hebrew means 'confused', and the episode is part of a larger narrative, God's division of mankind into warring groups with different languages so that they cannot challenge His omnipotence. Mankowitz's Nimrod is, at the start, anything but powerful. He accepts the gift of a smart hunting jacket and trousers from an old man who first greets him as he sits, poor and forsaken, in his desert-tent. The jacket makes him invincible in battle with the neighbouring tribes, but as his kingdom grows so does his self-pride.

The old man, who finally reveals himself as Adam, urges him to remember, at every stage of his aggrandizement, that he is 'only a man'; but Nimrod's ambition carries him to the point where it is he who starts building the Tower of Babel, which will have a council chamber in cedar-wood and sheet-gold, where he can debate with God the question of his mortality. Nimrod's humanitarian impulse to use his power to, as the old man puts it, 'build blocks of flats, with hot and cold running water, and kindergartens for the ruined children from ruined homes' has been transformed into a mad desire for total control and he finishes babbling in back slang. The old man finishes with the last of his Brecht-like addresses to the audience:

> A man is a man and it ain't very much
> Even a king is more or less
> The same kind of miserable, crawling thing.[30]

The piece was well enough received. Although the *Financial Times* considered it a decorated and laboured parable, the *Kensington News* found it a salutary modern parable that absolute power corrupts absolutely and noted the inventiveness of the set which had 'all the fascination and illogicality of a junk shop'. *Truth* thought it 'a brilliant little morality' and the *New Statesman* admired Warren Mitchell as a bowler-hatted and bearded Adam. The *Manchester Guardian* described Mitchell as 'a crazy old Jew in a topper hopping about a junk shop singing (to Geoffrey Wright's music) the sort of ballads which made the reputation of Brecht and Weill in the Berlin of the twenties'.[31]

No designer is credited in the programme for this non-naturalist set so we can presume that it was a collaboration between Mankowitz and the director/producer, Peter Zadek, here at the start of an illustrious Anglo-German career in avant-garde theatre, film and opera direction. He had already directed one of the earliest English productions of Jean Genet's *The Maids*, at the Royal Court in 1952 under the artistic directorship of Oscar Lewenstein, but four years before the English Stage Company took over the theatre. He would direct a successful production of Genet's *The Balcony* at the Arts Theatre in the following year, 1957.[32]

Mankowitz's play was part of a double bill with *Don't Destroy Me*, described by the *Weekly Sporting Review*'s critic (3 August 1956) as an examination of 'the motives of a group of characters in a low-life Brixton habitat'. Its author was an 18-year-old self-educated writer, Michael Hastings, who would write a number of well-received plays for the Royal Court over the next twenty-five years, culminating in his very successful dramatization of T.S. Eliot's marriage to Vivienne Haigh-Wood, *Tom and Viv* (1984). If we also note that Warren Mitchell was just at the start of a distinguished career in theatre and television, we can see that Mankowitz at this time was very much associated with young, adventurous talent in the theatre.

He was also continuing his close association with public media. He was everywhere. Nancy Spain had a half-page spread in the *Daily Express* of 17 May 1956, in which she interviewed Mankowitz and Eartha Kitt on the importance of their first names for the success of their careers. He was one of a male panel invited to speak their minds about women on the 16 July edition of the Home Service's 'Male Opinion'. The *Johannesburg Star* of 16 August ran an interview with this 'wonder boy of British entertainment' who was in South Africa to script and cast a film, *IDS*, on illicit diamond smuggling. The project was first publicized as a series of short stories in the *Daily Express,* which ran from October 1956 and eventually became an ATV series, 'The Killing Stones', which will be discussed in the next chapter.

Mankowitz was always good for a quote. In the *Star* interview he called Diana Dors 'the only advance civilisation has made on foam rubber', and Paul Tanfield's 'Quotebook' in the *Daily Mail* of 26 October 1956 records his view of the Angry Young Man movement as a 'cult like the *New Statesman* set to Rock 'n' Roll'. He was also good for controversy. His aggressive exchanges with Colin Wilson at the Royal Court meeting were eagerly reported the next day by Edward Goring in the *Daily Mail*; Penelope Mortimer's report of a rerun of the contest on ITA's 'This Week' figured Mankowitz as 'play[ing] with Master Wilson with the benevolence of a rogue elephant at cross purposes with a mouse'.[33] His interview-show for Associated-Rediffusion in early 1958 was aptly entitled 'Conflict'.

On the other hand, his ten-day trip to the Soviet Union in September/October of 1956, as a guest of the Union of Writers for the Shaw Centenary Celebrations, was not designed to endear him to the British public as a 'media personality'. His conclusions on Stalin, artistic freedom and Soviet youth were balanced and nuanced,[34] but his praise for Soviet film expertise was unequivocal: 'They are very advanced in gear, stages, equipment and technique' and their film colour is 'the best in the world'.[35] MI5 kept close watch on Mankowitz in this period. His public statements before and after his trip are preserved in the first Kew File, as are reports monitoring his movements to and from the Soviet Consulate. One entry for 25 September 1956 is typically thorough: '11.24 am. Visitor no. 6 (Mankowitz) entered from taxi SLL 51. Blue zip jacket, grey trousers.' By the end of October, as if to right the balance, he was installed as story editor for Columbia Pictures in their new London offices, Film House in Wardour Street.

He always had time for the press. The *Birmingham News* reported that he would be spending the Christmas of 1956 at home 'being driven mad by my three children – and write about it afterwards!' He always had time for a party or a luncheon. He chaired a Foyle's literary lunch at the Dorchester hotel just before Christmas to launch a book on musical comedy by W. Macqueen-Pope. He was a guest at a party at the beginning of December where, although the beautiful models kept their distance from media personalities such as Gilbert Harding and Nancy Spain, a trial marriage between these two worlds had already occurred in the shape of one Jean Dawnay, 'a beautifully groomed model-turned-TV-star'.[36]

It was not bizarre, therefore, that the face of the author of *The Bespoke Overcoat*, *A Kid For Two Farthings* and *Wedgwood* should appear in a vast photomontage of television personalities in the *TV Mirror* for 23 February 1957. The Assistant to Controller of BBC TV Programmes, Cecil Madden, and his daughter Mardie had created it to stimulate the exhausted public into yet another vote for various categories of television achievement. They stated their choices and nominated, for the 'Ideas Department Award', Mankowitz's 'A–Z'. He was thus at this point a successful bridge between the competing cultures, old and new, of the metropolis. We shall see to what extent this balancing act turned out to be a tightrope performance.

He was on firm ground, however, with his two major publications of 1957, *The Mendelman Fire*, published by Deutsch in June and by Atlantic-Little, Brown Books of Boston, and *The Concise Encyclopedia of English Pottery and Porcelain*, with R.G. Haggar, also published by Deutsch in September. They were a summation of his principal themes and interests over the last five years. *The Mendelman Fire* was also a selection of otherwise fugitive pieces for newspapers, primarily the *Evening Standard*, and journals such as the *Atlantic Monthly*. The long title-story dated back to October 1954 when it appeared in *Lilliput*.[37] It is set in the late 1920s, the beginning of the Depression, and is narrated by Leo Botvinnik, accountant and lifelong friend to Morris Mendelman, dealer in everything from ladies' raincoats to Army surplus bell tents. Like the absent father in *A Kid for Two Farthings* he does business in South Africa but, unlike that father, Mendelman returns, flourishes and devotes his wealth to a first-class education in music at conservatoires in London and Paris for his remaining child, Rosa. He also develops a love of learning for himself and is always pressing on Botvinnik the latest book which has enthused him. One of these is Dr Joseph Wolff's *Bokhara*, a work that Mankowitz's father greatly admired.

But Mendelman loses everything when he switches from exchange into production. He invests all his capital in an enterprise to make a small, vital part for a new sewing machine; the sewing-machine company collapses; and he is left with a factory and machinery that are useless. Morris, Botvinnik observes, is a brilliant salesman because he can convince the customer that he 'wants to give you something which he thinks will do you good',[38] but he is a failure when he has to produce the goods. He cooks up a scheme whereby he will write a libellous letter to Rosa accusing her of being a whore, burn down his factory, lose the subsequent libel case and pay Rosa with the insurance money from the fire. It's a mad scheme and Botvinnik finds himself manoeuvring between Rosa and her Parisian lover's wife, Mendelman and the insurance company. It all collapses: Rosa is alienated, Mendelman dies and the company won't pay out. The machinations of family and the machinations of business don't mix, appears to be the message; but Mankowitz also displays his characteristic fascination with the mechanics of tricksterdom.

The rest of the volume comprises two groups of short stories under the respective titles of 'A Village Like Yours' and 'Good Business With Sentiment'. The first recreates and pays homage to the Russian village-world of his great-grandfather, a world of Jewish craftsmen, rigid hierarchy and village fools, but one which, in 'The Day Aunt Chaya Died' is also threatened by revolutionary activists. These are not tales with a moral or a narrative twist at the end. They are virtuoso exercises in the rendition into English of a world which the author never knew at first hand. The lead story, 'The Finest Pipe-Maker in Russia' is notable as a close version of Mankowitz's first story broadcast by BBC radio on 1 July, 1946.

The second group describes and anatomizes the urban villages that Mankowitz knows at first hand, those of East and West End dealers or, in the case of 'Nature's Way', a village in rural Essex whose chemist patents and profits from the sale of his home-made laxative which he calls 'SAFELAX: Nature's Way'. As the narrator remarks: 'trade circulates and creates trade'.[39] The title-protagonist in 'The Blottick Monopoly' persuades 'modernizing' households to exchange their Victorian loos for brand-new toilets. He then creates a niche in the antiques market for these loos with a feature in *Vogue* and a book, *Famous Basins*.

In the lead story, 'A Life in Art', Arthur Pelk uses his position as a successful salesman in a Bond Street gallery to pass off as genuine his own copies of minor, fashionable artists such as Constantin Guys. He is not motivated by financial gain; the skill of his copies is his only proof he is a genuine artist. But they enter the market, he becomes rich, then impoverishes himself by buying them back out of guilt, then rich again as their price rises even higher. In Henry James's 'The Real Thing', first published in 1892, it is the artificiality of art that gives it value. The narrator prefers a vulgar cockney, Miss Churm, and an Italian vagabond as models for his representations of an English lady and gentleman, to Major and Mrs Monarch who are 'the real thing, but always the same thing'.[40] With Arthur Pelk – a Jamesian name if ever there was one – we are in the art world of the late twentieth century, where virtuoso copying and imitation are given as much value by the market as originality. 'He had tried to lose himself in the practice of his art', reflects Pelk, 'but it was useless.'[41]

Emanuel Litvinoff, reviewing the collection for the *Jewish Observer*, found the Mendelman story charming but less impressive than *Make Me an Offer* which had a distinctive 'astringent, sinewy authenticity'. The 'amiable humanity' of the other stories was attractive and he concluded that although 'one may not always fall for Mr Mankowitz's sales-talk ... one likes him to keep on talking'. The *TLS* reviewer preferred *The Mendelman Fire* for its 'revelation of wide-eyed innocence among the shrewd and the tough', and Gabriel Costa for the *Jewish Chronicle* praised the novella, in which 'every character is seen in the round, living, sentient beings, types you and I encounter every so often'.

Punch, however, was unimpressed by the literary personality revealed in this collection: 'his is a small wistful voice over-amplified by synthetic means until it pulses like an enlarged heart', and Dwight MacDonald, for *Encounter*, found the Russian stories 'pseudo-folk' and the London stories 'manufactured anecdotes, all slicked up for quick sale'. The *New Statesman* review gave a perceptive summary of Mankowitz's current identity in the literary culture, as a writer who 'used to be the rising hope of the stern and unbending younger Leavisites' and had now become 'a splendid vulgar entertainer, a kind of English Damon Runyon'.[42]

Mankowitz's other 1957 publication, the *Concise Encyclopedia of English Pottery and Porcelain*, was the very opposite of vulgar. Specialist critics in trade journals in the quality and local press praised its high standards of production and reproduction and noted that the volume was a joint enterprise between firms in England and Holland. The *Staffordshire Evening Sentinel* highlighted its '24 full-page colour plates showing fine examples of English ceramics, 160 pages of monochrome photographs, a double-spread of embossed potters' marks, and an embossed title-page reproduction of the Portland vase'. The *Encyclopedia* was also, for the reviewer in *Pottery and Glass*, a work of original scholarship, drawing on local records, diaries, literature in the field and a wealth of previously unpublished data, although the reviewer detected a slight bias towards yesterday's rather than today's pottery.[43]

The authors' foreword makes it clear that the book is aimed at both the connoisseur and the trader. It has been designed, they state, 'for the practical collector of, or dealer in, ceramic objects. The authors' intention is to supply all information which can lead to accurate identification.'[44] Mankowitz, at least, is here alluding to a more wide-ranging argument about use and exchange values expressed in the preface to his 1953 volume *Wedgwood*. He argued there that 'the *serious* dealer is a man with a *serious* interest in the objects as well as the values in which he deals' (italics in the original), and went on to claim that it was the 'informed taste' of both collectors and dealers which 'preserves the values other than monetary embodied in objects of virtue'.[45] Mankowitz's critical vocabulary may be neoclassical – 'taste', 'virtue' – but the debate on value, as we have seen, is central to post-war British culture.

The *Encyclopedia*'s authors conclude their foreword by stating that, as far as possible, the originals for all the illustrations have been drawn from public collections, such as the Victoria and Albert Museum, rather than from 'private sources where examples are not on view to the public'.[46] The book is therefore aimed at an elite, but at an elite of the knowledgeable, from whom, we presume, 'the people' can learn how to appreciate beautiful objects in museums with free access. We are reminded of the 11-year-old Charlie at the start of *Make Me an Offer* as he begins to learn how to 'see' the Portland Vase on his trips to the British Museum. A leather-bound copy of the *Encyclopedia* is still the standard reference work in its field in the British Library.

If 1955 was the year of Mankowitz's arrival, the late 1950s, particularly 1958 and 1959, were his *anni mirabiles*. The critical receptions of his satirical stage musicals *Expresso Bongo* (1958) and *Make Me an Offer* (1959) were favourable. The former ran for 316 performances in the Saville Theatre from 23 April, with Paul Scofield playing the lead role of the unscrupulous agent Johnnie. Phillip Hope-Wallace, for the *Guardian*, delighted in this attack on 'the cult of the moronic teenager'; and Scofield's characterization of what Alan Brien for the *Spectator* called 'one of those leather-skulled, dead-eyed agents who edge along the back-alleys of Soho like a tortoise with a leaking shell' was universally praised.[47] The reviewer for *The Times* declared: 'The new English musical at the Saville has the smooth drive and satirical bite hitherto regarded as exclusively American. It may be ranked perhaps a little lower than *Guys and Dolls*, a little higher than *Pal Joey*.'[48]

Make Me an Offer had a combined run at Stratford East and the New Theatre of 267 performances and won the *Evening Standard* award for the Best Musical of 1959. Mankowitz was unhappy with Joan Littlewood's improvisation methods at Stratford East but when it transferred to the West End there was, according to John Russell Taylor, 'little about either the cast, the production or the play itself which would have seemed at all exceptional had it come from an ordinary West End commercial management'.[49] In this production, young actors who would go on to have distinguished careers included Daniel Massey, Sheila Hancock, Victor Spinetti and Roy Kinnear. Oscar Lewenstein commented on the works produced by the joint Mankowitz-Lewenstein company for 1959 that they were 'all successful artistically and financially, and all socially and theatrically progressive'.[50]

Mankowitz himself also scripted the film version of *Expresso Bongo* (1959), wrote two six-episode series, 'East End, West End' and 'The Killing Stones' for ATV in 1958, and hosted his own interview series, 'Conflict', also for ATV, in the opening months of 1958. This body of work could be called a reprise of his major themes and concerns – value, class, Yiddish culture and new media – but its modes of representation, the satirical in particular, begin to drift to some indeterminate ground between the new and the outdated.

The guests on 'Conflict'[51] – a typical late 1950s title – represented precisely the mix of media, politics and academe, hitherto separate categories in the press and on radio, which the cool, participatory nature of television creates. Mankowitz interviewed, among others, Malcolm Muggeridge and Hugh Cudlipp (media), Frank Cousins and Morgan Phillips (politics), and Sir John Cockroft and Geoffrey Gorer (academe). Spike Milligan also made an appearance but seemed to have transferred his own satirical chaos to the technology. 'As the programme opened', according to the *Ilford Recorder*, 'there was vision – a picture of Mr Mankowitz facing an empty chair – but no sound.' Sound was restored but a few moments later 'the faces on the screen developed severe twitches and occasional spasms of flashing up and down in an alarming manner'.[52] The empty chair looks forward to the much-later 'Mastermind', but the occupied chair and one-to-one interrogation anticipate the famous 'Face To Face' interviews of John Freeman between 1960 and 1962.

The stage and film versions of *Expresso Bongo* were immediately seen as satires on a very contemporary issue, youth culture and its music. Both versions derived fairly directly from a Mankowitz short story published also in 1958 in the *Evening Standard* and the *Atlantic Monthly*. An anonymous narrator, a small-time Soho music agent, recounts the tale of his rise and fall as the owner and transformer of an amateur bongo-player, Bert Rudge, into an international record star, Bongo Herbert. The narrator has been astute enough to realize that this moment, 1958, is a moment of crossover and mix. His imaginary blurb for Bongo's first record advertises 'something that's new, a swaying calypso beat woven around a rock foundation'.[53] The older generation has been exhausted by the war. They are stuck in old-fashioned attitudes so 'the kids were in their own – except for their discs and their fancy dress, and scrappy bits of entertainment like Bongo'. Leon's modest coffee bar in Frith Street becomes The Tom-Tom, heaving with sweaty teenagers attracted by Bongo's 'elemental violent energy coupled to an inane but genuine gaiety'.

When Bongo from Hoxton moves up the artistic scale to a season at the Diplomatique Café he also moves up the class scale. He now mixes, much to the narrator's suspicious disgust, with 'these classy, kittenish debs, the doggy younger sons of dukes, and the tired old fashion-wise operators of neither sex'. He also meets Dixie Collins, an ageing variety star who has risen beyond her Brixton origins, built a career in America, and now returned to London and become 'a pillar and oracle of café society'. She renegotiates a fairer contract for Bongo than the 50 per cent split that the narrator had inveigled him into, and the story finishes with the narrator trying to get his stripper girlfriend Maisie the lead role in a musical version of the life of Omar Khayyam, to be made by Kakky Katz, an extinct Hollywood producer. The narrator is an agent and should have been master of the moment of exchange, the contract. But he has bungled it by not getting legal permission from Bongo's parents, and he has overreached the market by demanding 50 per cent of his client's earnings. He is alert to but unaware of the full power of the interested parties who swiftly gather round the developing property that is Bongo Herbert.

These parties were more fully developed in the stage and screen versions of *Expresso Bongo*. Mr Mayer, the successful producer for Garrick records, who signs up Bongo and has an instant hit, was played by Meier Tzelnicker on stage and screen. In the film he is small and rotund in a double-breasted suit with a Yiddish-inflected accent and a cigar. He moves at a stately pace which contrasts with the frantic speed, of walk and speech, of the agent, now named Johnny Jackson, played by Laurence Harvey.

Mayer loves opera and despises this new pop music but there is money in it and he is a producer. He gets one of the best songs in both versions, 'Nausea', where he expresses his contempt for teenage culture: 'When I see this little bleeder and compare him with Aida / When he gets his Austin-Healey / He'll think he's as great as Gigli/ Nausea ... nausea.'[54] The lyrics for both stage and screen were by Julian More, David Heneker and Monty Norman, with additions to the screen version from, among others, Norrie Paramor and the film's director and producer, Val Guest.

Other interested parties are Lady Rosemary, her daughter Cynthia, and Linda Laverick of the *Evening World*. A finely tuned sequence of alternate lines by them in the stage play adds up to the anatomy of a modern pop star:

> CYNTHIA: Me because I just adore the quaint way he speaks.
> LINDA: Me because I'm sure he'll make good copy for weeks
> DIXIE: Me because he knocks me out, he thrills me, I'm sent.
> JOHNNIE: And me because I love him, he pays the rent.[55]

But the most interested party in Bongo and his origins is television. In the first two versions of the story (short story and stage) it is a TV documentary called 'Teen-Age Rebellion', starring Bongo and other youths discussing their attitudes with various adult worthies, that makes Bongo a star. Extracts from the stage play, including 'Nausea', were shown on BBC TV on 11 December 1958. The film follows a more nuanced sequence. The first intrusion of television into these small, familiar Soho streets, with their coffee bars, newsagent and friendly whore, is outside the Intime club, where Johnny's girlfriend, Maisie (played by Sylvia Syms), works as a stripper, another Soho cliché. From the start the film camera has moved swiftly to keep up with Johnny as he zips through his 'manor' or pays lightning visits to Meyer's Garrick Records or the snarling bear pit of a working-class marriage which is Bongo's home in Hoxton.

The film is in black and white and the effect is of flipping through a series of well-known photographs. Even Johnny's dress is slightly out of date, with his Frank Sinatra tip-up trilby, bow tie and dress shirt. Cliff Richard's Bongo, singing his first number 'Love', is new, but the opening music for the film has been big-band, and Richard performs in a cellar called the Jazz Club. We seem, as in the outdoor jiving scenes in *A Kid for Two Farthings*, to be poised between the early and the late 1950s. The Intime, the Jazz Club and the Garrick office are separate cultural spaces, drawn into relationship by the frantic energy of Johnny. Then we have a middle-distance shot of a technician unrolling a long cable into the Intime from a small BBC van in long shot. Johnny asks him what he's doing. He says they're setting up the cameras for a documentary on the Intime which will be shown on BBC's 'Cosmorama' programme.

This cable announces that we are firmly in the late 1950s. Strippers – and they are, for the 1950s, very naked – can be shown on what Johnny calls 'the hot cod's eye which watches every home in Britain', as can Herbert Bongo, or Dixie Collins, or Johnny Jackson, or anybody or anything. Mankowitz knows this. He has been both sides of the TV cameras for the last five years, as writer and performer. Val Guest, as a highly experienced film-maker, knows it too. But if television can frame anything, why not have film frame television so as to preserve some media superiority? The next shots, therefore, are of Johnny coming into the club and nearly tripping on the cables, a sideways one of a camera team on a large camera filming the nude review, then one of a two-man crew further back, filming the same scene.

Mankowitz's fictions always interest themselves as much in process as in product. Johnny, of course, is only interested in getting his client on TV, so he approaches the programme's frontman, Gilbert Harding, and persuades him to bring his crew over to The Tom-Tom. He also persuades Maisie and the rest of the strippers to come over so as to swell the crowd. The street outside The Tom-Tom is now blocked by a large, white van with 'BBC – Telerecording Unit' printed boldly across its front. Cars are hooting, a policeman clears the way for a blocked taxi, and the Soho street is no longer a cosy, community thoroughfare. A thick TV cable already lies across the pavement and snakes down into the club where, surrounded by a mixed audience of strippers, teenagers and a rock group, Gilbert Harding gives a restrained, grumpy-old-man introduction about this new youth phenomenon and its music, and Cliff Richard sings 'Voice in the Wilderness' straight to camera. It is a thoroughly professional performance and by February 1960 the record was number two in the charts.[56]

Mr Mayer and Johnny then leave the club and perform the lyrics of 'Nausea' along the street. They are both hustlers and their sardonic song and dance act is more consonant with the variety traditions of Soho, as well as deliberately counterpointing the smooth accomplishment of Richard. Tzelnicker and Harvey are also professional actors. They are playing roles. Richard is just himself. He can't, unlike Frank Sinatra, act; he just sings, as well as he can, 'Voice in the Wilderness' and, later, a ballad of unctuous mother-love, 'The Shrine on the Second Floor'.

Gilbert Harding is also himself in the next-but-one scene where Johnny talks his way into the heart of the tentacular cable-beast, Television Centre, and duns Harding for £100, his fee for allowing Bongo to perform on TV. He also gets himself included as a panellist, along with a selection of adult worthies, on the documentary which discusses teenage rebellion. Johnny uses his spot to plug 'Voice in the Wilderness', which delights Bongo, Maisie and Beast back home, who are watching the small television screen while we are watching the small screen on the big screen.

Later in the film Dixie Collins welcomes Bongo on to her TV variety show, but he is such a success that it is he, not Dixie, who gets top billing for a forthcoming American tour. *Expresso Bongo*, therefore, proposes that television is the new solvent within which will be dissolved old categories of class, occupation, skills, entertainment, even fiction and reality. It was, as we have seen, in his 1956 address to the Arts Theatre Club, that he explained the financial strategy of the English Stage Company as subsidizing unpopular plays with popular ones: 'This is known as the balance of culture.'[57] Three years later he seems to predict a swing of the scales in favour of pop culture.

Mankowitz and Guest, however, also propose Johnny Jackson as a whirling centre of resistance to the bland conformity of TV. He appears in most scenes and dominates all of them. He too mixes old with new, stage variety with television variety, strippers with teenagers, Hoxton with the West End. But his mixing is individual, almost anarchic. Des Hickey and Gus Smith record in their biography of Laurence Harvey that he created an ersatz accent for Johnny, 'an incredible mixture of Cockney, Yiddish and mid-Atlantic' which then lapsed 'into the broad South African of his youth'.[58] Val Guest confirms this in his autobiography, *So You Want to Be in Pictures*, when he recalls telling Harvey that he thought Johnny's accent should be 'part Soho, part Jewish, and part middle class'. He then realized that this was Mankowitz's own accent and noted that, from time to time during shooting, Harvey would have a quick telephone chat with Mankowitz, then return to the set and say: 'Better roll before I forget it.'[59]

Johnny is fully engaged in making what he can from this new Soho scene, but he also maintains a sardonic distance from it. He has nothing but contempt for the singing abilities of his girlfriend Maisie and Herbert Bongo and he is highly suspicious of the crowd at the Diplomatique. Guest and Mankowitz have him meet Kakky Katz early on when Kakky declares he would never compromise himself by making pictures for television: at the end he is happy to propose Maisie for a lead role in Kakky's improbable musical epic. His artistic allegiances, if any, are with stage variety and the big-band music he used to perform, and his fraternity is the band of small-time tricksters and dealers which populates so many of Mankowitz's fictions and which is making its final stage appearance in the musical of *Make Me an Offer* concurrently running at the Theatre Royal, Stratford East.

Johnny Jackson, in brief, is an 'inside-outsider', a familiar figure in other works of the period such as *Lucky Jim*, *Look Back in Anger*, *Absolute Beginners* and *Room at the Top*, in the film version of which Harvey had starred the previous year. All the chief male protagonists of these works are displaced or displace themselves socially, a self-alienation which allows them a critical view of their situation. The first-person narrator of the *Expresso Bongo* short story maintains throughout a stance of sardonic mockery towards his actions. The film, without voice-over, has to rely on structure and scene to achieve the same effect. The most vivid example is when Johnny takes Maisie to The Tom Tom for the first time, seizes a teenager dancing on the floor and enacts a half-hunched, grotesque parody of jiving, the equivalent of Jim Dixon's grotesque face-pulling in *Lucky Jim*. Harvey, in fact, constructs Johnny throughout as a figure of exaggerated theatricality, with a repertoire of upturned palms, shrugging shoulders and rolling eyeballs that would be remarkable in Naples.

Contemporary critics noted the two-faced stance in the film's attitude towards its subject matter. Regan Redbarn for the *Record Mirror* praised the speed and brashness of the production but found that it 'never really decides whether it is going to be sentimental or vitriolic. Sometimes the film is satire, and sometimes it is routine comedy.' For Ivon Adams of the *Star*, 'the musical intrusions ... not only hold up the film but change the mood from bitter realism to fantasy'. Isabel Quigly's *Spectator* review welcomed the film as an exposé of a world which baffled her, a film which was 'fast, efficient, and often very funny, and because of its oddities of casting you can take its funniness in several ways, its jokes depending for what they mean to you on how far or close you are'. Peter John Dyer for *Sight and Sound* saw a 'broad enough surface fantasy of show-biz corruption to confound anyone who likes his satire in focus'. But he found the casting of Cliff Richard as Bongo incredible. 'It seems astonishing', he wrote, 'that anyone should confuse [his] authentic air of well-bred abstraction with virginal innocence or professional naivety.'[60]

Later academic criticism has emphasized the film's importance in foregrounding, as K.J. Donelly puts it, 'television's role in the promotion of pop music', satirizing a new breed of ruthless managers, and firmly situating 'the music's origin in coffee bars, with rock 'n' rollers as central figures in these cinematic coffee bars'.[61] Linda J. Sandhal best 'places' a film full of displacements: 'Like *The Girl Can't Help It*, this is an anti-rock diatribe disguised as a musical. The makers manage to have their cake and eat it too by despising the music while exploiting it to the hilt.' She admits, however, as did the bulk of reviewers at the time, that the film is slick and enjoyable and the whole cast give fine performances.[62]

The third reincarnation of *Make Me an Offer* was running in the West End from 12 December 1959 and was thus concurrent with *Expresso Bongo*. The familiar cast of Wendl, Sparta, Charlie, the Redhead and the Americans follows the same plot of double-dealing before and during the auction of the contents of the country house (here called Cramping Grange) and the 'knock-out' agreement is played out as a full-stage scene back in the Portobello Road market. Its dramatic potential is exploited to the full as, according to the stage directions, 'The seven of them form a circle with WENDL centre – fairly close – a conspiracy but an open one observed with interest and admiration by the other DEALERS.'[63]

Mankowitz's rewrite for this stage musical version has, however, sharpened the split between Charlie's domestic and business life, and his wife (renamed Sally) has several bitter songs (lyrics and music again by Monty Norman and David Heneker) about Charlie's lack of success and her role as housebound mother. 'If I was a man', she announces to her girlfriends in Act I, 'I would be adult and responsible / I'd accept a little blame for the facts of life / Wouldn't always take it out on my weary wife.' The girls chorus back: 'But the law of self-importance / Is all a man obeys' and Sally replies: 'A man's world they say / In their pompous way.'[64]

The Redhead's role, by contrast, is built up as that of a ruthless upper-class businesswoman called Lady Celia, who buys the shop behind Charlie's pitch in Portobello Road, owns Cramping Grange, seduces Charlie and only mixes with the street-traders to learn the tricks of their trade. She needs the money from the house-sale, she tells Charlie, in order to marry a sweet boy who won't inherit until his father dies. So she seduces Charlie in order to learn how to get the best price at the house-sale. Charlie affects disgust at her cynicism, which provokes the most complex statement of value in Mankowitz's work to date:

> CHARLIE: Never heard anything so immoral in my life. A girl with your background and looks could marry the richest in the land.
>
> REDHEAD: You mean sell myself to the highest bidder. Lot two hundred, a well-fitted sex-object with an excellent provenance.
>
> CHARLIE: You're so coarse.
>
> REDHEAD: I deal in things I don't value in order to be able to give away what I do.[65]

Charlie's idealism still flickers at the end of the play when he remembers looking out at night over his backyard and smelling the stocks his mother had planted. 'The air was deep green, just like that vase', he says. 'I knew then that a beautiful thing isn't just something you deal in.'[66] He is reconciled to Sally and another baby and limits his ambitions to a large lock-up on the Portobello Road.

This happy ending may accord with producer Joan Littlewood's desire to create plays that 'celebrated the power of laughter and the vitality of the excluded',[67] but the emotional balance of this play lies with the scathing wit of songs such as 'Business is Business' and 'Break Up'. We have already noted Mankowitz's resistance to improvisation of his scripts, and Robert Leach adds that *Make Me an Offer* 'was created with the specific purpose of transferring'.[68] Its East End provenance needed a West End home. Mankowitz's aim with this play was not to celebrate community strength and vitality but, as always, to dramatize the moment of exchange as the fulcrum of modern capitalism.

A strong American presence is therefore vital to this play in ways that it would not be for, say, *Sparrers Can't Sing*. Mindel and Sweeting, the American dealers for Californian and Chicago buyers, are far more integrated into the Portobello Road community (a West End community) of trickster-dealers than in previous versions. In the first scene of Act I, Wendel and Sparta sing a brief resume of historical theories of money from Bentham to Keynes. Sparta sings: 'According to Karl Marx the means of production and distribution', but Wendl cuts him off and reminds him he's talking to Americans.[69] This is meant as an oblique reference to the Cold War, but Sparta would have completed his verse with 'exchange', which, as Mindel and Sweeting's song 'Concerning Capital' demonstrates, is now an American province. The third verse, sung by both the Americans and the Dealers, begins 'You've got to have Capital / With a capital D [ollar]' and concludes: 'Then we fill up our ship / At the end of the trip / And pay with capital D / For culture with a Capital C.'[70] Culture, money and 'the people' now form a complex diagram of interacting forces.

NOTES

1. *Harper's Bazaar*, January 1956, pp.58–9.
2. *New Statesman*, 18 February 1956; *The Times*, 10 February 1956; *Spectator*, 17 February 1956.
3. *Daily Mail*, 17 May 1956.
4. John Osborne, *Almost a Gentleman: An Autobiography, Vol. 2, 1955–1966* (London: Faber & Faber, 1991), pp.20, 30.
5. *Evening Standard*, 31 October 1960.
6. John Barber, *Daily Express*, 21 October 1958; account in *The Author*, Autumn 1959, of meeting 12 July 1959; *Oxford Mail*, 28 July 1956.
7. *Encore*, 13, 5 (June–July 1957), pp.13–35. All subsequent quotations are from this reproduced text.
8. Dan Rebellato, *1956 and All That: The Making of Modern British Drama* (London and New York: Routledge, 1999), p.21.
9. Mankowitz, *My Old Man's A Dustman* (London: Barker Dragon Books, 1958), p.10. All subsequent citations are from this edition.
10. Ibid., p.96.
11. Karl Marx, from *Capital Vol. I*, in T.B. Bottomore and M. Rubel (eds), *Karl Marx: Selected Writings in Sociology and Philosophy* (Harmondsworth: Pelican, 1963), pp.148–51.
12. Mankowitz, *My Old Man's A Dustman*, pp.42–3.
13. Ibid., p.129.
14. Ibid., p.187.
15. Ibid., pp.11, 76.
16. Ibid., p.73.
17. Ibid., p.179.
18. The novella is set around 1945–46, the peak period for cinema attendance in Britain.
19. Ibid., p.182.
20. *Spectator*, 25 May 1956; *The Times*, 24 May 1956; *Manchester Guardian*, 22 May 1956; *TLS*, 22 July 1956; *Tatler*, 13 June 1956; *Sunday Times*, 27 May 1956.
21. John Metcalf, 'Wolf Mankowitz', *Atlantic Monthly*, October 1956, p.868.
22. Robert F. Moss, *The Films of Carol Reed* (Basingstoke: Macmillan, 1987), p.217.
23. Peter William Evans, *Carol Reed* (Manchester: Manchester University Press, 2005), pp.150–9.
24. *Daily Film Renter*, 10 August 1955; *New York Herald Tribune*, 5 August 1955; *Sight and Sound*, January 1956.
25. Sir Carol Reed Papers, BFI Scripts, no. 4890076, BFI National Archive, Berkhamsted.
26. Wolf Mankowitz, *The ABC of Show Business* (London: Oldbourne Press, n.d, probably 1956), pp.5, 29, 45, 49, 55.
27. Ibid., p.51.
28. Letter from Wolf Mankowitz to Cecil McGivern, 2 July 1958; and note from Cecil

McGivern to the Controller of Programmes, Television, CM/C.P. Tel, 3 July 1958, both T48/402, BBC Written Archives Centre, Caversham Park, Reading.
29. Philip Purser, *News Chronicle*, 3 March 1959.
30. Wolf Mankowitz, *Wolf Mankowitz: The Plays*, preface by Anthony Dunn (London: Oberon Books, 2006), pp.163–75.
31. *Financial Times*, 26 July 1956; *Kensington News*, 3 August 1956; *Truth*, 3 August 1956; *New Statesman*, 4 August 1956; *Manchester Guardian*, 27 July 1956.
32. Forty-nine performances between 22 April and 6 June 1957.
33. *Evening Standard*, 12 December 1956.
34. *Daily Worker*, 20 October 1956; *British Soviet Friendship*, February 1957.
35. *News Chronicle*, 9 October 1956.
36. *Daily Telegraph*, 20 December and December 1, 1956.
37. *Lillliput*, 35, 4 (October 1954), pp.49–63.
38. Wolf Mankowitz, *The Penguin Wolf Mankowitz* (Harmondsworth: Penguin, 1967), p.96.
39. Ibid., p.192.
40. *Henry James: Selected Tales*, edited by John Lyon, Penguin Classics series (London: Penguin, 2001), p.214.
41. Mankowitz, *Penguin Wolf Mankowitz*, p.180.
42. *Jewish Observer*, 5 July 1957; *TLS*, 5 July 1957; *Jewish Chronicle*, 12 July 1957; *Punch*, 4 September 1957; *Encounter*, September 1957; *New Statesman*, 27 July 1957.
43. *Staffordshire Evening Sentinel*, 1 October 1957; *Pottery and Glass*, November, 1957.
44. W. Mankowitz and R. Haggar (eds), *The Concise Encyclopedia of English Pottery and Porcelain* (London: André Deutsch, 1957), p.xi.
45. W. Mankowitz, *Wedgwood* (New York: E.P. Dutton, 1953), p.viii.
46. Mankowitz and Haggar (eds), *Concise Encyclopedia*, p.xi .
47. *Guardian*, 24 April 1958; *Spectator*, 2 May 1958.
48. *The Times*, 24 April 1958.
49. John Russell Taylor, *Anger and After* (Harmondsworth: Pelican Books, 1963), p.121.
50. Oscar Lewenstein, *Kicking against the Pricks* (London: Nick Hern Books, 1994), p.91.
51. Eleven fifteen-minute interviews between 3 January and 28 March 1958.
52. *Ilford Recorder*, 27 February 1958.
53. This, and all subsequent quotations, are from 'Expresso Bongo' in W. Mankowitz, *Make Me An Offer, Expresso Bongo and Other Stories* (London: Hutchinson Educational Ltd, 1961), pp.73–94.
54. W. Mankowitz, *Expresso Bongo: A Musical Play* (London: Evans Bros, 1960), p.16.
55. Ibid., p.51.
56. Dave McAleer (ed.), *Hit Singles: Top Twenty Charts* (London: Carlton Books, 2007). Cliff Richard had already established his Top Twenty reputation with 'Living Doll' (lyrics by Lionel Bart and produced by Norrie Paramor) in August 1959.
57. *Stage*, 21 June 1956.
58. D. Hickey and G. Smith, *The Prince: The Public and Private Life of Laurence Harvey* (London: Leslie Frewin, 1975), p.129.
59. Val Guest, *So You Want To Be in Pictures* (London: Reynolds & Hearn, 2001), pp.134–5.
60. *Record Mirror*, 28 November 1959; *Star*, 26 November 1959; *Spectator*, 4 December 1959; *Sight and Sound*, January 1960.
61. K.J. Donnelly, *Pop Music in British Cinema: A Chronicle* (London: BFI Publications, 2001), pp.5–6.
62. Linda J. Sandhal, *Encyclopedia of Rock Music on Film* (Poole: Blandford Press, 1987), p.38.
63. W. Mankowitz, *Make Me an Offer*, Act 2, Scene 5, p.32, stage musical version 1959, Mankowitz Family Archive.
64. Ibid., Act 1, Scene 1, p.24.
65. Ibid., Act 2, Scene 1, p.3.
66. Ibid., Act 2, Scene 6, p.40.
67. Robert Leach, *Theatre Workshop: Joan Littlewood and the Making of Modern British Theatre* (Exeter: University of Exeter Press, 2006), p.141.
68. Ibid., p.143.
69. Mankowitz, *Make Me an Offer*, Act 1, Scene 1, pp.31–2.
70. Ibid., pp.34–5.

1. Wolf Mankowitz's maternal grandparents. Aunt Ada's, Hampstead Garden Suburb. Mankowitz Family Archive (hereafter MFA).

2. Wedding of WM's parents. Great Alie Synagogue; 1921. MFA.

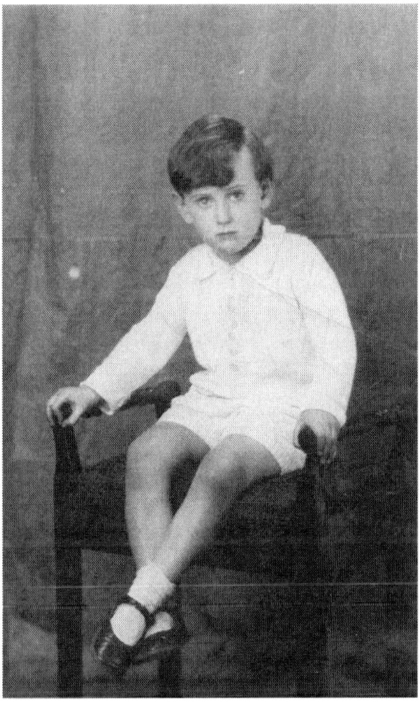

3. A very young Wolf Mankowitz. MFA.

4. Portrait of Wolf Mankowitz aged about 16. MFA.

5. Wolf Mankowiz (fourth from left) with group of East Ham Grammar School evacuees, Swindon 1943. MFA.

6. Portrait of Wolf Mankowitz, c. 1948. MFA.

7. Wolf Mankowitz with Portland Vases, 1953. MFA.

8. Mrs Ann Mankowitz at a charity event, November 1955. MFA.

9. Wolf Mankowitz on the film set of *Trapeze*, 1956. MFA.

10. Wolf Mankowitz on the set of *The Bespoke Overcoat*, 1955. MFA.

11. Wolf Mankowitz, together with Eamonn Andrews and Diana Dors' husband Dennis Hamilton, on Diana Dors' *This Is Your Life*, April 1957. MFA.

12. Wolf Mankowitz and Ken Tynan (centre) and unknown third person. MFA.

13. Wolf Mankowitz and Paul Scofield in a Soho café, 1958. MFA.

14. Wolf Mankowitz and Laurence Harvey on the set of *Expresso Bongo*, 1959. MFA.

15. Wolf Mankowitz with china in the basement of Gered (Antiques) Ltd, Piccadilly Arcade, late 1950s. Tom Blau – Camera Press Ltd.

16. Mrs Mankowitz (Snr) in East Ham shop, late 1950s. MFA.

17. Wolf Mankowitz (centre) on 'Press Conference', July 1957. MFA.

18. Wolf Mankowitz in Piccadilly Arcade office with LP and posters of productions, c.1959. Tom Blau – Camera Press Ltd.

19. Wolf Mankowitz and family, 1960. MFA.

20. Wolf Mankowitz and father, early 1960s. MFA.

21. Wolf Mankowitz at his typewriter, c. 1965. Gered Mankowitz.

22. Wolf Mankowitz with supporters at 'Israel 20', Albert Hall, 28 April 1968. MFA.

23. Wolf Mankowitz and Milo O'Shea on the set of *The Hebrew Lesson*, 1972. Gered Mankowitz.

24. Wolf Mankowitz as director on the set of *The Hebrew Lesson*, 1972. Gered Mankowitz.

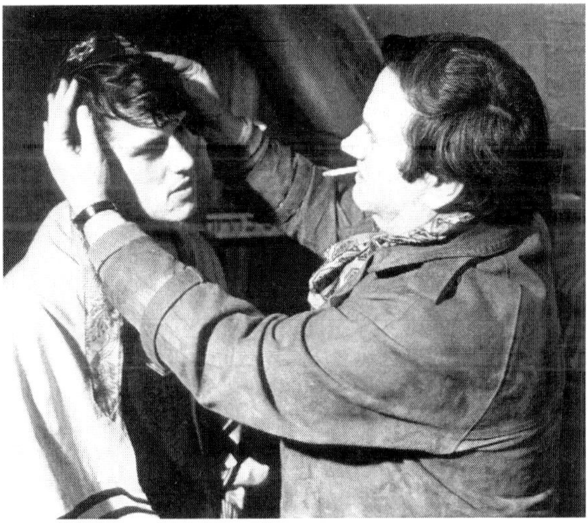

La Junta Provisional de Gobierno de la República de Panamá.

A todos los que las presentes vieren,

Salud.

Por cuanto que es conveniente a los intereses del Estado desarrollar las relaciones comerciales que felizmente existen entre la República de Panamá y la de Irlanda ha tenido a bien nombrar al señor Wolf Mankowitz por sus aptitudes y probidad Cónsul honorario de Panamá en Dublin, otorgándole la competencia necesaria reconocida por el Derecho Internacional.

Por tanto encarece al Gobierno de Irlanda reconocer al nombrado con el carácter expresado, prestarle su apoyo, concederle las prerrogativas inherentes a la jerarquía del cargo que se le confiere y permitirle ejercerlo libremente.

En fe de ello, hemos hecho expedir las presentes Letras Patentes firmadas, selladas con el escudo de la República y refrendadas por el Ministro de Relaciones Exteriores en el Palacio Presidencial, en Panamá, a los once (11) días del mes de mayo del año mil novecientos setenta y uno (1971).

Reg. No 2322.–

Refrendado.

Presidente de La Junta Provisional de Gobierno,

El Ministro de Relaciones Exteriores,

Miembro de La Junta Provisional de Gobierno,

25. Wolf Mankowitz's documentation as Honorary Panamanian Consul in Dublin, 1971. Gered Mankowitz.

26. *Wolf and Fork (2)*, 1970s. Gered Mankowitz.

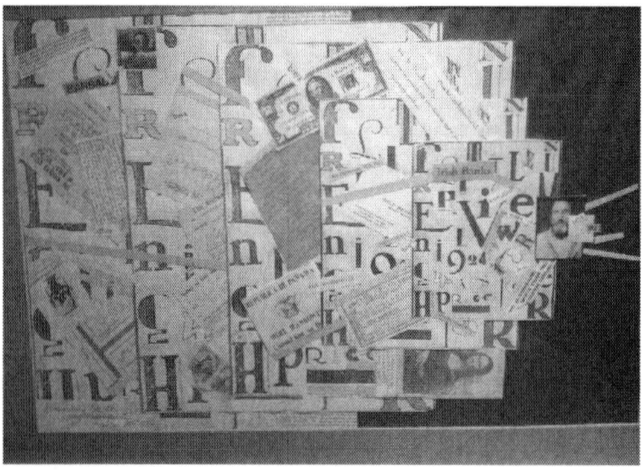

27. Wolf Mankowitz's collage *Diminishing Identity*, December 1989. Daniel Mankowitz.

28. Wolf Mankowitz's collage *Clues in the case of the theft of the Duchess of Devonshire*, 1990. Gered Mankowitz.

29. Wolf Mankowitz's collage *Mermaid Disintegrates*, 1990. Gered Mankowitz.

30. Wolf Mankowitz's collage *Socrates*, 1990. Gered Mankowitz.

CHAPTER SIX

Rebalancing Culture (1958–61)

Mankowitz's scripts for *Expresso Bongo* may have satirized television, but his scripts for his two series for Associated-Rediffusion, 'The Killing Stones' and 'East End, West End',[1] signal an intention to retain a significant presence in this new medium. David Griffiths's *TV Times* preview article[2] on 'The Killing Stones' notes that its director, Cecil Petty, had worked on Mankowitz's TV version of *Make Me an Offer* and that Sir Donald Wolfit would be the participant observer in this cycle of six tragic stories set in the murky underworld of South African illicit diamond-buying. Wolfit plays de Haan, a diamond polisher, who keeps a discreet distance from the circulation of uncut diamonds through the lives of a range of figures who add up to a cross section of South African society. The cast of characters who kill and are killed for what de Haan calls 'pebbles that last forever like death', includes Kleiber (an assayer), Ant Eater (a self-styled bishop and diamond fence), Suzie (a mixed-race aspirational model), Desai (an Indian trader in narcotics), Julius Hammerman, who is the spoilt son of a diamond tycoon, and his jealous employee, Coetzee. It is Coetzee who hands on the largest illegal diamond of all to de Haan, and it is de Haan who is finally tempted to sell it in Rothmark's Bar, the hub of the illegal trade. De Haan and an employee, Lou, haggle over the price for the diamond – 'a beauty. Pure Xdorp'[3] – but at the magical moment of exchange, the police intervene and arrest de Haan, Lou and Coetzee. The circle of destructive beauty is complete.

Press reaction to various episodes varied from mild enthusiasm to downright distaste. *Reynolds News* found the flurry of action at Johannesburg Airport at the end of the first episode too quick even for the cameras and hoped that 'for Sir Donald's sake ... Mr Mankowitz has thought up something more convincing for future instalments'. The *Sunday Dispatch* thought it was a comedown for a classical actor like

Wolfit to be in a TV play about illicit diamond smuggling but the first episode 'made a refreshing change from the usual Saturday routine – for which millions must give thanks'. The *Stage*'s reviewer, D.E.H., found the first episode 'pretty grim. This is not Mankowitz at his best. Surely he is above this sort of cheap, novelettish story.' For the *Liverpool Evening Express* the second episode was one of '[two] clever little pieces well up to the standard we expect of the fabulous Mankowitz', but the third episode 'featured above anything else our old friend Sex and therefore hardly qualified for Sunday night entertainment'. The *Sunday Dispatch*'s comment on the last episode sums up the mixed reaction: 'I reckon Mr Mankowitz made his point – illicit diamonds spell trouble – at the first turn of the cycle. But he held my interest with his plot twists.'[4]

In retrospect, and with only the dialogue scripts as evidence, the series seems prescient in that it presents the violence of the diamond trade as symptomatic of the violence endemic in an apartheid society. There can be no valid exchanges between anyone, black or white, in such a society. The Sharpeville massacre was perpetrated two years later. *Blood Diamond*, Leonardo Di Caprio's 2006 movie set against the background of the civil war in Sierra Leone, has made the same point. The only true value in the film is the Zulu music, which had been created in the townships and which reached, with 'The Killing Stones', a far wider audience. The theme tune, 'Tom Hark', recorded in Johannesburg's modern recording studios by Elias and his Zig-Zag Jive Flutes, reached number four in the May 1958 UK charts and number three in June.

The series also seems adventurous cinematographically. Most television series of the period confined themselves to a few domestic sets. 'The Killing Stones' has action set in an international airport at the end of Episode 1, and a long car drive up-country, with violent action inside and outside the car, to the farm of Coetzee's father, and then outdoor scenes on the farm. With Wolfit as the star, the new commercial channel of Associated-Rediffusion was ready to spend serious money on a Mankowitz series.

It also invested heavily in 'East End, West End', the six-part prime-time series that preceded 'The Killing Stones'. Sid James played himself, in his first lead role, as a dealer at the bottom of the antiques chain with a basement full of junk in Gerrard Street, Soho. The supporting cast for the first episode reads like a round-up of Mankowitz regulars, with Meier Tzelnicker as Mr Rosen, whose showroom of dresses in Great Portland Street is a cut above Sid's basement, and Sidney Tafler as Sammy Shmutters, who auctions off his stock of dresses from a market stall. Miriam Karlin, the prominent Jewish actress, appeared throughout as Donna, Sid's fiancée and then his wife, and daughter of Mr Rosen. Alfie Bass appeared in the fourth episode as Alfie Crate, a hapless antiques packer for the American market. There was also great press interest in Sid James's lead debut, since the very popular radio show 'Hancock's Half Hour', in which he played the unscrupulous sidekick to Hancock's idealistic dreamer, was now in its fifth series and, in fact, running almost concurrently with 'East End, West End', on Tuesdays between 8.00 and 8.30 pm. The equally popular television series of 'Hancock's Half Hour' would not resume until December 1958.[5]

London newspaper readers would also have been familiar with the plots and characterization of at least four of the episodes, since they had already appeared as short stories in the *Evening Standard* over the last two years. In their TV adaptations the plots remain ingenious enough, but the cynical observer of the *Standard* has mutated into a Sid James who is alert to the main chance but content with his lowly position in the dealers' pecking order. He is a man divided against himself, with a split-screen or voice-over alter ego frequently warning him against over-ambition. He refuses a credit-line from Mr Rosen and has to accept his useless dresses in lieu of a dowry for his daughter. He is suspicious of his wife's social climbing in Episode 3 and is outmanoeuvred by the bankrupt Hollywood producer, K. Arnold Krinkel (played by Warren Mitchell) in Episode 5. He is most successful in the last episode when, by a series of ingenious sales of non-existent property, he obtains the position of Grand Vizier and Treasurer to the Sultan of Baderabad, a godforsaken country in the Middle East which has just gained its independence from Britain. His triumph seems complete and his new social position assured when Tony Hancock, disguised as a beggar and led by a goat, wanders into the penultimate scene. Sid gives him a coin and Hancock says to camera: 'It makes a change for him to be slipping me the guptas. Still it's his dream after all.'[6]

Hancock's comment must have seemed, at the time, no more than a good-humoured exchange between two established stars but, in retrospect, it sounds like an ominous warning for both Sid James and Wolf Mankowitz. The humour of 'East End, West End' is plot-driven, with a central character, a small-time Jewish dealer, who is yet another version of Charlie. Sid even repeats Charlie's observation in *Make Me an Offer* (1952) at the start of the series: 'It's a funny game this dealing.

Nothing's worth anything until you sell it. Then it's worth whatever you can get for it.'[7] The language has its moments of wit but, as the *News Chronicle* critic remarked, the first episode was 'not quite a situation comedy, certainly not a laugh show' and its humour was 'the wry Jewish sort, its story-telling ... as simple as strip cartoons.[8] The 'Hancock' series are language-driven. The situations are amusing enough but they are only vehicles to bring into interplay the very different registers of accent, tone and cultural reference of the bizarre inmates of 23 Railway Cuttings, East Cheam. The characters are their language, and scriptwriters Alan Galton and Ray Simpson intuited that mid-1950's Britain would embrace their cultured demotic as it had embraced the linguistic surrealism of 'The Goon Show'.

Episode 3 of 'East End, West End' and the radio episode of 'Hancock', which Roger Wilmut entitled 'The Publicity Photograph', contrast these two satirical approaches. The radio programme was broadcast half an hour before the television programme on the same evening, 18 February 1958. In Mankowitz's script, Sid James is dazzled by the selling techniques of his American colleague, Shaps Ginegar. 'Sell the sucker the story', says Shaps to Sid. 'The story is what they're buying.' Shaps proves his point. Everything he touches yields him a profit. But he wants his money to be gilded by breeding, so, much to Sid's disgust, he marries into the aristocracy. This is represented as a class of effete hangers-on, with names such as Lord Ffolliot, Lady Deadbeat and the Count from the Scrofula branch of the Monte Cristos, in the aptronymic tradition of classical satire. They live off Shaps's wealth until Sid suggests that Shaps lose his fortune by loaning it to the government of Perivania, an earthquake-stricken country in South America. But he prospers even here and is awarded its import monopoly for any products. Sid's wife, Donna, has meanwhile been following Shaps's social rise in the society columns and succeeds in getting Shaps and his wife, now the Princess of Perivania, to come to dinner. A gaggle of upper-class vultures also turns up, but Donna is happy with her social elevation and so is Sid, since the only meal they can offer them is hamburgers and potatoes.

The 'Hancock' episode also pivots, as does all English comedy, on cultural distinctions, but here it is Hancock whose dreams outrun reality and Sid who persuades him that he can make them come true. Miss Pugh (Hattie Jacques) and Sid decide that Hancock isn't getting work as an actor because his publicity photos are unflattering. Hancock says they're fine. Sid asks him who his photographer is. Hancock replies,

'Dufflecoat Charlie in Horseguards' Parade.'[9] Miss Pugh asks him where he does his developing. 'He borrows a guardsman's busby and does it under that', replies a nettled Hancock. Sid carts him off to Hilary St Clair (Kenneth Williams), who doesn't do 'snaps' but 'paints in pure light' and who finds Hancock a most unpromising subject.

However, when the photos come back, Hancock is delighted to see he has been transformed into a handsome, manly beachcomber. But Sid and Tub (Bill Kerr) now have to get the man to resemble the image, and there follows a regime of DIY makeover with bricks on his ears and a mud-pack from the garden, followed by plastic surgery at the hospital. When Miss Pugh sees the result she is ecstatic; her Anthony is more handsome than she ever knew a man could be. But Hancock fights her off: 'Don't start all that over again. Go and sit in the fridge.' Sid thinks his made-over client can command £10,000 a picture as Rock Hancock, but the American producer, Mr Guggenheimer, says public taste has changed, comedy is what is needed, and he wants to engage the little fat guy in goggles and flying-jacket on the wing of a Spitfire in an old publicity photograph. Sid says they'd better get back to the drawing board and 'get this boy unstitched'. 'Oh, me Grecian hooter' wails Hancock.

This is satire by riposte. The exchanges are swift and pointed. They are often cruel, as in the best satire. By 1958 the cast of secondary 'Hancock' characters was well established. Tub (Bill Kerr) was the thick Aussie, Miss Pugh the fat secretary and Kenneth Williams the flamboyant queen. Galton and Simpson's task was to devise situations where this eccentric 'family', as with all families, could stab each other to exhaustion. Then, like true actors, they can rise again for another round. The scripts are full of contemporary references. 'The Publicity Photograph' guys society photographers, whose status and scope were about to be extended by the rise of East Enders David Bailey and Terence Donovan. Hancock observes that he can't be a rock 'n' roll star because he's more than 12 years old, and when he answers the door with his mudpack still on, the milkman asks him if he's Harry Belafonte. Galton and Simpson give Hancock a line which is both in character and demonstrates the cultural mix of the period. Hilary St Clair wants his legs exposed for the beachcomber photograph. Sid tears off his trousers at the knee. 'Oh, well', sighs Hancock, 'so much for me clerical grey drainpipes.'

Galton and Simpson's next satirical vehicle would be 'Steptoe and Son', starring Harry H. Corbett and Wilfred Bramble as a lowbrow Vladimir and Estragon in their junkyard in Shepherd's Bush. The warring couple first appeared in a pilot episode as part of Galton and Simpson's 'Comedy Playhouse' on 5 January 1962. It was entitled 'The Offer', which reads now like their appropriation of Mankowitz territory for a new species of language-based London comedy.

Mankowitz's version of working-class Jewishness was also being contested by a new generation of playwrights. Harold Pinter's *The Birthday Party*, which ran for only eight performances at the Lyric in 1958, and Arnold Wesker's *Chicken Soup with Barley*, which also had a run of only eight performances at the Royal Court in the same year, had lukewarm, even hostile, critical receptions compared with the enthusiastic notices for *Expresso Bongo*. But by 1960 Wesker was the successful author of a trilogy of plays which dramatized the development and decline of socialist commitment in successive generations of a Jewish East End family; and Pinter's next full-length play, *The Caretaker*, transferred, after a month at the Arts Theatre, to a year-long run at the Duchess Theatre. They had arrived, and with their own versions of Yiddish, the East End and the British working class. Exchange, for them, was dialogic not commercial, so the art of their plays countered, and still counters, their commodification as product. Mankowitz expressed an interest in Wesker's work due, perhaps, to his own residual leftism and his father's socialist past. But the scrambling of cultural levels in the language of Pinter's characters and the menacing actions that this scrambling generates make Pinter more a contemporary of Galton and Simpson than of Wolf Mankowitz.

Bryan Cheyette analyses in some depth the character of Goldberg, the most Jewish character in Pinter's oeuvre, and fellow-thug to the Irishman McCann in *The Birthday Party*. They have come to Petey and Meg's seaside boarding house to remove their long-term guest Stanley for some undefined crime. Goldberg ingratiates himself with Meg by praising her running of the house and presenting himself as a gentleman of old-style courtesy. Cheyette details both his references to Jewish religion and to an idealized English past of Boots lending library and tea in Fullers. Cheyette calls these self-contradictions 'specious fabrications' which indicate 'a refusal to come to terms with the past' and a desire to create the two communities as flawless images of each other.[10]

It is a plausible analysis but over-solemn about Goldberg's aims and function within the play. Goldberg is a conman who, like a character in a Ben Jonson play, constructs himself through a farrago of cultural idioms. In Act I he praises his uncle Barney to McCann with an exuberance of random cliché:

> he was an impeccable dresser. One of the old school. He had a house just outside Basingstoke at the time. Respected by the whole community. Culture? Don't talk to me about culture. He was an all-round man, what do you mean? He was a cosmopolitan.'

This process reaches its climax in Goldberg's last, extended speech where he asks McCann to look into his mouth and then addresses the assembled company:

> All my life I've said the same. Play up, play up, and play the game. Honour thy father and thy mother. All along the line. Follow the line, the line, McCann, and you can't go wrong. What do you think, I'm a self-made man? No! I sat where I was told to sit. I kept my eye on the ball. School? Don't talk to me about school. Top in all subjects ...[11]

He continues in the same vein until he collapses into incoherence with a parody of the Old Testament's endless genealogies.

This is comedy, blacker than Hancock's, but generated by the same mishmash of cultural registers. Goldberg certainly isn't a self-made man. He is a man made by language, he is nothing more than language; but because that language is a collection of clichés he is finally speechless. Pinter's art lies in the selection and rhythmic positioning of those clichés and the contrast between them and Goldberg's sinister mission. Pinter's particular talent is always to charge with meaning the most banal of units in the language – the workaday verbs 'get' and 'have' underpin the ruthless battle for possession and ownership which is *The Homecoming* – and the silences between them. English departments in the 1970s got very excited about the 'linguistic turn' in philosophy and criticism which posited that meaning and existence were created in and through language. Pinter was there long before the professors.

By 1960, Mankowitz saw himself as neither a professor nor a Pinter. His break with Oscar Lewenstein in the summer of that year released him for a career, for the next few years, as producer/writer of musical theatre and as scriptwriter for the commercial film industry. He made it clear where his balance of culture now lay in an interview for the *Stage* in October, where he praised the theatre as a place of popular entertainment and star roles. 'I am in the theatre for entertainment', he said, 'to please as many people as possible, and not as an idealist.'[12] It is not surprising, therefore, to find him compèring an Associated Rediffusion TV tribute to the life and lyrics of Oscar Hammerstein, in the company of Prince Littler, Dennis Lotis and Edmund Hockridge.[13]

In the Davis interview he talks about his fascination with the technical challenges of musicals. The 'book' has far less wordage than a play, but creating a musical's collage, its mix of words, music and spectacle, demands great skill. 'It's like trying to get a daisy-chain of 100 people to come off simultaneously ... practically impossible but a remarkable explosion if you could do it.' He is far more critical of the constraints on the script-writer in that period. Straight narrative was demanded by directors and any experimentation with voice-overlays or strange intercutting or expressionist techniques was vetoed. But screenwriting, after all, is 'a service not an art'; the audience is there to be entertained, and the writer then 'was rather like a French letter, essential protection but completely disposable'. Writing for film, rather than the theatre, provoked the elitist in Mankowitz.

His break from Lewenstein, however, also cut him off from a symbiosis of theatre and film writing which created the most critically respected British cinema of the period. A brief notice in the *Tatler* for November 1960 gave details of Lewenstein's career at Glasgow Unity Theatre and the Royal Court and then announced that his first show after the split with Mankowitz was Keith Waterhouse and Willis Hall's stage hit *Billy Liar*, and that he was now a partner with John Osborne and Tony Richardson in stage and film companies.[14] The film company was Woodfall Films, formed by Osborne and Richardson to produce the film version of Osborne's *Look Back in Anger* (1959) and the production company for film versions in the early 1960s of, among others, *The Entertainer* (1960), *Saturday Night and Sunday Morning* and *A Taste of Honey* (both 1961) and *The Loneliness of the Long Distance Runner* (1962).

New Wave directors and actors such as Lindsay Anderson and Albert Finney switched back and forth between theatre and film in this period, between new scripts and adaptations of the classics. Richardson directed Osborne's screen adaptation of Henry Fielding's picaresque masterpiece *Tom Jones* (1963), with Finney in the title role, for a film which won four Academy Awards and, on the calculations of John Heilpern, made the present-day equivalent of $247.7 million on a budget of half a million pounds. Woodfall Films received 50 per cent of the film's profits, which made millionaires of Osborne, Richardson and Finney. Heilpern also notes that Lewenstein, the film's associate producer, 'received riches beyond belief' for a modest role in the film's production.[15]

Lewenstein had, in effect, stayed with his conviction, quoted earlier in relation to the *Evening Standard* Theatre Awards for 1959, that artistic success and commercial success were also compatible in the film industry, and that audiences would watch films with socially progressive content. Woodfall Films, along with other films such as *Room at the Top* (1958) and *This Sporting Life* (1963), bridged the gap between elite and popular cultures by, as Heilpern puts it, 'elevat[ing] working-class life from the sideshow of character parts to the centre of the action'. This life was not the dogged, rooted community of Hoggart and Williams; it was aggressive, satirical, individualistic and sexual. New Wave cinema would seem to be a cinema to which Mankowitz's temperament and scripting abilities were ideally suited.

He must, with his Royal Court and media associations, have known about the formation and direction of Woodfall films. He certainly knew the documentary work of Lindsay Anderson for the 'Free Cinema' movement and, in a 1959 talk for 'Comment' on the Third Programme, he makes sensible observations about the danger of middle-class film-makers, with their 'keen ear for authentic working-class vernacular and sweat-beads', producing a 'kind of nostalgia for the lumpen-proletariat which the Welfare State has made a class of the past'. He also notes that 'Free Cinema' was produced on a shoestring by amateurs and wonders how free its practitioners will be when they have to deal with finance and the unions in the arena of the commercial cinema. But he finishes with praise for Richardson and Anderson as theatre directors and for Jack Clayton as a cinema director of honesty and sincerity.

He focuses on Richardson's direction of *Look Back in Anger* for Woodfall in another 'Comment' report later the same year. Richard Burton is too masculine for the narcissistic Jimmy Porter of the stage play and the film version, because the women's characters have been more fleshed out, which skews the audience's sympathies more towards them than towards the men. Richardson cannot reproduce the effect of the stage play – 'the moving helplessness he made out of Osborne's words' – but he remains, for Mankowitz, a director of unflagging invention and stamina and an essential aid to and interpreter of Osborne's work.[16]

In the absence of documentary evidence we can only infer the reasons for Mankowitz's lack of interest in Woodfall films. In their biography of Laurence Harvey, Des Hickey and Gus Smith record Harvey's friendship with Mankowitz, based on what he conceived of as their common Lithuanian Jewish inheritance. When Harvey was being considered for the role of Joe Lampton in the film version of John Braine's Yorkshire novel *Room at the Top*, Mankowitz was approached by the director Jack Clayton to write the film script. But he declined. As a 'citizen of cosmopolitan London, [he] was out of sympathy with regional writing'.[17] His people were London dealers, not Northern workers. He would also, presumably, have been uninterested in scripting early Woodfall films set in Salford and the Midlands.

Osborne, Richardson and Lewenstein were also metropolitan figures, but their years of struggle at the Royal Court had created a collectivist, almost club-like mentality, which they transferred to their film company. Heilpern records that Osborne gave George Devine, Artistic Director at the Royal Court, a valuable share in the profits of *Tom Jones*, even though Devine had played no part in the production. 'It would make nothing but sense', wrote Osborne, 'and no one need know except us.'[18]

Lindsay Anderson, who directed *Billy Liar*, set in the North of England, also catches this spirit of a common endeavour in a diary entry for 1 January 1961. Anderson, only a year older than Mankowitz and with an upbringing of colonial India, Cheltenham and Oxford, sees himself as part of this Royal Court group and muses about the film he'd like to make 'about all this, all of us, and the problems and meanings of our lives now – of Karel (Reisz) and Albie (Finney) and Zoe (Caldwell) and Jill (Bennett) and Willis (Hall) and Oscar (Lewenstein) and where we are going, and the aspirations and the egoism and the unhappiness'.[19] This group was an unstable mix of generations and backgrounds but for Anderson, an arch individualist and loner, it represented an artistic home.

Mankowitz, however, was by now (1960) determined to prove his individualism by way of independent theatre and film production in the commercial sector, and to deploy his artistic talents in screenwriting. It is unusual for one person to combine two such diverse functions, and almost impossible for them to be combined successfully. It is as if, in the actual practice of production, Mankowitz is determined to succeed where so many of his fictional creations fail. But he had no significant success with his productions of Shelagh Delaney's second play, *The Lion in Love* (in late 1960), nor with Jack Ronder's *This Year, Next Year* (a six-week run from 20 October at the Vaudeville), also in late 1960, and, as we shall see, his 1961 production of the musical *Belle*, for which he also wrote the 'book', was panned by the critics.

This Year, Next Year could, however, be said to have produced Mankowitz himself. The central chapters of the novel *First Act* by Anne

Christie, Jack Ronder's wife, are a fictionalized account, through the first-person narrative of Kate Mandel, of the trials and tribulations of her husband's play, here renamed *Personal*, as it makes its way from Edinburgh down to Manchester and then London's West End. Chapter 24 contains an incisively ironic account of a press conference before the play's Manchester opening. Mankowitz appears as Abe Bramstein, an ebullient impresario who is also noted for his antiques business, luxurious offices and boundless energy. He is first described by Pete, one of Kate's fellow-students at art college in Edinburgh, as a big, fat man with a very cruel face who appears on telly panel games about antiques; but Kate finds him charming and generous although she, like her husband Ben, disagrees with Bramstein's decision to upgrade the play's class-setting from lower middle-class Edinburgh to middle-class Home Counties.

The play, like Bramstein's sister-production, an unnamed second play by the Manchester writer Mary O'Donovan, has a short run. The young couple are happy enough with their first London production, but Bramstein has, 'as he succinctly put it, all but lost his balls with his two flops, so he didn't intend to be an impresario for some time to come'. He has admired an African mask that Kate rescued and reconstructed and made her several offers for it, but she doesn't want to sell. Nonetheless, Abe concludes: 'Ethnic sculptures are more secure than theatre management.'[20]

Mankowitz's screenwriting, however, contributed to the success in this period of two very different films, *The Millionairess* (premiere 20 October 1960) and *The Long and the Short and the Tall* (premiere 16 February 1961), and played a significant part in the hostile critical reception to his third film of this period, *The Two Faces of Dr Jekyll* (premiere 7 October 1960). Their range of genres – romantic comedy, war movie and horror – exemplifies the versatility demanded of a scriptwriter in the open market, and their directors (Anthony Asquith, Leslie Norman and Terence Fisher) read like a paradigm of highbrow, middlebrow and lowbrow taste in British cinema of the period. All three were adaptations, the first two from plays by, respectively, George Bernard Shaw and Willis Hall, the third a virtual rewrite of Robert Louis Stevenson's famous novella. Mankowitz, although sharing screenplay credits with two other writers, Frederic Gotfurt and T.J. Morrison, is certainly the principal writer for *The Long and the Short and the Tall* and thereby could be said to continue his association with the Royal Court where Lewenstein/Mankowitz productions had mounted the very successful stage play. Mankowitz's mark, however, is clearly stamped on *The Millionairess*, with invented cameos for Alfie Bass and Miriam Karlin, some Shavian-type epigrams, and a running debate between bureaucratic modernity and humanized community.

The film also played a part in Mankowitz's first venture into film production. It starred Sophia Loren as Epifania Parerga, the headstrong inheritor of her father's fortune, and Peter Sellers as Dr Ahmed El Kabir, an Indian doctor who works selflessly for the London poor. It was Mankowitz, as quoted in Roger Lewis's biography of Sellers, who suggested that Loren and Sellers co-star in a version of Shaw's play, and who negotiated a contract with the producer Anatole de Grunwald of £37,500 for Sellers's performance and £12,500 for Mankowitz's screenplay.[21] This put Sellers, for the first time, in the international league of star earners. But Mankowitz had a larger vision for Sellers and himself. He wanted them to be joint partners in a production company, Sellers Mankowitz Productions Ltd, modelled on the early United Artists Company whose stars made and distributed their own films. Actors from the new generation – another Sellers biography names them as Peter O'Toole, Albert Finney, Sean Connery and Diane Cilento[22] – would be associated with the company, and in the Memorandum of Association, dated 22 April 1960, just a month before shooting began on *The Millionairess*, the company's first productions were mooted: adaptations of Frederic Raphael's novel *Memoirs of a Cross-Eyed Man*, and Mankowitz's *My Old Man's a Dustman*.

Mankowitz also negotiated a deal with American backers and distributors, Continental Distributing Inc., but at this point Sellers withdrew from the partnership with Mankowitz, citing investment costs and his desire to concentrate on his career as an actor. Lewis cites a 'Counsel's Opinion' which suggests that the Sellers-Mankowitz Company become a holding company for project development by either or both of the parties' independent companies. Mankowitz was angry and astounded at Sellers's withdrawal from their joint agreement and approached any future collaboration with great caution. He considered Sellers professionally unreliable and emotionally unstable, especially since, during the shooting of *The Millionairess*, Sellers had confided to him that he had fallen in love with Loren and that he was sure she had fallen in love with him. Mankowitz, who knew how deep the attachment was between Loren and her lover, Carlo Ponti, ridiculed the idea, but Sellers persisted and Mankowitz dated his megalomania from this time.

Lewis is harsh on Sellers's break-up with Mankowitz, calling it spiteful, jealous and arbitrary, but there is some truth in Sellers's assertion that Mankowitz was trying to fulfil too many roles at the same time. Sellers thought he should concentrate 'more on one thing, like screen-writing, and leave the impresario business alone'. Mankowitz would seem to have agreed. In a letter of 22 September 1960, to the head of Continental Distributing Inc., he recounts and apologizes for the dissolution of the partnership with Sellers, then adds: 'I fear that I lack some finally essential quality necessary to a producer. I don't know that I mind not having it.' Production had, again, proved hazardous for him.

Mankowitz certainly showed his skills as a professional scriptwriter with *The Millionairess*. He focussed much more than did Shaw's play of 1936 on the conflict between Epifania's relentless production of profit and Dr Kabir's selfless service to the underprivileged. He wrote in scenes where London's polyglot poor – of many nationalities – crowd the doctor's surgery, a run-down building on London's Thameside. The patients are another version of Mankowitz's 'little people', as is Alfie Bass as a kipper-curer in another invented scene. He allows Epifania to use his riverside hut to dry out her clothes after she has been consoled by Dr Kabir after her suicide attempt. As one of the most voluptuous bodies in post-war cinema gradually undresses behind a flimsy screen, Alfie Bass continues an imperturbable account of his unique process – 'a smoking mixture which gives them the quality and flavour of the best smoked salmon' – for curing kippers.

Shaw's Epifania has inherited from her father not only money but also the faculty to see how money can be made. In Act III she reorganizes the finances of a sweatshop in the East End, bypassing the distributors of the finished garments and offering a slice of the profits to the delivery man, whom she has deliver directly to the retailer. Epifania manages opportunity. In Mankowitz's version the garment business becomes a pasta business. Epifania has its management (Vittorio de Sica as Joe and Miriam Karlin as his wife Maria) invest in modern machinery which raises productivity, which enables them to raise the workers' wages. The wage-incentive will produce still greater productivity which, as Epifania points out, will enable management to reduce the work-force.

Joe is unhappy with this modernization. He misses the informal camaraderie between boss and female workers. But this Epifania has a relentless drive for efficiency. She is a modernizing manager. She is accordingly impatient with the human scale of Dr Kabir's surgery. She buys up the leases of all the buildings in its block, has it demolished, and builds a large, glass block of a hospital, equipped with the most advanced medical technology. She offers it to Kabir as proof of her love for him, but Kabir is as confused and repelled as his patients by its inhuman size and impersonal processing.

Sellers had starred the previous year in *The Battle of the Sexes*, where his Edinburgh tweed-maker's accountant had been driven to try and kill the female American time-and-motion expert, hired to update the firm's archaic practices. But London afforded Asquith and director of photography Jack Hildyard a far bigger stage on which to contrast soaring buildings of shining glass and plastic with humble rooms with scuffed green paint and patients jammed side by side on rickety chairs. The film's plot ends with the unlikely mating of business (Loren) with idealism (Sellers), a version of the 'modernising of Britain' debate, which had begun in the late 1950s and would be propelled forward with the Labour victory of 1964. But it is clear that the sympathies of Asquith and Mankowitz lie with the human-scale perspectives of Kabir and Joe. Shaw's pre-war play was another version of his perennial juggling of the relationship between morality and money. Mankowitz's version dramatizes a dominant post-war concern, human alienation.

The popular press was enchanted by the Loren-Sellers partnership. For Harold Conway, Loren was a sexy comedienne, in and out of her Balmain dresses and skirts. Sellers counterpointed her exuberance with a restrained performance 'quiet, sing-song voiced, whimsically reducing riches to mockery'. For Alexander Walker, writing for the *Nottingham Journal*, this was the best film of a Bernard Shaw play since 'Pygmalion', and Anthony Asquith's refurbishment of the play 'fizzes with effrontery and dances a jig with absurdity'. Regan Redbarn of the *Record Show Mirror* found the film 'gay and witty [with] the benefit of an intelligent script drawn from a play by a great writer' and F. Maurice Speed, for *What's On*, was impressed by a superb supporting cast including Alastair Sim as the lady's lawyer Sagamore, and Dennis Price who 'contributes a deft, satirical cameo as a psychiatrist'. The verdict of the trade-press *Kinematograph Weekly* (20 October 1960) was the characters' antics 'stimulate the imagination and give audiences plenty to read between the lines', and Elspeth Grant, writing for the upmarket magazine *Tatler*, praised Mankowitz's screenplay, Loren's performance as a 'goddess, by Mammon out of Venus' and Sellers's ability to make the line 'I have fallen in love with your pulse' sound like exquisite poetry.[23]

The quality press was more circumspect and more inclined to praise Sellers than Loren. For C.A. Lejeune, the *Observer*'s doyenne film critic,

Loren's performance could not match those of Edith Evans and Katharine Hepburn in the stage play. She had a film presence, but not the skill to interpret a Shavian woman. The quiet authority of Sellers, however, marked him out as a Shavian, even a Shakespearean actor. For the *Guardian*'s film critic, Loren did well in her familiar hyperbolic style, but Sellers turned in 'a really remarkable character study' which gave some cohesion to a film that did not 'add up to a cogent unity'. Dilys Powell in the *Sunday Times* was ecstatic over Sellers's mimesis of the Indian doctor – 'the gesture of the whole body has an alien composure' – but found that Loren, for all her elegance, lacked comic authority and the overbearing self-confidence that was the mainspring of Shaw's character. The *New Statesman*'s critic was impressed by Sellers's Dr Kabir, 'one of his most brilliant impersonations', but unimpressed by Loren, whose lure and skill were largely wasted, and by the film as a whole – 'too vague, pointless, and episodic to be the romp it is meant to be'. The reviewer for the *Queen* was vitriolic, largely because the film's representation of wealth was corny and perfunctory and Mankowitz's screenplay had concentrated on the superficial whimsy of Shaw's play. Not even Sellers's touching performance could save it.[24]

New York and Washington critics also favoured Sellers over Loren. Archer Winsten of the *New York Post* thought Sellers did 'more than one would think possible to one of his British facility', but regretted that Shaw's arguments had been lost with Asquith's emphasis on Loren's looks and outfits: 'A play of ideas has been laced with high fashion modelled by Sophia Loren.' *Time*'s reviewer dismissed Loren with a quip – '[she] puts her breast a foot forward' – but considered Sellers a true actor, 'not a professional show-off who attracts attention to what he is doing, but an artist who reveals what he is'. The hugely influential Bosley Crowther of the *New York Times* characterized Loren's performance as that of a wily vamp whose elegant posturing only distracted from the Shavian arguments about money and happiness, and whose Neapolitan accent obscured the lines of a play which was 'inferior material supplemented with some equally inferior material conceived by Wolf Mankowitz'.

Variety New York was kinder to Loren, a fascinating, predatory figure of many moods, and well-matched by Sellers' convincing character-study of an Indian doctor and Alastair Sim's unctuous, scheming lawyer. But Richard Coe's review for the *Washington Post* damned the film entirely. It had jettisoned Shaw's original point about money-making being only destructive of the State, and substituted Loren in

100 gowns by Balmain and a syrupy True Love ending. He concluded that 'even with a halfway good thing, those idiot movie-makers (British) didn't have a clue what to do with it. Stay away.' The public did and the film had very poor takings in the US.[25]

* * *

Alexander Walker concluded his positive review of *The Millionairess* by referring back to his 'atrocity report' on Mankowitz's script for *The Two Faces of Dr Jekyll*, a Hammer Film directed by Terence Fisher and produced by Michael Carreras, which had opened some two weeks before, on 7 October, at the London Pavilion. In Mankowitz's version of Stevenson's minor classic, Mr Hyde (Paul Massie) becomes an amoral, debonair, man about town, who samples the fleshpots of London in the company of Paul Allen (Christopher Lee), a languid wastrel and the lover of Dr Jekyll's bored, promiscuous wife, Kitty (Dawn Addams). Neither of these characters appears in Stevenson's novella; nor does Mr Hyde's mistress, Maria (Norma Marla), an exotic snake-dancer in The Sphinx, a West End nightclub. They are all, however, murdered by the elegant Mr Hyde, who thus revenges himself on his unfaithful wife and her lover, and exercises a kind of Nietszchean power over his mistress. For Walker, these injections of sex into Stevenson's austere narrative were simply an exercise in sadistic titillation and an adaptation to the Hammer norms of blood and female masochism. Mankowitz's screenplay was, he concluded, 'preposterous, unpleasant and pretentious'.[26]

A majority of Walker's fellow-critics in the popular press agreed with him. For Paul Dehn of the *News Chronicle*, Mankowitz's script 'has not a wisp either of moral wisdom or literary distinction'; for Harold Conway of the *Daily Sketch*, Paul Massie is debonair and demonic but Mankowitz spoils everything by 'the introduction of sex at its silliest'; for Dick Richards of the *Daily Mirror*, the film is reasonable escapist stuff, not an exposé of Victorian moral hypocrisy, but full of 'enough murder, seduction and sadism to justify the censor's profitable "X" certificate'.[27] The quality press was equally uncomplimentary. The critic of *The Times* saw a film which 'works itself into a state of artificial and unconvincing violence' and the *Daily Telegraph*'s critic had praise for Paul Massie's performance in a film that was, however, intentionally 'unpleasant and tasteless'.[28]

Independent magazines were more charitable. The critic of the

Illustrated London News compared Massie favourably with five previous actors in the role and considered his virtuosity a saving grace in otherwise absurd scenes of 'decadence' in nightclubs and bedrooms. Elspeth Grant, for *Tatler*, congratulated the writing and production team on an 'adult and subtle presentation of Hyde as a handsome young man, whose beastliness is all within'; and the *Jewish Chronicle* praised Mankowitz's original treatment of Stevenson's story as well as Jack Asher's staging and photography of Victorian London, and David Kossoff's portrayal of Litauer, Dr Jekyll's kindly medical colleague.[29] The negative reviews did not prevent a degree of box-office success. *Kinematograph Weekly* reported that by the end of October the film had grossed the highest Saturday takings for a film premiere at the London Pavilion.[30]

Mankowitz would have been pleased by these takings, as he was pleased by the £5,000 Hammer paid him for the script which was 'more than twice what Hammer was used to paying to the likes of Jimmy Sangster to write *Dracula*'.[31] He sent a sardonic telegram to Alexander Walker at the *Evening Standard*, wondering why the critic hadn't blamed him, in addition to everything else, for the colour quality of the film, but he would not have been surprised that his mix of elite and popular cultures aroused critical hostility on both sides of the fence. His injection of sex into Stevenson's sombre morality tale – though it had precedents in nineteenth-century music-hall productions – would also provoke the deep-seated prurience of the British press.

Cultural boundaries are now more indistinct than in 1960. The history and ideology of Hammer Films has been the subject of several academic studies and the sex in their films has been subsumed into larger studies of sexuality in film. Andrew Spicer's study of masculinity in British film has a brief section on *The Two Faces of Dr Jekyll* where he quotes Mankowitz's desire to make evil attractive and to write not a horror film, but a psychological thriller which would be a comment on the two-facedness of respectable society. Spicer is unconvinced: 'this modern ambiguity fails to work because there is no counterpoint to Hyde's corruption'. We are led on an interesting journey round London's underworld of boxing clubs and opium dens but in the end 'it matters little what Hyde or anyone else does'.[32]

Jonathan Rigby, in his comprehensive study of horror cinema, devotes several pages to the film. He finds the rape of Kitty and the murder of the mistress Maria (in Kitty's bed) a 'cinematic splurge of misogynist violence', but he admires Mankowitz's dialogue, particularly for the way in which it accurately characterizes Christopher Lee's Paul Allen as 'the perfect embodiment of the "superfluous man" in Victorian society', a sponger who talks all the time about his 'honour'. Rigby also praises the design and photography work of Bernard Robinson and Jack Ashe. They 'smother Kitty's bedroom in cold tones of blue while staining Maria's boudoir blood red' and then have the two colours collide 'in an opium den wreathed in blue smoke, but lit in one corner by a hellish crimson'.[33]

The most extended reappraisal of the film, however, is by Denis Meikle in the *Little Shoppe of Horrors* article cited above. He details the battles and concessions over sex scenes and strong language between producer Michael Carreras and, in England, the Board of British Film Censors and, in America, the distributors Columbia Pictures. Columbia, in fact, sold the film on to American-International, who gave it a new title, *Jekyll's Inferno*. This version received a 'B' rating from the Catholic Legion of Decency so it was then cut back to eighty minutes, retitled *House of Fright* and finally released in the USA on 3 May 1961 – that is, almost sixteen months after what the producer and director (Terence Fisher) thought was the conclusion of the film's principal photography.

These were the years of the *Lady Chatterley* trial and the contestations of authorized literary language being made by such American writers as Alan Ginsberg and William Burroughs. Mankowitz was well aware that Anglo-American culture was at a moral turning point. 'We were on the edge of a sexual explosion', Meikle quotes him as saying, 'and I wanted to go as far as possible in this film. I wanted to have very convincing bordello sequences – I wanted the whores to be like whores.'[34] Michael Carreras agreed. He didn't want the film's characters to be black and white. He approved of the moral ambivalence Mankowitz created by making Hyde a glamorous man about town.

Meikle acknowledges the film's faults – its garish make-up, Massie's wooden acting, its stagey, artificial look – but he argues that in the end Mankowitz and Hammer films was a clash of irreconcilable opposites. The morality of Hammer movies was a simple opposition between good and evil. Dialogue was functional and budgets were tight. Mankowitz, in Meikle's account was seen, in 1960, as a man of many and prodigious talents, 'one of the foremost intellectuals of his day', and a screenwriter of a calibre far above the usual Hammer journeyman. Mankowitz, in a statement that sounds like another attempt to link East and West End, says that his script tried to 'utilise the whole of the London scene as described by the contemporary writers about London'. He later describes his mode of thinking as dialectical and Freudian and interprets Jekyll as 'Victorian bourgeois society – his disorders are not just his personal disorders, they reflect a whole disordered materialism in that society'. *The Two Faces of Dr Jekyll* were the faces of two opposite cultural styles – 'highbrow concept, lowbrow execution' as Meikle says – and the film can be read as another attempt by Mankowitz to balance his two-way pull between populism and elitism as well as an opportunity to dramatize the most extreme of personality exchanges.

Mankowitz's film-script changes to Willis Hall's original play-text of *The Long and the Short and the Tall* are chiefly dictated by the differences between stage and filmic conventions. The dramatic situation is the same in both versions. A patrol of British soldiers, far from base in the Malayan jungle during the campaign against the Japanese in the Second World War, capture a Japanese soldier and have to decide whether or not to execute him when they attempt to break through an encircling ring of enemy troops. The patrol is a cross section of men from all parts of the United Kingdom and all classes. Bickering and dissent are fanned throughout by Private Bamforth, played by Laurence Harvey, the archetypal barrack-room lawyer and foul-mouthed East Ender, who proves, however, to be the only defender of Tojo, the Japanese prisoner. In the end, Tojo is accidentally shot by the radio operator Private Whitaker (David McCallum) who dies in his turn as the Japanese move in and wipe out the patrol. Only Corporal Johnstone (Richard Harris) is left standing as he staggers across the clearing towards the Japanese with his white flag aloft.

Where the stage action was confined to a hut in a clearing, Mankowitz opens out the action to include fording a dangerous stream, jungle manoeuvres against the Japanese, and herding a line of pack-mules through the jungle. They are carrying heavy sonic equipment whose signals are intended to deceive the enemy as to the true position of the main body of the army. The ruse – Mankowitz's invention for the screenplay – doesn't work and it is the Japanese who communicate with the patrol through a series of eerie messages in broken English, warning them that they are coming to kill them. Mankowitz throughout reduces many expository passages in the play to brief statements of information,[35] and, together with director Leslie Norman and director of photography Erwin Hillier, devises an iconic death for Bamforth.

He is buried under a fall of rock but an arm, straight and strong and grasping his rifle, thrusts defiantly out of the debris.

The balance of critical opinion was in favour of the film. While both the quality and the popular press had their criticisms of the studio-set for the external shots of the jungle and questioned the success of this film adaptation of a stage play, Laurence Harvey's performance as Bamforth was judged a character success and the moral ambiguity of the original was seen to be retained in the film. Dominic Le Foe, writing in *John O'London's Weekly*, thought the plot 'had more genuine and spirited arguments than would be read in a dozen tracts' and the *Guardian*'s critic concluded that it was because of its horrid events and brutal language that this was one of the better war films, although 'it might have been better had it stuck closer to the play'. C.A. Lejeune, writing in *Films and Filming*, admitted that the war was not her favourite topic but she had found, in this dramatization of it, 'dignity, humanity, and utter honesty and under the rough exterior a very tender heart'.

The trade press was enthusiastic, with the *Daily Cinema*'s critic declaring that 'No British film has ever punched over the message that war is a shoddy, demoralising, despicable business so tellingly' and *Kinematograph Weekly* summing up the film as 'a "Journey's End" of the jungle [which] will grip all classes and both sexes'.[36] Mankowitz's script was not universally praised but he had, at the very least, done a workmanlike job for a film that was almost the last, and certainly the most sardonic, of that very popular post-war genre, the war movie.

Mankowitz's second important film script performed in 1961 was his contribution to *The Day the Earth Caught Fire*, a sci-fi movie of considerable depth and subtlety which was produced, directed and part-written by Val Guest. It opened in late November 1961 and was a box-office success on both sides of the Atlantic. The plot proposes that simultaneous nuclear explosions by the USA and USSR have tilted the earth off its axis so that it is heading for collision with the sun. The consequent meteorological changes are disastrous for the planet, with London – the principal setting for the movie – suffering rapid and intolerable shifts from rain to sweltering heat to fog to hurricane.

The nuclear issue, as I.Q. Hunter points out in an article-length analysis of the film, was much debated at the time, with 100 nuclear tests by all countries recorded in 1958, and Bertrand Russell and other members of the anti-nuclear Committee of 100 arrested two months before the film's release.[37] Footage of a CND meeting in Trafalgar

Square is included in the film and – another contemporary touch – beatniks parade through Chelsea, headed up by a jazz band, then overturn cars and invade the flat of Jeannie Craig (played by Janet Munro) before being turfed out by her lover, *Daily Express* journalist Peter Stenning (Edward Judd). Jeannie, a telephonist with access to government information, has been Stenning's source for the nuclear explosions.

Hunter reads the beatnik scene as indicative not just of riotous, irresponsible youth, but of a youth that has lost all faith in society's leaders. But, in the context of Mankowitz's film-writing, it reads as a development of the rock 'n'roll scenes in *A Kid for Two Farthings*. There the music signalled a working-class possession of the street; here the music signals a countercultural Bohemianism, a riposte to traditional upper-class English restraint in a time of national emergency. A jazz parade through the stricken streets 'is a sign, first, that consensus is over, and, second, that the national self-image is frayed and unravelling'.[38]

It is difficult, however, to decide whether Guest or Mankowitz should take credit for the central idea of the film. Guest is quite clear that he had been obsessed with making it for seven or eight years until, with the help of Michael Balcon, he was able to finance it. He used as collateral the considerable profits from *Expresso Bongo*, and engaged Mankowitz as scriptwriter whom he calls, in interview, 'a writer with *bite*; he will churn you out twenty pages which you can whittle down to three *brilliant* pages' (italics in the original). [39] He expands on this account in his autobiography, describing how he cornered Mankowitz in his Wedgwood office in Piccadilly and persuaded him to script the film: 'he signed the swiftest contract he'd ever signed and worked the longest hours he'd ever worked ... until we had completed our second lucky screenplay together'.[40]

Mankowitz, however, in the Davis interview, recalls that the idea came to him in a flash, of Russia and America letting off something in the upper atmosphere which would throw the earth off course and cause the earth's temperature to increase rapidly: 'I put the idea to Val Guest and we developed it and I wrote the script and he wrote the scenario, the shooting-script ... and the whole operation took us, I think, three weeks to write.' Hunter confirms this as their probable division of labour when he says that Mankowitz 'appears to have contributed the dialogue and details of the journalistic milieu'.[41]

Guest had begun his career as a film journalist so it seems likely that it was his idea to structure his film as an extended flashback focussed through journalist Peter Stenning. The film begins with him in the deserted newsroom of the *Daily Express*, dictating a last story on the future of mankind. He does not yet know of the success or failure of a desperate plan, agreed by all nations, to restore the earth's axis by simultaneously exploding four nuclear bombs. Then follows the main story, or rather several main stories, since the film, as Hunter observes, is a narrative hybrid of several genres: 'the disaster epic with romantic melodrama and the social problem film'.[42] At the end the *Express* has prepared two front pages, one with a 'World Doomed' headline and the other with 'World Saved'. With the last shots panning up to St Paul's and bells ringing over the final credits, the implication is that the world has been saved – largely thanks to the *Daily Express*, as several reviewers for other publications acidly remarked.

But Mankowitz also had his interest in popular journalism. He contributed short stories, articles and reviews to a range of newspapers throughout the 1950s. He would dedicate *The Blue Arabian Nights*, a collection of such work published in 1973, to Charles Wintour, editor of the *Evening Standard*, then part of the Beaverbrook Press, which also published the *Daily Express*. Mankowitz was not a professional journalist but he enjoyed being part of the news-making process, just as he enjoyed being part of the news itself. It is not surprising, therefore, to find that the sub-story, as it were, to the apocalypse of the film is the production process of the news about it. We are shown every stage of the story, from Jeannie's leak to Stenning, through editorial conferences about it, Stenning's attempts at official verification, the writing and printing of the story and its distribution to all parts of London by the *Express*'s famous delivery vans.

We are even shown the picture library and how it operates when Jeannie, sacked from her government post, is given a job there on the instructions of Stenning's cynical but sentimental colleague, Bill McGuire, superbly played by Leo McKern. Production is, as we have seen, a precarious concept for Mankowitz at this stage in his career, and the two alternative headlines at the end of the film could be read as an expression of his unease. Val Guest had no doubts. He had produced, directed and co-scripted a film which was a commercial success and was awarded a joint prize, along with *A Taste of Honey*, for Best British Screenplay of 1961 by the British Film Academy in 1962.

The critics endorsed, with reservations, the public. *The Times* was caustic about Arthur Christiansen, ex-editor of the *Express*, playing the editor in the film, but praised Leo McKern's performance and pronounced that 'script and direction make the film a good example of its kind'. The *Guardian* found the film 'remarkable for its realism and the tireless, exhausting quality of its machine-gun dialogue'. The *Observer*'s Penelope Gilliat, after noting the 'giggling viciousness' of the beatniks and the accurate presentation of the 'Fleet St. creep' with his relentless flippancy, suggested that the film's scriptwriters had engineered an unholy thematic alliance between the ethics of nuclear fission and 'the shiftier aspects of popular newspaper ethics'. *Tribune* called the film a 'glorification of the popular press' which perpetuated the values of the *Daily Express*, but the *New Statesman*'s John Coleman found the film a 'rich and plausible Science Fiction idea' which had been doused in a 'bucketful of Fleet St ethics'. Coleman added that the script carried Mankowitz's 'characteristic flavour of schmaltz-and-bitters'.[43]

Between his film-script successes of 1961, however, Mankowitz had suffered his most disastrous failure in the theatre with his production of *Belle or the Ballad of Dr Crippen*. He and Monty Norman, like John Osborne and Joan Littlewood, wanted to make a musical which would draw on the traditions of the great music-hall era in Britain of the late nineteenth and early twentieth centuries. The provocation lay in making the principal figure one of the most notorious murderers in British history. The music and lyrics were by Monty Norman and the 'book' was adapted by Mankowitz from a play by Beverley Cross. Val May directed and Loudon Sainthill designed the set. The play opened on 4 May 1961 at the Strand Theatre. It was subtitled 'A Music Hall Musical' and the whole action of Crippen's (George Benson) affair with his secretary Ethel le Neve (Virginia Vernon), the poisoning of his mediocre actress wife Belle Elmore (Rose Hill), the flight by ship across the Atlantic and Crippen's identity and arrest through a Morse code message was played as a series of music-hall 'turns' by vaudeville artists, as if recreating the old Bedford Theatre in Camden about 1910.

Mankowitz was thus attempting to dramatize his fascination with the theatricality of theatre in a popular cultural form. George Lasher (Jerry Desmonde) and Mighty Mick (Davy Kaye) introduce the turns with the wisecracking of the period; the poisoning of Belle is a farce and maybe unintentional; and the Morse code arrest provokes the best sing in the show, 'The Dit Dit Song' (later recorded by Tommy Steel) where the lovers tap out with their handcuffs on the railing of the ship 'I Love You' in Morse code.

This was also another London-centred work by East Enders

Mankowitz and Norman. *Make Me an Offer* was devised in the East End, moved to the West End and its main action took place on the Portobello Road. *Belle* is set in Camden but it is the centre of the West End that is lovingly itemized as a playground where toffs and poor theatricals can mingle. Jenny (Nicolette Roeg), a Vesta Tilley figure, Belle and the music-hall chorus take us round the West End of a poor actor's night out:

> On a toff's night out
> Then you'll soon know what London town
> Is all about ...
> The Gaiety the Tivoli the
> Empire the Criterion ...[44]

Belle finishes with a company chorus to the criminal heroes of England which counterpoints the earlier traditional music-hall paean to traditional heroes such as Drake and Britannia. The criminal heroes include Captain Kidd, Dick Turpin, Guy Fawkes, Sweeney Todd, Jack the Ripper and ... Dr Crippen. The Finale, sung by Crippen and the Ladies, is 'You Can't Beat a British Crime'.

Mankowitz and Norman's provocation was deliberate and should be read in the context of the then anti-Establishment satire of *Beyond the Fringe*, which opened in London in the same month as *Belle*, 'The Goon Show' and *Private Eye* (first issue at the end of October 1961). The critics took up the challenge. Not all the notices were unfavourable. Fergus Cashin for the *Daily Sketch* considered it 'the most delightful, bawdy, wonderful, amoral, immoral, indecent, sweetest and naughtiest love story ever told' and *The Times* found gaiety, the burlesque and pathos skilfully intermingled. T.C. Worsley for the *Financial Times*, despite criticizing the awkward mixture of moods, did register the audience's great enjoyment and praised the work's ingenuity and native spirit. R.B. Marriott for the *Stage and Television Today* admired the skill and pastiche of the book and lyrics, and the *Punch* critic praised the performance of George Benson as Crippen and the ingenious set of Loudon Sainthill. Nathaniel Field for the *Sunday Express* used the poor critical reception of the musical to castigate the critics for advocating Wesker and Ionesco instead of rejoicing, like the opening-night audience for *Belle*, in a music-hall succession from sentimental tears to melodrama to slapstick.[45]

But the majority of critics, led by Bernard Levin of the *Daily Express* and Robert Muller of the *Daily Mail*, damned the musical for poor taste, uninspiring lyrics and uninspired music. Felix Barker for the *Evening News* summed up the poor taste case: 'Quite simply murder is not funny and real people alive or dead (and remember Miss le Neve is said to be still living) should not be guyed on stage.' Richard Findlater, a champion of Mankowitz from the start of his career, criticized the musical's 'fundamental failure to mix the artificial and the real, the sweet and the sour' and the feebleness of the lyrics and the dialogue. For the *Observer*'s critic, the musical was 'aurally an embarrassment', although Sainthill's set was 'the very ecstasy of Victoriana'; for J.C. Trewin, writing for *Illustrated London News*, the story was absurd, the comedy embarrassing and 'as music-hall pastiche it is not noticeably expert'.

The headline to Robert Muller's review was 'A sick joke with music but dismally flat' and he went on to castigate the occasion as one where 'Boisterous music-hall numbers were interspersed with naturalistic plot scenes played straight and falling dismally flat.' Davy Kaye, as Mighty Mick, 'revived our sagging spirits with a round dozen burlesqued appearances', but a final critique of the decor as 'straightforward Music-Hall-Ugly' completed his demolition of the play. Bernard Levin also found the musical flat, 'with the sad flatness of flat champagne', and it 'peters out in a penultimate scene of shattering vulgarity', a vulgarity maintained throughout by a chorus which 'relentlessly shows so much thigh that I was eventually constrained to murmur "Thigh no more, ladies." '[46]

Mankowitz, always pugnacious, hit back. He addressed the audience from the stage after the show and after this critical onslaught. He encouraged them to ignore the critics and encourage their friends to attend. It was one of those periodic spats between writers and critics in the theatre. As audiences fell away he took the battle to the enemy camp. The *Evening Standard* for 9 May reported that earlier that day six girls in *Belle* costumes, escorted by Mankowitz, had carried a pinewood coffin down Fleet Street and into the lobby of the *Daily Express* building. Two notices were on top of the coffin. One read: 'Dear Bernie. This is your size, not mine. Signed Wolfie.' The other said: 'To Bernard Levin. With best wishes from the Belle company.' On the back was a label saying: 'Please return the empties.' Mankowitz said in interview: 'This is the moment we have all been waiting for. To send a midget coffin for a midget critic.' Levin, when informed of the coffin's delivery, remarked: 'Send not to ask for whom the bell tolls.' Despite these metropolitan theatrics, *Belle* closed a month later on 10

July, although it had a brief, truncated revival as a forty-five-minute production for ATV's 'Big Night Out' series on 12 August of the same year. Mankowitz's musical had run for six weeks and cost him and his backers £20,000. This wasn't a favourable exchange for a man who valued exchange so much.

Adrian Wright's recent detailed survey of the post-war British musical, however, offers a revisionist account of *Belle*. He suggests that local factors, such as the discovery that Ethel le Neve was still living and the current debate about the death penalty for murder, obscured such merits of the musical as Monty Norman's wide range of musical modes, from heartfelt sentiment to Edwardian parody, and Mankowitz's use of self-reflexive theatre. The result is a 'mix of melodrama, history, music hall jokes and murder' which was unique in the popular theatre of the past and the present. The musical was also unique in the writing careers of Norman and Mankowitz. Neither they, nor anyone else, wrote anything prior to or after *Belle* which equalled this 'strange conflagration of affection and satire, cruelty and love, this anarchic distortion of history, this effrontery'. Wright's final, sardonic, note is that Mankowitz would have been interested to learn that 'in 2009 DNA evidence suggested that Crippen was innocent of his wife's murder'.[47]

Mankowitz, however, continued to build his reputation as a public figure in other spheres throughout 1961. He was the guest of honour at the Club of London Gala in late March and was announced in May as one of the founder-members of The Lucky Ones, a charitable association set up by successful Jewish East Enders to help their less fortunate co-religionists. The *Jewish Chronicle* of 27 October reported his participation in a recent London Symposium on Soviet Jewry which protested against renewed anti-Semitism in the Soviet Union and highlighted a precipitous decline in Yiddish speakers and writers in the country. He was co-signatory, along with – among others – Bernard Kops, Emanuel Litvinoff and Frederic Raphael, of an open letter to the Secretary-General of the Union of Soviet Writers in September which protested against anti-Jewish stereotypes commonly utilized in the Soviet press and again deplored the virtual elimination of Yiddish language and culture.[48]

He was the subject of a laudatory profile in the *Hackney Gazette* (30 April) where he was bracketed along with Pinter, Kops and Wesker as a popular public writer who 'break[s] through the barriers of accepted etiquette with shattering impact'. He was also the subject of a lengthy interview in the *Leicester Evening Mail* (29 May), part of a series including Lord Boothby, Peter Sellers and John Betjeman, in which he declared that the Angry Young Man movement was a fashionable bandwagon, stated that 'necessity' had been the main inspiration of his career, and said he admired Mark Twain and James Joyce more than any of his contemporaries.

He was also happy to share his domestic life with the public. The readers of the January number of *House and Garden* were taken on a guided tour of his converted sixteenth-century Kentish tithe barn with its mess of children's toys and its resistance to four vigorous boys. These same sons, aged 14, 11, 7 and nine months are the addressees of 'Letter to My Four Sons', the Home Service 'Tuesday Talk' on 18 April. This is a rather sombre talk in which he disclaims any profound paternal wisdom and claims only to have tried to realize as best he can his talent for writing and selling stories of heroic quests for talismanic objects. He recommends that his sons pursue their current obsessions with exams, chess and the recorder with the same concern for quality and achievement. He has little faith in religious prescriptions for the good life which, for him, is a matter of aesthetics rather than ethics.

His talks about his growing family for 'Woman's Hour' some eight years earlier had been more light-hearted, as titles such as 'How to Keep Hamsters' (25 November 1953), 'My Life with the Indians' (19 April 1954) and 'The Bonehead Revisited' (24 October 1954) indicate. He constructs himself here as a father, overwhelmed by children and women, who just manages from time to time to assert his authority. It is all very good-humoured and there is no resentment expressed about his writing career being undermined by domestic trivia. Radio was an important source of income and publicity in Mankowitz's early career and he gave talks on both obscure (Matthew Prior) and well-known (Kafka) writers as well as a six-part series for the Forces Educational Broadcast (Light Programme) on 'Heroes'.[49] These were not unusual topics for a Cambridge graduate making his way in the world of post-war media, but his self-exposure in these charming sagas of family life was unusual for the period and these accounts of his wife and children are the product of a sensitive and inquisitive imagination.

The press was also invited to share the saga of this family's move to Barbados at the end of November, 1961. It was advertised as temporary, a six-month respite from London's rush and gloom, but the *Evening Standard* of 21 September announced that Mankowitz had put the family's town house in St John's Wood – 'studio room ... three bathrooms ... children's wing with nursery' – on the market for £25,000, and the *Barbados Advocate* announced, shortly before the family's arrival in the Caribbean, a new twenty-part short-story series in their Sunday edition. Mankowitz himself announced he would be working on a new novel about the film industry, provisionally entitled *The Other Is for You*, which was eventually published in 1963 as *Cockatrice*. There was a plan for Mankowitz and his eldest son Gered to collaborate on a book about the West Indian islands, for which Mankowitz would write the script to Gered's photographs, a profession he had already decided on at the age of 15, and one in which he would achieve considerable distinction.

Mankowitz was, as always, full of plans and projects but, as he and his wife settled their children into their new home – a spacious mansion called Marlborough, opposite the Governor's House, with a darkroom and studio for Gered – he may have wondered about the fate of his latest film script. It also had a Caribbean setting and was the first in what would become a very successful film genre. But the history of this script and its importance for Mankowitz's career are complicated and debateable and best reserved for a new chapter.

NOTES

1. 'The Killing Stones', six consecutive episodes on Associated-Rediffusion between 15 March and 19 April 1958, 8.00–8.30 pm on Saturday nights; 'East End, West End', six consecutive episodes on Associated-Rediffusion between 4 February and 11 March 1958, 8.30–9.00 pm, except the first episode, 10.00–10.30 pm, on Tuesday nights.
2. *TV Times*, 7 March 1958.
3. 'Killing Stones', Episode 6: 'The Retirement of de Haan', Dialogue Script, Mankowitz Family Archive, p.14.
4. *Reynolds News*, 12 March 1958; *Sunday Dispatch*, 16 March 1958; *Stage*, 30 March 1958; *Liverpool Evening Express*, 31 March 1958, 7 April 1958; *Sunday Dispatch*, 20 April 1958.
5. These and subsequent details are from Roger Wilmut, *Tony Hancock – 'Artiste': A Tony Hancock Companion*, paperback reprint edn (London: Methuen 1985).
6. 'East End, West End', Episode 6, p.28, Mankowitz Family Archive.
7. Ibid., Episode 1, p.1.
8. *News Chronicle*, 5 February 1958.
9. This and all subsequent quotes from 'The Publicity Photograph' are from the audiotape *Hancock's Half Hour: Number 8*, in the BBC Radio Collection (BBC Worldwide, 1999).
10. Bryan Cheyette (ed.), *Contemporary Jewish Writing in Britain and Ireland: An Anthology* (London: Peter Halban, 1998), p.xxxiii.
11. Harold Pinter, *The Birthday Party*, Methuen Modern Plays (London: Eyre Methuen, 1980), pp.27–8, 77. (First published in 1960.)
12. *Stage*, 27 October 1960.
13. *Coventry Evening Telegraph*, 21 September 1960.
14. *Tatler*, 2 November 1960.
15. John Heilpern, *John Osborne: A Patriot For Us*, paperback edn (London: Vintage Books, 2007), pp.289, 180–1.

16. 'Comment', 12 February and 3 June 1959, Box T-85, Radio Talks Scripts, BBC Written Archives Centre, Caversham Park, Reading.
17. D. Hickey and G. Smith, *The Prince: The Public and Private Life of Laurence Harvey* (London: Leslie Frewin, 1975), p.128.
18. Heilpern, *John Osborne*, p.289.
19. Lindsay Anderson, *The Diaries*, paperback edn (London: Methuen, 2005), p.70.
20. Anne Christie, *First Act* (Loughton: Judy Piatkus Books, 1983), p.194. Anne Christie has confirmed, in a personal communication, that Abe Bramstein is based on Wolf Mankowitz and that the production saga of *Personal* is closely based on that of *This Year, Next Year*.
21. This reference, and all subsequent summaries and quotes, excluding the following Alexander Walker quote n.22, are from Roger Lewis, *The Life and Death of Peter Sellers* (London: Century, 1994), pp.452–8.
22. Alexander Walker, *Peter Sellers: The Authorised Biography* (London: Weidenfeld, 1981), p.107.
23. Harold Conway, *Daily Sketch*, 21 October 1960; *Nottingham Journal*, 22 October 1960; *Record Show Mirror*, 22 October 1960; *What's On*, 21 October 1960; *Tatler*, 11 November 1960.
24. *Observer*, 23 October 1960; *Guardian*, 22 October 1960; *Sunday Times*, 23 October 1960; *New Statesman*, 22 October 1960; *Queen*, 26 October 1960.
25. *New York Post*, 1 January 1961; *Time*, 3 February 1961; *New York Times*, 2 February 1961; *Variety New York*, 26 October 1960; *Washington Post*, 23 March 1961.
26. *Evening Standard*, 6 October 1960.
27. *News Chronicle*, 7 October 1960; *Daily Sketch*, 7 October 1960; *Daily Mirror*, 7 October 1960.
28. *The Times*, 10 October 1960; *Daily Telegraph*, 8 October 1960.
29. *Illustrated London News*, 28 October 1960; *Tatler*, 19 October 1960; *Jewish Chronicle*, 14 October 1960.
30. *Kinematograph Weekly*, 27 October 1960.
31. Denis Meikle, 'Fisher's Folly or The One That Got Away – The Two Faces of Dr Jekyll', *Little Shoppe of Horrors*, 19 (2007), p.84.
32. Andrew Spicer, *Typical Men: The Representation of Masculinity in Popular British Cinema* (London and New York: I.B. Taurus, 2001), p.179.
33. Jonathan Rigby, *English Gothic: A Century of Horror Cinema*, 3rd edn (London: Reynolds & Hearn, 2004), pp.93–5.
34. This and all subsequent quotations are from Meikle, 'Fisher's Folly', pp.82–9.
35. Compare, for example, Sergeant Mitchem's lengthy marching orders to his men in Act I of the play, in Tom Maschler (ed.), *New English Dramatists 3* (Harmondsworth, Penguin, 1961), p.36; and the much more condensed film version in BFI Scripts, BFI National Archive, Berkhamsted, Release Script S13395, Reel 5, p.4.
36. *John O'London's*, 23 February 1961; *Guardian*, 18 February 1961; *Films and Filming*, March 1961; *Daily Cinema*, 27 January 1961; *Kinematograph Weekly*, 26 January 1961.
37. I.Q. Hunter, 'The Day the Earth Caught Fire', in I.Q. Hunter (ed.), *British Science Fiction Cinema* (London and New York: Routledge, 1999), p.102.
38. Ibid., p.108.
39. Tom Weaver, *Attack of the Monster Movie Makers: Interviews with Twentieth Century Genre Giants* (Jefferson, NC, and London: McFarland, 1994), pp.113–14.
40. Val Guest, *So You Want To Be in Pictures* (London: Reynolds & Hearn, 2001), p.140.
41. Hunter, 'Day the Earth Caught Fire', p.100.
42. Ibid., p.99.
43. *The Times*, 24 November 1961; *Manchester Guardian*, 25 November 1961; *Observer*, 26 November 1961; *Tribune*, 8 December 1961, cited in Hunter, 'Day the Earth Caught Fire'; *New Statesman*, 1 December 1961.
44. W. Mankowitz, *Belle or the Ballad of Dr Crippen*, Lord Chamberlain's File, Ref. LCP 1961/28, p.6, British Library, London.
45. *Daily Sketch*, 5 May 1961; *The Times*, 5 May 1961; *Financial Times*, 5 May 1961; *Stage and TV Today*, 11 May 1961; *Punch*, 10 May 1961; *Sunday Express*, 7 May 1961.
46. *Evening News*, 5 May 1961; *Time and Tide*, 11 May 1961; *Observer*, 7 May 1961; *Illustrated London News*, 20 May 1961; *Daily Mail*, 5 May 1961; *Daily Express*, 5 May 1961.

47. Adrian Wright, *A Tanner's Worth of Tune: Rediscovering the Post-War British Musical* (Woodbridge: Boydell Press, 2010), p.186.
48. The letter, with signatories, is reproduced in the *Birmingham Post*, 11 September 1961.
49. 'Matthew Prior', 28 June 1949, West of England Home Service; talks on 'The Tablets of the Law' (Thomas Mann) and 'Franz Kafka' (Max Brod), 6 June 1947, Home Service; 'Heroes' 16 November to 12 December 1950.

CHAPTER SEVEN

The Scriptwriter (1961–67)

In *Licence to Thrill: A Cultural History of the James Bond Films*,[1] James Chapman traces with scholarly precision the convoluted genesis of the script for the first Bond film, *Dr No*. He quotes *Kine Weekly*'s report in their July 1961 number that Mankowitz has been signed by the producers Harry Salzman and 'Cubby' Broccoli to write the film's screenplay. Broccoli confirms in his autobiography, *When the Snow Melts*, that Mankowitz introduced him to Saltzman, who had an option on Fleming's novel. When the two producers finally secured the necessary finance from United Artists, Broccoli thought it only fair to let Mankowitz have a crack at the screenplay, since 'he was a fine writer and had acted as marriage broker in our partnership'.[2]

Mankowitz was teamed with the experienced American producer and screenwriter Richard Maibaum, but the first treatment they came up with horrified Broccoli, who quotes Maibaum as saying that they found Fleming's villain so ludicrous that they decided he 'would be a villain who always had a little marmoset monkey sitting on his shoulder, and the monkey would be Dr No'.[3] Broccoli found the scriptwriters' concept even more ludicrous and they retreated, Mankowitz more reluctantly than Maibaum, to write scripts closer to Fleming's novel.

They were not, however, according to Chapman, the only writers. He cites the claim of the film's director, Terence Young, that he and his script girl, Joanna Harwood, polished up one version, and Maibaum's claim that a novelist with the pseudonym of Aubrey (probably Berkeley) Mather and Harwood did some work on his first draft of the screenplay. Chapman concludes that, despite these rival claims, the Maibaum-Mankowitz team was probably responsible for the final shape of the story and notes that the fourth draft screenplay, dated 12 December 1961, bears both their names. To this can be added an entry in the British Film Institute's catalogue of a fifth draft screenplay, dated 8 January

1961, whose authors are Maibaum, Mankowitz and Harwood. What is indisputable is that when *Dr No* opened on 5 October 1962, the accredited screenwriters were Maibaum, Harwood and Berkely (*sic*) Mather. Broccoli records that early on in the scriptwriting process Mankowitz decided that it was 'a piece of crap' and wanted nothing to do with the film. When he saw the rushes he asked Broccoli if he could have his name back on the credits. Broccoli agreed, provided Mankowitz paid the considerable costs involved. 'The hell with it!' said Mankowitz and so threw away the best deal he could ever have made in the film industry.[4]

It is true that no one involved with the film could have forecast that United Artists' initial investment of one million dollars would, at this time of writing, have realized worldwide gross box-office takings of $59.6m, nor that the screenwriters, between them, had created, in James Bond, a new post-war cinema hero. Monty Norman had written the music and lyrics for Mankowitz's disastrous production of *Belle* the previous year, but Broccoli had been one of its backers and had thought it much better than the critics did. He had been impressed by Norman's work and invited him to write the theme tune for *Dr No*. It became the most famous signature tune in film history and made Norman a very rich man. Broccoli himself does not criticize Mankowitz for his decision and remarks in his autobiography that misjudgement of audience reaction is an occupational hazard in the film industry.

But Mankowitz's see-sawing between rejection and acceptance of his film credit is symptomatic of a larger cultural struggle. It is one of the prime examples in his career of the two-way pull in his sensibility between elite and popular cultures. An *Observer* article of March 1962 shrewdly categorizes Mankowitz and his Cambridge friend John Metcalf, a prominent figure in the advertising world, as 'lapsed Leavisites'.[5] With regard to the writing credit for *Dr No*, the Leavisite in Mankowitz revolts against the clichés of a *Boys' Own* adventure movie; the dealer in him tries to renegotiate his price. The result is deadlock and Mankowitz walks away from the clash. Maybe he realizes that 'credit', in its fundamental sense of 'believability', is the concept in play here. It's certainly the concept he plays around with in *Cockatrice*, a compact satire on the film industry, published in April 1963, whose young hero, Danny Pisarov, spends his nights and days running around London and up and down the Home Counties in search of a film credit, the prize that will authenticate his life.

But now, in early 1962, Mankowitz had to look to his own credibility in London cultural life since, as noted above, he and his family were primarily resident in Barbados for the first six months of the year. Photos of the family in the sun (*Woman's Own*, 29 September) and news of a Mankowitz interest in a local pottery firm, Christopher Russell Potteries, were balanced by an *Evening Standard* item of 9 March that he was back in London on a ten-day business trip; a *Daily Mirror* notice of 4 April that he had returned to Barbados; and a *Barbados Advocate* announcement of 6 June that he was returning to the Caribbean after a month in the UK arranging contracts. The *Daily Express* noted on 12 July that the Mankowitz family had returned to London from their six-month stay in Barbados and that this would be an ongoing arrangement.

His association with Christopher Russell also extended and flourished. The *Barbados Advocate* for 3 November 1962 had a front-page spread on the firm, announcing its plans to move into mass production of high-class pottery due to the discovery in the area of a species of clay which, when mixed with salt-free sand, could provide the material for Devon-type pottery. Mankowitz made available technical advice from Wedgwood, and the *Lancashire Evening Post* a year later (17 April 1963) notes that the firm now employs twenty people, with realistic prospects of still further expansion. Mankowitz's encouragement of Russell's individual work bore later fruit. Lucien Meyers wrote up his work in an article, 'Variety and Vitality in Ceramic Tiles', for *Design Journal* in 1965 where he praises Russell's 'unusual and striking glaze effects, fused glass and metals, [which] create pictorial and abstract panels'. Russell, by this time, was running a highly regarded craft pottery centre in Swanage.

With these hectic criss-crossings of the Atlantic it is unlikely that Mankowitz was able to attend the premiere of *Waltz of the Toreadors* which opened on 12 April 1962. The film, transposed to an English Edwardian setting, starred Peter Sellers as the ageing roué now renamed General Fitzjohn, French actress Dany Robin as his sentimental love Ghislaine and Margaret Leighton as his termagant wife Emily. With a largely positive critical reception, it was a great popular hit and within a month was playing simultaneously in four London Odeon cinemas. Mankowitz must have been writing the screenplay for this adaptation of Jean Anouilh's successful French stage play during the same period as he and his collaborators were struggling to finalize the screenplay of *Dr No*, and this may have further exacerbated his irritation with that project.

By the early 1960s, Anouilh was considered by audiences and critics as a classy, modern writer, who posed intelligent questions about the theatricality of theatre. He was of the generation of playwrights before Beckett and Ionesco and lacked their sombre surrealism, but he supported their early works, and was himself praised by Sartre. Both Peter Brook and Peter Hall, Britain's most radical young theatre directors in the post-war period, had long-running successes with their respective productions of *Ring Round the Moon* (*L'invitation au chateau*) in 1950 and *Waltz of the Toreadors* from February 1956 at the Arts Theatre, London. Hall's previous production there had been the first English performance of *Waiting for Godot* which opened on 3 August 1955. To engage with Anouilh was, therefore, to engage with a writer somewhere between middlebrow and avant-garde. To engage with Ian Fleming, Mankowitz may have thought, was to engage with a pulp-fictioneer.

Anouilh's play poses serious questions about ageing, self-delusion and marriage. His General, St Pé, is a serial lecher after the maidservants in his chateau, much to the disgusted contempt of his wife, Emily, who has taken to her bed to try and provoke pity and concern on the part of her husband. The General, however, has an unconsummated love for a much younger woman, Ghislaine, with whom he danced the 'Waltz of the Toreadors' at a military ball seventeen years ago. Ghislaine now turns up at the chateau and demands that the General leave his wife and marry her. In the end, after various farcical plot-twists, and despite a scene of scarifying candour about their mutual hatred, husband and wife cannot let go of each other. The General has left it too late. He is locked into codependency until death. Ghislaine gives herself to the General's secretary, Gaston, who turns out to be St Pé's illegitimate son. The General can only console himself with flirting with the new maid.

Mankowitz's script broadens the farce. His General falls through the balcony and into a water butt as he tries to get into Ghislaine's (Dany Robin) room at the local inn; his doctor-friend (Cyril Cusack) drives round in an early Edwardian car which is always banging to a halt in a massive cloud of black smoke; his naive secretary, played by John Fraser, hooks off Ghislaine's dress, while he is fly-fishing and she is trying to commit suicide; his Emily (Margaret Leighton) cycles maniacally in her white nightdress across the countryside to try and get to the railway crossing in order that she can commit suicide; his General and doctor-friend fight an absurd duel over Emily with a sabre and an umbrella. For some critics the intercutting of the hate-filled exchanges between the General and his wife with the slapstick pursuit of Ghislaine by the secretary through the meadows of a ruined abbey diluted the awful pathos of the aged couple. But the director, John Guillermin, in a *Daily Sketch* interview (13 April 1962), claims that this sequence was the result of a re-editing forced on him by the philistines of the Rank Organisation. The Sellers/Leighton confrontation should have lasted twenty minutes.

Nonetheless, Sellers carries the film. Dilys Powell for the *Sunday Times* (15 April 1962) notes well how the expression of Sellers's face can switch between amorous desire and 'settle into the folds of despair, even hatred'. It is Sellers, for her, who coheres the film's differing strands of bravado and pathos. Penelope Gilliatt, for the *Observer* on the same Sunday, catches the effect of Sellers' eyes: 'clenched as though he were used to wearing a monocle in both of them'. The *Guardian* (14 April 1962) is less happy with Mankowitz's adaptation – Anouilh's delicacy has been submerged in a 'kind of fury of knockabout farce' – but Sellers brings an authority to his scenes, which encompasses both laughter and acrimony.

The film critic of the *Middlesex County Times* (12 April 1962) gives the lengthiest analysis of the film and points out its technical debts to Ophuls and its quotations from the poetic fantasies of Renoir and Jean Vigo. 'It is a measure of the film's adultness', the review concludes, 'that the story doesn't lead to a facile, final rapprochement.' Roger Lewis, in his biography of Sellers, quotes from a scene with the doctor, when the General admits that despite all his bravado, he's empty inside, alone and afraid. 'Sellers' head', Lewis continues, 'is held close-up, and in profile, and it is one of those moments in his films when his own personal conflicts are being confided.' He then adds in parenthesis that Mankowitz wrote the screenplay for the film and that 'he knew exactly what to get Sellers to draw on'.[6]

Mankowitz, in this period, was less successful in judging the mood and taste of BBC TV executives. Correspondence in the BBC's Caversham archives shows a decreasing enthusiasm by the bureaucrats for various Mankowitz projects. He proposes, in the summer of 1959, a series, 'The Story of the Bible', to Ronnie Waldman of the BBC Film Section, but there is no further mention of this idea.[7] He has also suggested, a year earlier, to Eric Maschwitz, Head of TV Light Entertainment, a TV-scripted series, 'The New Arabian Nights', adapted from a series of short stories dramatizing the demi-monde of a fictitious Soho night-club, The Blue Arabian.[8] He writes to Dennis Norden at BBC TV on 18

September 1961, enclosing a copy of *The Mendelman Fire*, which includes several Blue Arabian stories, and says he intends to write one more series of ten Blue Arabian night stories. Maschwitz is interested and in a letter of 24 November 1961 he asks for a specimen script but, in an ominous rider, he warns: ' "Wolf Mankowitz does not do auditions" were your words on Friday last. On this occasion I feel Wolf Mankowitz really must.' The stories have already gone the rounds and a scathing letter from Donald Wilson, the Head of Script TV, to 'G.M.Tel.P.' ('General Manager, Television Promotions' and Ronnie Waldman's new post) warns him to steer clear of them because although Mankowitz thinks he's a latter-day Damon Runyon, he hasn't got Runyan's gift of 'turning the sharp tail of an otherwise slightly sentimental tale'.[9]

Mankowitz did write the pilot, a treatment of the story 'A Cure for Tin Ear', because the correspondence shows his company was paid the second portion of his fee, £120.20 on 20 March 1962. But the BBC was not happy with what they got. The rest of the correspondence is a barrage of criticism. Ronald Waldman would disapprove if the whole series were set in the 'cheap, shady atmosphere Wolf seems to favour' and he laments that Mankowitz 'can't avoid his leanings towards illicit sex', but he admits that 'this is clearly a matter for domestic programmes first of all'. A few days later, Donald Baverstock, Assistant Controller of Programmes, writes to Eric Maschwitz that the story is 'fake romantic, the characters are cardboard, the writing is undramatic'.

The next day Maschwitz gets an even more devastating broadside from David Whitaker, Light Entertainment Script Editor. The story's 'cynicism is absolute and Mankowitz illustrates in this that he is the complete iconoclast ... The writing has at moments an edge and possesses some illustration of the author's talent for Jewish humour and characterisation.' However, Whitaker goes on: 'I believe it is destructive to every avenue opened up and mined by us so successfully, and will lose for us an amount of public affection we cannot afford.'[10] Maschwitz wrote to all interested parties at the BBC on 6 April, informing them that the 'Blue Arabian' series had been turned down for domestic programmes, and a later letter to Mankowitz (2 September 1963) pleads scheduling difficulties for the abandonment of the project. A Maschwitz letter of 4 June 1962 to Mankowitz's agent, John Heyman, courteously returns a stack of scripts, including 'A Cure for Tin Ear', submitted over the last few years.

That script is not now available but it must have had a close resemblance to the script of the later ATV broadcast of the play on 22 November 1965 which, as we shall see, caused no moral panic among the critics. This teleplay was, as with the one for the BBC, based on an original short story by Mankowitz included in *The Blue Arabian Nights* collection published in 1973. It is a slight, sentimental tale about the love affair between Tilly Nickels, a vacuous, beautiful, end-of-the pier singer with a tin ear, and Theo Sandman, her much older lover and a shrewd musical impresario with a house in Mayfair. Tilly has pretensions to being an artiste and Theo gets her a London engagement. She is a disaster, but only for three days, because she then discovers she is pregnant and withdraws from the show. She changes her name to Sandman by deed poll and has a beautiful baby girl, but is told by the doctor that her pregnancy has affected her glands and it's unlikely she will ever sing again. Sandman is relieved but is so delighted by the birth that he fails to notice that his daughter's cry is as off-key as her mother's crooning voice. His problem with female 'artistes' is by no means over.

It is difficult now to comprehend why such an innocuous tale outraged the BBC executives. Hugh Carleton Green had been appointed BBC Director General in January 1960 and he was soon to become the target of moralists at large whose outrage was similar to that of Waldman, Whitaker and others, with his backing for the satirical news show 'TW3' ('That Was The Week That Was') whose first extended run began on 4 November 1962, and with his appointment of Sydney Newman, as Head of Drama in April 1963. Newman, in his previous post as producer of commercial TV's ABC, had, from 1958, created his very successful 'Armchair Theatre' series featuring a combination of absurdist and social-realist writers such as Harold Pinter, Alun Owen and Giles Cooper. Now he switched over to the BBC where he created his equally successful series 'The Wednesday Play', for which he produced original screenplays by David Mercer, Alun Owen, and Nell Dunn. Ken Loach directed Nell Dunn's *Up the Junction* and, most famously, Jeremy Sandford's exposé of the young homeless, *Cathy Come Home*, in 1966. In 1964 he told the BBC Board of Governors that morals and politics had changed radically in post-war Britain. Extramarital sex had increased; homosexuality and abortion were subject to parliamentary debate; the divorce rate had gone up; and relations between capital and labour were changing. 'All these [changes]', he stated, 'are food for the hungry and aware playwright.'[11]

The timing of Mankowitz's submission of his unpretentious play was, perhaps, its main problem. Carleton Greene had only been in post for a couple of years and traditional BBC attitudes towards public morality would have still been in place. The most vituperative criticisms of Mankowitz's play-script come some six months before the launch of 'TW3', whose inconoclasm would far outstrip Mankowitz's, and a year before Newman took up his post. Its setting, a louche club in Soho, would be beginning to seem outdated, spivvy rather than affluent post-war. The Tom-Tom club in *Expresso Bongo* or the Establishment Club in Greek Street, opened in October 1961, were much more contemporary settings. Mankowitz seems here, as on other occasions, to be culturally situated both too early and too late, an awkward position to maintain without considerable social finesse.

Newman's reorganization of the BBC drama group into three sections – series, serials and individual plays – might, however, have advanced the prospects of 'A Cure for Tin Ear'. Mankowitz's script, for whatever reasons, was received and circulated, as we have seen, by Eric Maschwitz, the Head of Light Entertainment, among whose flagship TV shows were 'This Is Your Life', 'What's My Line?' and 'Dixon of Dock Green', and who oversaw radio's Light Programme whose tone, in Sandbrook's words, was 'domestic, middle-class, feminine and individual'. Its programmes included 'Woman's Hour', 'The Archers', 'Hancock's Half Hour' and 'Family Favourites'.[12] Mankowitz had featured on a number of editions of 'Woman's Hour' in the 1950s, but these were rueful, whimsical reflections on his role as father to a growing family of boys.

His proposed TV script dramatized very different family origins and circumstances. David Whitaker was right, in this context, to read it as undermining the affectionate family values espoused by BBC light entertainment, particularly at this time when the BBC was in a ratings war with the new commercial TV channels. Programmes such as ATV's 'Sunday Night at the London Palladium' (from 1955) and Granada's 'Coronation Street' (from 1960) had been strongly contesting the BBC's definitions of 'the people' and 'the family' and the entertainment appropriate for them in this affluent post-war period.

Maschwitz himself – something of a culture-shifter, with a public school and Cambridge background, a long career in musical theatre, scriptwriter for *Goodbye Mr Chips* and composer of 'A Nightingale Sang in Berkeley Square' – was an unashamed populist. 'We've got to please the people' was his mantra, and, however meaningless the slogan, he certainly fought commercial television successfully on its own ground in this crucial period from the mid-1950s to the early 1960s. In a neat illustration of how fluid were allegiances and how precarious were cultural definitions in these new media worlds, Maschwitz left the BBC to join ITV in 1963, the same year that Sidney Newman made the reverse journey to the BBC.

Maschwitz appears to have been an emollient and diplomatic character. Mankowitz was neither. The headline to Fergus Cashin's interview with him, at the midpoint of his life, for the *Daily Sketch* (11 April 1962) is 'Who's afraid of the big brash Wolf', and Cashin describes him as 'shrewd in his dealings, and careless about wealth. He is loud. He is brash. He gives the impression of a complete egotist – aggressive, confident.' The interview is to publicize Mankowitz's next London show, Harry Secombe in an adaptation of *Pickwick Papers*, and his forthcoming satire on the film industry, then entitled *The Other Is For You*, but Mankowitz also expatiates on his career: 'I am a professional writer. I like writing. All forms. I don't want to be a genius. I'm thirty eight and at this time in my life I've decided to live in the sun.' He projects himself as a loner, unafraid of being hated, confident in the love of a select few. He admits, as these popular narratives of self-sufficiency always do, to needing reassurance from time to time, in this case through psychoanalysis, but Cashin sums him up as a happily married family man and an enemy of humbug and hypocrisy.

Cashin's article is a masterclass in the popular press's ability to reconcile opposites without analysis, but it does highlight Mankowitz's overbearing nature. Frederic Raphael, of the Pinter/Wesker generation but public school and Oxford educated, confirmed this in the course of the telephone interview of 11 August 2009, already cited in the 'Introduction'. He describes Mankowitz as a 'fuckem Jew', aggressive about and unashamed of his Jewishness. He could be a bully if you gave him the chance, but behind the assertiveness there was a 'kind of self-loathing'. He was the type of man who never wanted to be caught out and, despite all his frantic production, Raphael 'never read a book that summed him up'. He would, Raphael added, have made a very good East End taxi-driver or American.

The brash, American-style impresario side of Mankowitz is well caught in Raphael's fictional representation of Mankowitz as Jake Nathanson in his short story 'Quixote/Schmixote'. The narrator, a would-be screenwriter, is ushered into Nathanson's office and notices that the matchbox from which Nathanson lights his cigar is crammed with five-pound notes. He is then told, as an example of the storyline

Nathanson is after, a ludicrous tale involving apes on the Rock of Gibraltar, a nice Jewish girl from Dalston mistaken for an Arab princess, and an ugly suitor with depths. Nathanson's last injunction is: 'I can't afford to piss about with somebody who can't give me the crap I want ... I want a hundred and twenty pages, tops, and it's got to be a knicker-wetter.' The story is based on Raphael's experience of being engaged as a tyro scriptwriter for Mankowitz's ill-fated joint production company with Peter Sellers in 1960.[13]

But Sellers did do the Mankowitz family a good turn. Gered, the eldest boy, was unhappy with conventional schooling and Sellers suggested he take up photography. This proved to be his ideal métier and by early 1963, at the age of 16, he was a partner in a company, Gered Mankowitz Photography Ltd, along with his father, Jeff Vickers, an older and more experienced colleague who had his own photography company, and Mark Stone, founder of a leading London press and public relations agency. Gered and Jeff Vickers found a location for a new studio at 9 Mason's Yard, very close to where his father had a flat at 100 Jermyn Street, just round the corner from the Wedgwood showrooms on Piccadilly. His father put up the premium for a lease on the property and the three parties formed another company, GM Studios Ltd.

Mason's Yard, however, was about to reinvent itself as a centre for 1960s countercultural and rock music activity. A couple of doors down from Gered's studio was a club, The Scotch of St James, which, in Gered's words, was 'the preferred hangout for just about every major music personality of the time',[14] including The Rolling Stones and Jimi Hendrix. Gered found that the subjects for his photography were his neighbours and he became the photographer of The Rolling Stones during the mid-1960s. The photo of Jimi Hendrix that everyone of that epoch knows, the tightly framed, slightly elevated portrait of the rock guitarist, dressed in a hussar's gold-tasselled jacket and purple scarf and staring straight at camera, is by Gered Mankowitz and assured his reputation as one of the finest practitioners of this new genre of rock photography.

His other significant neighbour was at 6 Mason's Yard where John Dunbar, married to Marianne Faithfull (whom Gered knew because of his close association with The Rolling Stones), opened an art gallery called Indica. His partners in the enterprise were Barry Miles, who would later run the countercultural bookshop, also called Indica, in Southampton Row, and Peter Asher, brother of Jane Asher, at that time the girlfriend of Paul McCartney. It was at Indica that Dunbar introduced John Lennon to Yoko Ono in 1966 when she was presenting her first solo show at the gallery. By chance, therefore, Mankowitz's eldest son set himself up professionally in a space where, at that precise moment, new lines of connection between class and culture were being rapidly drawn. Faithfull and Jagger, Asher and McCartney, Lennon and Yoko were all unlikely pairings even five years before.

It was a time, Gered recalls, when 'bands didn't have posses or staff. There were no assistants, press agents, stylists or makeup people.' They were making it up as they went along, but the role of Gered's father in all this was also important. It's unlikely that his musical tastes were those of his son's generation – *Expresso Bongo* has ill-concealed contempt for late-1950s rock 'n' roll – but he did provide not only vital encouragement and business expertise, but also an example of how to inhabit with confidence the richest zones of the metropolis. Mankowitz Senior was a Jew from Fortune Street, who had a flat in Jermyn Street and an office in Piccadilly Arcade. He doesn't seem to have made much of this to his son, but a son in Mason's Yard looks like a confirmation of the East End's arrival in the West End. Mankowitz's 'balance of culture' begins now to look more like an 'intersection of cultures'.

Mankowitz Senior's own significant writings for 1963 were *Cockatrice*, a scathing satire on the film industry, published by Longmans on 8 April; and his 'book' for *Pickwick*, a musical version of Dickens's episodic narrative of the famous clubman and his friends, which opened at the Saville Theatre on 4 July and ran there for 694 performances until 27 February 1965. Bernard Delfont was the producer, Harry Secombe played the lead and the lyrics were by Leslie Bricusse, a long-time associate of Mankowitz, and one of his partners in the launch of the Pickwick Club in Great Newport Street, off Charing Cross Road, at the same time as the musical's launch at the Covent Garden end of Shaftesbury Avenue.

The Saville Theatre would be bought by Beatles manager Brian Epstein in 1965, shortly after the end of *Pickwick*'s run, and would become more famous for its Sunday night rock concerts, featuring such as Chuck Berry, the Cream, Pink Floyd and the Jimi Hendrix Experience, than for its play productions, which included works by Arnold Wesker and Berthold Brecht. The Saville was converted into a two-screen cinema in 1970, and can thus be read as a display site for the various versions of popular culture – musical/variety, rock music, cinema and New Wave theatre – with which both Mankowitzes had a central involvement.

Cockatrice, however, through its cynical, treacherous first-person narrator, one Danny Pisarov, personal assistant to the movie tycoon Arno Borian, disabuses the reader of any romantic notions of the film industry. While his boss is away, Danny uses Borian's contacts, residence, actresses and secretarial help, to try and set up a production deal for which he will take full credit. In the lead-up time to Christmas he scours central London and the Home Counties, gradually acquiring a property, a star, a writer and finance. En route he has sex with an ageing actress, Marcia Darling; with an upcoming actress, Billie Robinson; and with Monique, secretary to Raoul, who is the agent of the French star, Mignon Destret. He does not have sex with his ex-wife, Marion, who loves money as much as Danny loves production. 'Sleeping with her', he remembers, 'was like entering into union with the Mint.'[15] But they are parents to an 11-year-old son, and Danny, now aged 35, shows some sense of responsibility by detouring from his race round London and the Home Counties to stop by Marion's house to see his son and leave him a Christmas present.

Danny's best present would be to see his name credited as producer of a film. The text of *Cockatrice* is studded with the words 'credit' and 'production', like emblems of wishful success. Towards the end of the novella, Danny prays: 'Dear lady bitch-goddess, patroness of producers, protect me now and in the production period to come.'[16] He has his 'property', *The Vision of Maria Baldi*, a pamphlet on the divine visions of a simple Sicilian peasant girl, written by an alcoholic journalist, James Malloy. Maria is, in his scheme, to be played by Mignon Destret; Danny will engage Angela Lenten (a satirical portrait of Joan Littlewood) to direct the film. He has lined up his writer and he is confident of his finance. He fails, of course. Production is once more a blighted goal for a Mankowitz hero. Borian returns, takes back his apartment, takes over the Baldi story, takes Billie Robinson and plans to produce the film with Billie playing Maria, since Destret has just tried to commit suicide.

Danny's only Christmas present is from Borian. It is a bloodied bullfighter's sword from Barcelona. Mankowitz here refers back to the novella's opening where Danny recalls a dream in which he finds Borian dying from a self-inflicted stab wound in his chest. There is an open Russian leather case on his desk containing two identical short swords, handle to tip. A note propped on the case reads: 'Dearest Danny, to succeed in our business you need these. One is for them, the other is for you.'[17] Mankowitz tells the same story in the Davis interview, where it is attributed to Alexander Korda, for whom Mankowitz had great affection and respect. Korda helped Mankowitz out of financial difficulties on several occasions and treated talented writers like sons whom he wanted to do well. Korda was witty even on his death bed. He was living in an apartment near the House of Commons. Mankowitz recalls him remarking, towards the end: 'It's interesting. I, a Hungarian Jew who stole Big Ben as a trademark, am now kept awake by it.' Such figures, Danny concludes, are better suited than him to the film business. They are simple, competitive capitalists and will always outmanoeuvre an artist like Danny.

A number of critics cited Mankowitz's definition of a cockatrice as the frontispiece of this satirical novella – 'a fabulous serpent-like monster, hatched against nature out of the egg of a cock ... its breath was deadly, its glare fatal to human beings'. For Mankowitz this seemed 'an appropriate heraldic beast for the film industry' but for some critics it symbolized the author's love–hate relationship with the industry. Julian Jebb of the *Sunday Times* (7 April 1963) found this relationship lurid and unpleasant, but the 'keyhole information is put across with terrific verve'. Arthur Pottersman of the *Daily Sketch* (8 April 1963) criticizes the work as 'guilty of all the excesses it is supposed to condemn', but the critic for *The Times* (11 April 1963) cites Ben Jonson's *Volpone* as Mankowitz's model with Pisarov as 'a Mosca who fails to have even a moment of triumph over his Volpone', and the *TLS* (12 April 1963) compares Mankowitz's satire favourably with that of Nathaniel West. The most cutting observation is by Nina Hibbin in the 20 May 1963 number of the *Daily Worker*: 'in his heart he is secretly proud of being on nodding terms with these naughty people and their promiscuous goings-on'.

But, for our purposes, the most illuminating remark is by Anthony Burgess in his review for the *Observer* (7 April 1963), where he suggests that *My Old Man's A Dustman* showed [Mankowitz] to be 'a sort of East End Joyce; here there is a glaze of sophisticated parody and experiment ... a brilliant performance, a kind of intellectual sulphate of baryta producing admirable, if unlovable, jasper ware'. Burgess was, by the early 1960s, a novelist and critic of considerable stature, with his Malayan trilogy already published and *A Clockwork Orange* having appeared the year before, in 1962. A commendation from him, which also alluded to Mankowitz's ceramics scholarship, was prestigious and the public seemed to agree with Burgess's critical estimate. *Cockatrice* came fifth in the *News of the World*'s list (14 April 1963) of fiction top sellers. It was preceded by, among others, Henry Miller's *Tropic of Cancer* and James Baldwin's *Another Country*, controversial American artistic company. A *Sunday Express* round-up on 21 April listed Fleming and Mankowitz as top fiction bestsellers and a week later (28 April 1963) *Cockatrice* had advanced to fourth place in the *News of the World* list, with Ian Fleming's *On Her Majesty's Secret Service* still topping it and Henry Miller in second place.

Mankowitz's next popular success was, as mentioned above, his adaptation as a stage musical of Dickens's *Pickwick Papers*. This was an unashamed grab for the public heart, and the public and the critics, judging by the length of the musical's run, were happy to be taken. 'If I Ruled the World' and 'Look into Your Heart' became recording hits. Mankowitz filleted Dickens's episodic sprawl into a tightly coherent narrative which begins with Pickwick about to enter the debtors' prison, The Fleet, and then recounts, among other incidents, the duel between Dr Slammer and Mr Winkle, Mr Jingles's elopement with Rachael Wardle, and Pickwick's trial for breach of promise. Sam Weller is a Mankowitz-type trickster and Bricusse gives him Mankowitz-type sentiments in the number 'Talk', whose refrain is that in any tight situation you have to 'Talk your way out of it ... Talk around a bit / But talk!'[18]

Bricusse and Mankowitz's other collaboration at this time, as founder-members of the Pickwick Club, has already been noted. It was located opposite the Arts Club in Great Newport Street – thereby, we may conjecture, seeking to distance itself from the more familiarly louche clubland of Soho. Its publicity advertises it as an exclusive club for professionals in the entertainment industry. The *Free Trade Review* for September 1963 notes its lush Dickensian decor with 'candle flanked gilt mirrors, deeply padded brass studded banquet seating, a well stocked bar and, as a magnificent centre piece, a set of four brass gas lamps'. On the menus are such delicacies as Mrs Bardell's chicken in wine, Mr Jingle's peppered steak and Mr Pickwick's boiled dinner.

The club's third founder-member was Desmond Cavanagh, married to the sister of Jeanne Moreau. According to various sources, the club attracted the new generation of actors, producers, writers and pop stars. In a biography of Michael Caine, *70 Not Out*, William Hall quotes Caine as calling the club 'the hub of the so-called Swinging Sixties', with a roll-call of star customers, including Francois Truffaut, The Beatles, Terence Stamp and Harry Salzman, who offered Caine the lead in *The Ipcress File* when dining at The Pickwick with Mankowitz.[19]

Another Caine biographer, Michael Freedland, describes the Pickwick Club as 'a symbolic place, an institution haunted by those in show-business who could afford to be there. It was one of the signs he [Caine] had arrived.'[20] Caine himself describes the club in much the same terms when he recalls it as having no dress code but a cliquey membership: 'Terry [Stamp] and I of course loved it. We now had a brand new place where we could dance, and one where we could eat.'[21] Edina Ronay, daughter of the food-writer Egon Ronay, and also the girlfriend of Terence Stamp and then Michael Caine, recalls in the *Observer* that when she was a young actress in London in the 1960s, The Pickwick was one of the clubs to be seen in: 'All we seemed to eat was steak – steak and salad or steak and vegetables.'[22] With this venture Mankowitz was at least maintaining a presence among the new generation of actors and producers, as he was among the new generation of rock musicians and photographers with his support for his son Gered's enterprise in Mason's Yard.

He was also maintaining a media presence at large. His and his family's journeyings between London and the West Indies received press attention, and a project to turn a biography of the Rothschild family into a musical was widely publicized. He also participated in a momentous occasion for post-war British theatre, the six-day-long International Drama Conference at the Edinburgh Festival, 2–7 September 1963. It was organized by the distinguished critic Kenneth Tynan, the young fringe theatre producer Jim Haynes and, most significantly, the independent publisher John Calder, the main conduit into British culture for such American and continental avant-garde writers as William Burroughs, Adam Adamov and Alain Robbe-Grillet, all of whom contributed to readings and debates.

The British New Wave was most forcefully represented by Pinter, Wesker and Arden, all of whom deplored the refusal of the British government to grant visas to Brecht's widow Helen Weigel and their company, the Berliner Ensemble, to attend the conference. Mankowitz's main contributions were a proposal for a Writers' Union which would protect them against unauthorized textual changes, and a shouting match with his old foe Bernard Levin over the relative importance of critics and artists. The terms of professional engagement were his concern, rather than the nature of theatrical representation. Brecht would have been happy to speak to both.

Other media appearances in this period included a film and novel discussion with presenter Vanessa Thornton on Southern TV in August, and a heated confrontation on BBC's 'Juke Box Jury' (5 October 1963) with popular composer Bunny Lewis about the value of pop music past and present. Mankowitz's comment on Gerry and the Pacemakers' version of 'You'll Never Walk Alone', adapted from the Rogers and Hammerstein musical 'Carousel', was 'a turgid voice which failed to move me to anything but nausea',[23] an implicit contrast to Harry Secombe's soaring baritone rendering of 'If I Ruled The World'. Both recordings were Top Twenty hits that year.

A more bruising media encounter was Mankowitz's suit for libel against *Private Eye*. The fortnightly satirical magazine had established itself, in the two years of its existence, as an incisive and sardonic commentator on the vanities and hypocrisies of cultural and political London. It was now owned by Peter Cook, a comic genius of his generation, and frequent contributors included Spike Milligan, Ralph Steadman, Christopher Logue and Willie Rushton. Rushton wrote and drew a cartoon strip entitled 'Aesop's Fables' in which prominent public figures, such as Winston Churchill and Laurence Olivier, had been lampooned. In the 31 May 1963 edition (number 38), it was Mankowitz's turn. As 'Wolf Mankyscripts' he is portrayed as a money-obsessed Jew; an opportunistic adaptor of others' work; and a juggler of the values of high art, inculcated at Cambridge by his tutor 'Barren Leavis', with those of popular musicals adapted from Dickens. The last panel shows his head emerging out of a dragon's body and tail with an egg beside it entitled 'The Cockatrice'. The balloon from Mankowitz's mouth reads: 'A LOT OF COCK WRITTEN IN A TRICE'.[24]

As with all good satire there are truths here – Mankowitz's conflict between elite and popular values and his focus on money and exchange – but not the whole truth. Mankowitz could have decided that, as a satirical target, he was in august company and ignored the provocation. But perhaps he saw Rushton, who was then also a star performer and writer for the new satirical television show 'That Was The Week That Was', and *Private Eye* as part of a new cultural complex, including New Wave theatre and cinema and rock 'n' roll, with which he had little sympathy.

He clearly felt his professional reputation had been impugned. Both quality and popular press carried notices, on 12 and 13 June, that a High Court writ for libel had been issued against *Private Eye*'s editorial board, publishers and printers. The *New Daily* (18 June 1963) quotes him, with approval, saying that 'at present not enough people are making enough fuss about the enormous amount of defamatory material appearing in one medium or another'. Mankowitz's stand was vindicated when, at the High Court hearing on 19 December 1963, the magazine conceded that the cartoon's material could have defamatory implications that were wholly untrue, apologized and agreed to pay an appropriate sum of money to the defendant, plus his costs. The action was reported across a broad spectrum of the press, thus confirming Mankowitz's prominence as a public figure.

The critics reported, not defamation, but a certain confusion of aims in the material that made up 'The Uneasy Crown', scripted by Mankowitz from an A.J.P. Taylor narrative and broadcast on 11 October 1963 on BBC-TV. Anthony Burgess, reviewing for the *Listener* (17 October), felt himself subjected to a 'dyspepsia of facts' which rushes the viewer from Philip II to Alfonso XIII with Richard Burton's voice-over as a confusing gabble. The film was a missed opportunity to analyse the national character of Spain's Catholicism, indeed to unravel 'the soul of the most paradoxical, enigmatic and lovable race in Europe'. The reviewer for *Variety*, New York (23 October), reports much the same experience, with the programme giving only a sketchy history of the monarchy and devoting most of its time to exploring the nature of Franco's fascism. 'The script', the review concludes, 'was tepid and fence-sitting, as if afraid to offend.'

A follow-up review for the *Listener* a year later (24 September 1964) reiterates this critique of confused aims and gabbled history and detects 'a guarded but unmistakeably friendly account of Franco's last-minute economic achievements', although it praises the programme, as did the *Variety* review, for unfamiliar newsreel of the Civil War. We have to conclude (without access to either script or film) that this was journeyman work for Mankowitz, significant only for this association with Richard Burton, which would be renewed when Mankowitz collaborated on two scripts for Burton films, *Dr Faustus* (1967) and *The Fifth Offensive* (1973).

His chief scripting commitments, however, during 1964 were to musicals. A show based on the life of the alleged German spy Mata Hari, with music and lyrics by his old collaborators Monty Norman and David Heneker, was extensively trailed in the press in the second half of the year. Lena Horne, Shirley Bassey and, finally, Georgia Browne were suggested for the lead but, in the event, none of these actresses was available so the project never got to the stage. His second musical, based on the novel of the same title by Rosalind Erskine, *Passion Flower Hotel*, had a reasonably successful run in London in late 1965 and will be considered in more detail later.

He was still writing for the press, his most exotic piece being a report on the architecture of San Juan, Puerto Rico, in which he characterized himself as 'a sort of satirical anthropologist'.[25] The press was still writing about him. There were frequent reports on the guests and the cuisine at the Pickwick Club where the *Daily Express* for 3 March 1964 reported a meeting made in showbiz heaven between Sammy Davis Jnr and The Beatles; and where, in the basement music space, Peter (Asher) and Gordon, new, young musicians, made their public debuts. Their recording of 'A World Without Love', written by Paul McCartney, topped the hit parade in April 1964. McCartney and Peter's sister Jane were still a couple and Paul occupied a small, attic room in the Ashers' family home, an elegant Georgian town house in Wimpole Street. He and John Lennon wrote the Beatles breakthrough hit 'I Want to Hold Your Hand' in the little music room where Jane Asher's mother, Margaret, gave tuition in the recorder and the oboe. Different cultures certainly intersected at 57 Wimpole Street in the mid-1960s.

The younger Mankowitz generation also featured. Edina Ronay may have recalled the Pickwick as a restaurant where you ate nothing but steak and chips, but she was also one of the most beautiful girls in London. Gered Mankowitz, according to the *Evening News* of 4 December 1964, was determined to photograph her and 'tracked her down like a sleuth from TV studio to film studio, from Pickwick Club to White Elephant Club'. He snapped her slightly from below and facing the camera, her arms outstretched and flat against a wall, a NO PARKING sign at head level, camera right, with a haughty look on her face. It was a portrait to put beside the far more famous one, shot in the same year, of Marianne Faithfull. She sits with her arms outstretched along a plush banquette in The Salisbury pub in St Martin's Lane below a huge wall mirror lined with brass statuettes of Diana the huntress. She wears a simple dress caught in at the waist and white, knee-high socks. She looks straight at the camera. Mankowitz has caught a gaze that is both frank and wistful, as if she is looking through the camera and glimpsing, in the near future, a life in which her beauty will prompt both triumph and degradation. As Gered Mankowitz himself commented years later: 'She exudes sexuality, and yet she's completely chaste.'[26]

Mankowitz Senior was less enamoured of purity. An article on Barbados for *Holiday* magazine which was, it appears, critical of lingering colonial attitudes on the island, the lack of a nightlife, and the island's overdependence on British subsidies, provoked heated correspondence in the local press. The *Barbados Daily News* for 24 January 1964 accused him of 'colossal conceit ... smug superiority ... impertinent half-truths', but a column by Ian Gale in the same paper's edition of 2 February 1964 praised the wit of the *Holiday* article and detected the persistence among the English in Barbados of a 'rigid and peculiar stance corresponding to the teapot or chamber pot of his fantasy'.

Mankowitz defended himself against what he perceived as half-truths in a long statement printed in the *Barbados Advocate* and the controversy bubbled along for the next couple of weeks. Shortly after his return from his winter break he told the *News of the World* (6 September 1964) that he had decided to sell the family's winter home because his work schedule would keep him in England for at least the next two years. But, to the interviewer from the *Sun* of 17 September 1964, he gave a slightly different, more discerning reason. Barbados, he said, was a paradise, but it didn't have a snake and 'when you have worked in show business as long as I have you miss the snakes'.

The year 1964 ended with Mankowitz himself accused of being a snake. The 10 December edition of Hansard records that the Conservative MP for Richmond, Anthony Royle, informed the Attorney General that Mankowitz and a colleague, on Associated Rediffusion's 'This Week', had stated that he had taken part in illegal practices with regard to antique sales and intended to do so in the future. The reference was to 'the Ring' whose techniques, as Mankowitz later pointed out, he had exposed in *Make Me an Offer*. Quality and popular press reported the accusation; Mankowitz strenuously denied it in open letters to the *Daily Mail* and the *Daily Telegraph* a week later; the Attorney General promised to investigate, Rediffusion refused to release the programme transcript and the scandal appears to have fizzled out.

What with questions in the House about his antiques dealings, appearances on 'The Eamonn Andrews Show' with The Beatles in April and on 'Juke Box Jury' in July 1965, and the premiere of his new musical *Passion Flower Hotel* in August of the same year, Mankowitz was moving, with great pleasure, forth and back from elite to popular, along the cultural spectrum. The *Sun* reported on 2 September 1965 that Bertrand Russell had asked Mankowitz, Christopher Logue (*Private Eye* contributor and translator of Homer) and Lionel Bart if they would like to make a musical out of his short-story collection *Satan in the Suburbs*. Mankowitz's comment was that he had the greatest admiration for Russell but 'it would be easier to attain world peace than to get the three of us to collaborate'.

Mankowitz had no difficulties with his colleagues on *Passion Flower Hotel*. His 'book', adapted from the 1962 novel of the same name by Rosalind Erskine (a pseudonym for Roger Longrigg), was interspersed with music and lyrics by John Barry and Trevor Peacock. This was the producer Gene Gutowski's first venture into theatre production, but he already had considerable TV experience and his production of fellow-Pole Roman Polanski's film *Repulsion* had been released two months earlier. The musical did decent enough business, with a two-and-a-half-week run at Manchester's Palace Theatre from 30 July 1965, then a four-month run of 148 performances at London's Prince of Wales theatre. The *Manchester Daily Mail* for 13 July 1965 quoted Mankowitz's view that the message of the musical is 'teenagers ought to have more sexual freedom', but such remarks caused nothing like the hysteria of BBC executives over the script for 'A Cure for Tin Ear' three years earlier. The *Evening Standard*'s critic (25 August 1965) found, in fact, the musical's representation of adolescent sexual experimentation to be 'square, dated, coy, gauche and juvenile'.

If the youngsters came across as gauche, they were meant to be. The plot concerns a group of five virginal fifth-formers at a posh girls' boarding school who form a syndicate to sell their sexual services to the nearest boys' school some twelve miles away. When push comes to shove, everyone is ignorant and embarrassed and the nearest they get to sex is a kiss under the gym-stage, which the girls have rigged up with cushions and shaded lights to resemble their idea of a brothel.

Such innocence may have seemed outdated to a metropolitan audience, but we should also remember that 1965 was still pre-Pill, and boarding schools were still fortresses of Spartan self-control in the more remote areas of England. Sarah Callender (played by Karin Fernald), the leader of the Syndicate, puts the business on a contractual basis by drawing up a 'Document'. This prices the services the girls offer into categories such as 'Seeing' or 'Touching'. These are then subdivided into 'Above Waist Only', 'Below Waist Only', 'Entire Operative', 'Nothing Barred Short of La Penetration' and 'Nothing Barred'.[27] Most libidinous males of the period trekked through similarly ferocious cartographies of the English female body.

The four members of the syndicate were played by actresses at the start of distinguished careers: Francesca Annis, Jean Muir, Pauline Collins and Jane Birkin. Annis had already played one of Cleopatra's handmaidens in the Burton/Taylor film and Birkin had an uncredited appearance as a motorcycle girl in the film version of Ann Jellicoe's *The Knack*. The critic for the *Sunday Times* (29 August 1965) notes 'spider-monkey Jane Birkin' and 'a beanpole blonde called Lucille Gaye [Lady Callender] who all too briefly blazes with exuberance', but, in common with several others critics, laments the actresses' amateur standards of dancing and singing. For Penelope Gilliatt (*Observer*, 29 August 1965) the plot loses its nerve and renders the sex 'comically mechanistic', while the best dance is 'a thwacking mixed hockey match' halfway through the show. *Plays and Players* (5 October 1965) is the most relaxed, in a very English way, about the musical's themes and actions: 'Wolf Mankowitz's script is hilariously dirty, and if its punches are bantam-weight, at least Mr Mankowitz rarely pulls them.'

Mankowitz's adaptation of the novel, a first-person narrative by Sarah Callender, does not seek to reproduce her Gwendolen Fairfax-like tone of icy self-appraisal – 'I will keep [this poem] and improve it suddenly when I am twenty'[28] – but he must have been attracted by the novel's application of business principles to sex. He makes two significant additions in the available theatre text. The girls meet the boys in a café, which Mankowitz rewrites as The Ton Up, where the boys finish up fighting and defeating a gang of Rockers. The meeting has been called to discuss the terms and conditions of the syndicate's services. Before Sarah produces the Document, there is a discussion about costs. Colin, the boys' leader, asks why money need be involved: 'Isn't the educational objective sufficient in itself?' His aggressive lieutenant Ellis then adds: 'After all, it's a purely bourgeois convention that you're giving and we're taking. In fact, it's fairer to consider the whole arrangement a sort of barter. After all, each had something the other hasn't got.'[29] Ellis's last sentence is Mankowitz's addition. It elides the worlds of the Portobello Road and Longcombe Public School into each other. Exchange levels gender distinctions; the Offer is all.

Make Me an Offer would, in fact, have yet another outing as the BBC's 'Play of the Month', a TV version of the stage musical, broadcast on 12 April 1966. There were no significant changes in the text, and Peter Gilmore as Charlie, James Grout as Sparta and Meier Tzelniker as Wendl formed a strong cast. The critic for *The Times* (13 April 1966) found that a televised musical could not reproduce the realism of a stage production, but that this production did catch its sardonic tone and that Tzelniker's was a dazzling performance. The *Daily Telegraph* (13 April 1966), by contrast, praised producer Cedric Messina and designer Eileen Diss for their convincing screen-reproduction of the energetic bustle of the Portobello Road.

But this *Offer* is best considered as only one in a group of works in the second half of the 1960s which reprises modes and themes that had preoccupied Mankowitz during his career to date. The BBC TV adaptation by James Gilbert and Jimmy Grafton of his stage musical *Pickwick*, transmitted on 11 June and 29 December 1969, is another, later, example of 'the repeat'. Secombe remained centre-stage as Mr Pickwick, and other roles were played by such distinguished television stars as Roy Castle (Sam Weller) and Hattie Jacques (Mrs Bardell). It is as if, to complement his new, thriving role as a film scriptwriter, Mankowitz wants also to lay down a marker for the importance of his work to date, as an original writer and a skilled adapter in those other fields of live theatre and television.

There was no strategy. Mankowitz insists, on several occasions in the Davis interview, that everything important in his career happened by chance. But there was a pattern. He finally got a production of 'A Cure for Tin Ear' in the ITV series 'Love Story' on 22 November 1965. Leo McKern as Leo Sandman probably helped to give it a positive critical reception, but the critic for the *Financial Times* (1 December 1965) also praised the play's 'concise, allusive, witty dialogue' and its structure that was 'beautifully turned and exactly judged'. Another ITV production of a Mankowitz short story, 'The Battersea Miracle', featured the next year (26 March 1966) in ITV's 'Armchair Theatre' series. It is an amusing fable of a talking flea, concealed in his clown owner's ear, who preaches world peace, without effect, to his audience, prime ministers and the United Nations. It is a satire, not just on political hypocrisy, but also, with a pop group called The Screamers who cut a record 'My Battersea Miracle Was You', on teenage youth culture. Critics were not particularly convinced by the messianic flea but they were impressed by the performance of Charlie Drake, a very popular knockabout comic of the period, who in his first straight role, played Joey the clown who owns the flea.

Critics were more impressed by *The Biggest Pig in Barbados*, another slight, but charming children's story published by Longman's in October 1965. Mankowitz shows here the same skill at representing the fantasy mind of a child as he had done ten years earlier in *Majollica and Company*. The setting is realist, the aspirant working-class life that Mankowitz had observed, and now left behind, during his family's winter breaks on the island. The novella, indeed, can be read as an envoi to that period of his life. Its language is a skilful mix of standard English and local patois, but the sporting dreams and fantasies of the boy-hero, Belgrave Batchford, show a shrewd insight into the psychology of an 11-year-old. Colin Reid of the *Daily Mail* links skilfully together plot and character when he describes the Batchford family's enormous pig 'half black and half white and the envy of the islanders' which is 'spirited away by the evil eye of the Obeah' and how it was that a small boy won it back with only his courage and a cricket bat. Ann Duchene, reviewing in the *Guardian*, focuses more on Mankowitz's linguistic virtuosity, when she admires the 'fracturing and flowering of the language' of the novella, conveyed as skilfully as the 'Yiddisher-English in his early, more earnest period'.[30]

Barbadan, Yiddish and other styles of English are all represented in *The Penguin Wolf Mankowitz*, a selection from his prose fictions and plays over the last twenty years, published by Penguin in October 1967. It ranges from 'The Finest Pipe-Maker in Russia', his first broadcast story for the BBC in July 1946, through *Laugh Till You Cry*, *The Mendelman Fire and Other Stories* and 'The Inspector', to *The Biggest Pig in Barbados*. *The Bespoke Overcoat* and *It Should Happen to a Dog* are the chosen plays. A Penguin selection was an honour. It established the significance of a writer's range, preserving early or neglected works for a new readership.

The writer who emerges from this selection is a Jewish writer, but not only a Jewish writer. He can deploy a variety of cultural voices, moves with confidence between the differing narrative modes of short story, novella and dramatic dialogue, and varies his milieux from a Russian village to an Essex village to Barbados to a Jewish Heaven with central heating and Kosher food. There is, however, no extract in this compilation from his best-known works, the 'Make Me an Offer' sequence. Mankowitz may have estimated he had become over-identified with the clichéd character of the Jewish dealer. He may have judged that the TV musical repeat the previous year had given the theme, the very phrase, its last bearable exposure.

The Penguin compilation was a tribute, but a tribute can turn into a monument, freezing development when the time is ripe for change. Mankowitz was now 42 and devoting increasing attention to film scriptwriting, at that time considered as no more than a journeyman craft, and certainly not eligible for extracts in a Penguin compilation. It was, however, a lucrative craft and appealed to the populist in Mankowitz. He had argued for a Writers' Union at the Edinburgh

Festival in 1963 but he had also suggested, later that year, as chair of a round table on the relationship between television scriptwriters and their editors, that the writer's product was a commodity sold to a capitalist corporation at the highest price he could negotiate. It was sentimental to believe that aesthetic value could trump exchange value in the mass-media market. Writers needed a strong guild just to prevent their work being edited without permission.

Mankowitz himself had some involvement, major or minor, in the scripts of at least four films in popular genres in this period of the mid-to-late 1960s. He had credits for two spy-thriller films: *Where The Spies Are* (UK general release 27 March 1966), directed and co-scripted with Val Guest; and *Casino Royale* (28 April 1967), the multi-scripted, multi-directed spoof of the James Bond movies. He made a significant script contribution to the war movie *The 25th Hour* (London premiere 9 March 1967), directed by Henri Verneuil and starring Anthony Quinn and Virna Lisi, and he is credited with additional dialogue for Basil Dearden's comedy thriller *The Assassination Bureau* (10 March 1969), starring Oliver Reed, Diana Rigg and Telly Savalas, adapted from Jack London's unfinished novel, *The Assassination Bureau, Ltd.* But he also made a contribution to what, in this context, we must call an 'art movie', when he collaborated with the Oxford don and Chaucer scholar, Neville Coghill, on the script for the film of *Dr Faustus* (10 October 1967) produced by, and starring, Richard Burton, and also starring Elizabeth Taylor as Helen of Troy.

The joint script of *Where the Spies Are*, with some additions by James Leasor, author of the novel *Passport to Oblivion* (the original source of the film), is competent as far as it goes, which is not very far. It introduces some mild parody of the James Bond conventions, with exploding pens, a nightmare plane journey for the hero, James Love (David Niven), in the hands of thuggish Russians and a beautiful double agent and fashion model, Vikki, played by Francoise Dorleac. Alexander Walker, who gives the most appreciative critique of the film for the *Evening Standard* (3 March 1966), sums up the narrative as a 'Rusky plot to assassinate an oil sheik on a State visit to Beirut during a Vogue fashion photography shoot'. With John Le Mesurier playing the head of MI6 with his customary air of exhausted disgust, there is no chance that Love's mission can be anything but ludicrous. Niven and Dorleac go through the motions of seduction, but an English gentleman and a French sex kitten are worlds apart. The best line in the script, picked out by the *Jewish Chronicle*'s reviewer (14 March 1966) and surely by

Mankowitz, is when the Russian interrogator on the plane screams at Niven to tell them where MI6's London message-drop centre is. 'Cohen's smoked salmon shop in the Edgware Road', replies Niven with studied calm.

David Niven is also the most prominent star, as the original 'old school' James Bond brought out of retirement to fight a collective of beautiful women called SMERSH, in the star-filled cast of *Casino Royale*. Orson Welles plays Le Chiffre, a master of baccarat and illusionism; Peter Sellers is a latter-day James Bond; Woody Allen is a cousin, Jimmy Bond; Deborah Kerr is superb as a demented aristocratic vamp; and Joanna Pettet is Mata Bond and daughter of the original James Bond and Mata Hari. Ursula Andress is spy Vesper Lynd and Jacqueline Bisset has a bit part as the luscious Giovanna Goodthighs. James Chapman calls the film a 'messy extravaganza', but he does point out that it was produced, not by Saltzman and Broccoli, but by Charles K. Feldman, a lawyer turned producer, who intended it as a spoof of the spy film genre.[31] It is full of gags and allusions, not only to German Expressionism, but also to the surrealism of 'The Goon Show' and the Richard Lester Beatles films.

Mankowitz's contribution to the final script is difficult to disentangle from a team, credited or not, that also comprised, among others, John Law, Michael Sayers, Ben Hecht, Terry Southern and Joseph Heller. But he would seem best placed to have been responsible for Ronnie Corbett's very English portrayal of Eno, butler to the SMERSH training school, whose ticker is powered by a dicky battery and who is besotted as much by Mata Hari's daughter as he was by Mata Hari herself. Mankowitz, while happy to work with Welles, was still hostile to Sellers. Ed Sikov, in his biography of Sellers, quotes Mankowitz as saying that Sellers would 'fuck everything up' and that he was '*terrified* of playing with Orson before he even met Orson' (emphasis in the original). Sellers insisted that all his scenes with Welles should be single cuts, so that they didn't have to work together.[32] But, despite all the incoherence of plot, backstage squabbles and bad reviews – Richard Roud, for the *Guardian*, called the film a 'big, colourful, noisy, star-studded, plot-less, junk-pile of a mess'[33] – it was a financial success. Chapman cites $17 million dollars for rentals by cinemas, and Roger Eglin and Iain Murray, in a piece for *The Observer* some years later on the occasion of the release of *Diamonds Are Forever*, quoted an estimated figure of $40.8 million for *Casino Royale*'s worldwide takings. On this Bond occasion Mankowitz did not insist his name be removed from the credits.

He also, along with director Henri Verneuil and Françoise Boyer, had a writer credit for *The 25th Hour*, which opened in London the month before *Casino Royale*. The script, adapted from the novel of the same name by the Rumanian C. Virgil Gheorgiu, focuses on a minor figure in the novel, Johann Moritz. He is a dim peasant from the village of Fontana who is denounced as a Jew (which he is not) by the village chief of police, Nicolai Dobresco, who wants Moritz imprisoned so he can make love to his wife, Suzanna, played with muted beauty by Virna Lisi. Moritz, played by Anthony Quinn throughout as a man of imperturbable stupidity, is bounced back and forth between Nazi and Allied forces, country and city, and, above all, Jewish and non-Jewish identity. To the Rumanian authorities he is a Jew; to the Jews who help him escape from prison camp he is a Gentile; to a crazed Nazi race scientist – a superb cameo by Marius Goring – he is an example of the perfect Aryan. He finishes up as one of the accused at the Nuremberg Trials but is, improbably, released on compassionate grounds following a letter from Susanna read out to the court.

When, at the start, Moritz complains to his fellow-villager Marco Goldberg that he isn't a Jew, Goldberg makes the key observation of the film: 'We're living in a world where any human being can become a Jew at any moment.' But reviewers also saw Moritz as a modern version of Candide, or Don Quixote. Quinn plays him with such imperturbable stoicism that any archetype, including Odysseus the Wandering Jew, could be read into his stolid face. Bosley Crowther for the *New York Times* (17 February 1967) criticizes this characterization as 'one of utter insensitivity', but Richard Davis for the *Daily Telegraph* (3 March 1967) commends the black farce of plot and character, although he wonders whether monochrome would have been a more effective medium than colour for this genre. Molly Plowright of the *Glasgow Herald* (29 May 1967) attributes to Mankowitz additional, very funny dialogue, and there are many occasions when we seem to be in a crueller version of the world of Sholem Aleichem rather than a middle-European version of *The Long and the Short and the Tall*. But it was in this same year, 1967, that, as we shall see, another war caused him to re-examine his own Jewish identity.

Michael Relph is credited with the production as well as the screenplay of *The Assassination Bureau*, proof that the two roles can combine to create a successful commercial film. Dearden and Relph retain the central conceit of London's novel, that there exists an age-old private organization which has arrogated to itself the power of assassinating corrupt leaders for the greater good. The Bureau's leader, Ivan Dragomiloff, by now a very wealthy man, accepts (as in the novel) to be the latest quarry of his own organization, as much for the thrill of the chase as for any sense of a guilty misuse of power. But his main pursuer here is not, as in the novel, a rich young man called Winter Hall, who is in love with Dragomiloff's daughter, but a young, feminist woman reporter in the early 1900s, Sonya Winter, played by Diana Rigg.

The film takes us on a picaresque tour of explosions in various European capitals as Dragomiloff (Oliver Reed) destroys all his pursuers. Here is excellent copy for a cub reporter but Sonya doesn't file a single story. She falls in love with Dragomiloff but resists his advances until, scrawny and shivering on a bed in a Venetian hotel, she is seduced by Reed's vulpine charm. 'Surrender', murmurs Reed. She hesitates and then, with English briskness, says the best lines in the script: 'Why not? To surrender is no defeat for a woman.' This is the observation of a witty woman of the world, a persona quite at odds with Sonya's blue-stocking primness, morally outraged by the female licence she has witnessed in Paris and Vienna. The line, knowing and pragmatic, sounds very Mankowitz and may well have been one of his additions.

An unusual postscript links *Where the Spies Are* and *The Assassination Bureau*. In 2009, the *Observer* put out a call to its readers to identify the subject of a photograph by Jane Bown, whose work they were currently celebrating. The photo was of a seated old lady, with white hair, large black-rimmed spectacles, a long necklace, rings and bangles. She was swiftly identified as Beatrice 'Bumble' Dawson, a much-respected film and theatre costume designer. One correspondent, Vernon Dobtcheff, Baron Muntzov in *The Assassination Bureau*, recalls her as a fun theatre companion and a generous and elegant hostess when they worked together on the film. Another correspondent, Louise Hartman, recounts an adventurous journey by taxi across the desert from Aleppo to Beirut that Dawson and her mother had to make, all planes being grounded because of fog. But 'Bumbles' was back punctually on the set of *Where the Spies Are* the next morning, the consummate professional.[34]

The history of Mankowitz's involvement with the film-script version of *Dr Faustus* is, if not tragical, certainly somewhat mysterious. The film premiered in Oxford on 10 October 1967 and starred Richard Burton as Faustus and Elizabeth Taylor as Helen of Troy. Burton was also co-producer with Richard McWhorter and co-director with Neville Coghill. One of the production copyrights was for Oxford

University Screen Productions (OUDS), and the film was presented by Columbia Pictures. This film of Faustus was, in effect, a follow-up to the OUDS production of the play at Oxford Playhouse, in February of the previous year, which had also starred Burton and Taylor. All profits from both productions went to the University Theatre Appeal Fund, and Burton and Taylor waived their usual fees – £300,000 each in the case of the film – for both productions. Burton had always recalled his brief time at Oxford as an idyll of intellectual and personal exploration and had an especial affection for Coghill, his tutor at the time. The largely undergraduate cast of the original stage production was flown over in the late summer of 1966 to De Laurentiis's studios in Rome at the Burtons' expense and the couple also financed the film.

By early 1967, then, it can be assumed that *Dr Faustus* had been scripted, at least in part by Mankowitz, shot and edited. That is certainly the impression given by Mankowitz in an interview for the *Los Angeles Times Calendar* (22 January 1967) on the occasion of his holding a series of seminars on plays, including *Dr Faustus*, and screen-writing at the University College of Santa Barbara. He is quoted as saying: 'I created eight more scenes for Elizabeth [in the film of *Dr Faustus*], though she still has no lines. But after all, if one is getting Elizabeth Taylor for nothing, one had best use her.' The interviewer adds: 'Since she is the one vision Faustus wants to retain, the additional scenes, says Mankowitz, strengthen the motivation.'

It is Coghill and Burton, however, who are named as the co-authors of this composite Marlowe text – with scenes from *Tamburlaine*, *Edward II* and *The Jew of Malta* amalgamated into the 1604 text of *Faustus* – in a biography of Burton by John Cottrell and Fergus Cashin. Coghill is apologetic about the hybrid nature of the final script but he makes it clear that it was primarily devised as a vehicle for Burton. There is no mention of any Mankowitz contribution, nor does he receive any attribution, in the accounts of the genesis and reception of the stage play and the film in biographies by Penny Junor and Melvyn Bragg.[35] His name does not appear in the list of credits.

A letter in the Family Archive lays out Mankowitz's reasons for disavowing the film. He finds that technically the film is a compendium of traditional special effects which defeat their aim of treating *Faustus* as 'a modern examination of the problems of sexual obsession'. He had not, contrary to their agreement, been consulted at any stage about cuts, rewrites or changes and does not agree with the treatment of the picture. He congratulates Burton on a magnificent performance and wishes all involved in it every success, but, with regret, asks them to withdraw his name from the credits of a film 'to which I feel I have contributed very little beyond that of a hired journeyman'.[36]

The critical reaction to the film was poor and it was a box-office disaster. Mankowitz made, it would seem, the wrong call with *Dr No*, but the right call with *Dr Faustus*. Bragg attempts to defend it, when he admits that although it is not a good film, more a student romp, it is nonetheless made in a good cause. Burton is 'not wholly terrible' but he carries the film too much and is 'badly constrained by the over-significance of the part'.[37] Cottrell and Cashin[38] quote Alexander Walker's positive review for the *Evening Standard*: '[Burton's] performance swells to fill the screen more movingly than it did on the stage', but he concludes that 'this was always going to be a film for a minority audience'.

Penelope Mortimer for the *Observer* finds the film a bore, largely because Marlowe's language and imagination aren't 'really up to the searching analysis of modern cinema'. Hell is just a hole in the ground and Elizabeth Taylor 'would not look out of place in a provincial draper's shop window'.[39] Michael Billington, for *The Times* (10 October 1967), categorizes the film as 'a weird unhappy hybrid' and for Margaret Hintman (*Sunday Telegraph*, 23 October 1967) its decor is 'mostly early Dracula'. Vast crowds greeted Burton and Taylor at the New York premiere in February 1968 but the critics were damning. For the *New York Times* the film 'is of an awfulness that bends the mind' and *Time* describes Elizabeth Taylor's Helen, as she seduces Faust to Hell, as a woman whose 'eyeballs and teeth are dripping pink in what seems a hellish combination of conjunctivitis and trench mouth'.[40]

NOTES

1. James Chapman, *Licence to Thrill: A Cultural History of the James Bond Films*, 2nd rev. edn (London and New York: I.B. Tauris, 2007), pp.57–8.
2. Albert R. Broccoli with Donald Zec, *When the Snow Melts: The Autobiography of Cubby Broccoli* (London: Boxtree, 1998), p.157.
3. Ibid., p.158.
4. Ibid., p.163.
5. *Observer*, 11 March 1962.
6. Roger Lewis, *The Life and Death of Peter Sellers* (London: Century, 1994), p.324.
7. Letter from Wolf Mankowitz to Ronnie Waldman, 9 June 1959, T48/402, BBC Written Archives Centre, Caversham Park, Reading [hereafter WAC].
8. Letter from Wolf Mankowitz to Eric Maschwitz, 5 June 1958, T48/402, WAC.
9. Letter from Donald Wilson to G.M.Tel.P. (General Manager, Television Promotions), 31 October 1961, T48/402, WAC.

10. Letter from Ronald Waldman to Wolf Mankowitz, 21 March 1962; letter from Donald Baverstock to Eric Maschwitz, 'Baverstock to Mashchwitz', 26 March 1962; letter from David Whitaker to Eric Maschwitz, 27 March, 1962; all T48/402, WAC.
11. Quoted in Dominic Sandbrook, *Never Had It So Good: A History of Britain from Suez to the Beatles*, paperback edn (London: Abacus 2006), pp.397–8.
12. Ibid., p.381.
13. Lewis, *Life and Death*, p.454.
14. This, and all subsequent quotations and all information about Mason's Yard, are taken from Gered Mankowitz, 'Introduction: Mason's Yard', in Gered Mankowitz, *The Experience: Jimi Hendrix at Mason's Yard* (San Rafael, CA: Insight Editions, 2010), pp.18–25.
15. W. Mankowitz, *Cockatrice* (London: Longmans, 1963), p.40.
16 . Ibid., p.162.
17. Ibid., p.8.
18. Script of *Pickwick*, Act I, Scene II, pp.7–9, Mankowitz Family Archive.
19. William Hall, *70 Not Out: The Biography of Sir Michael Caine* (London: John Blake, 2003), pp.117, 125.
20. M. Freedland, *Michael Caine*, paperback edn (London: Orion 2000), p.116.
21. M. Caine, *What's It All About?* (London: Century, 1992), p.135.
22. Edina Ronay, 'When George Harrison Came To Supper', *Observer*, 7 December 2003, p.35. The *Daily Telegraph* of 8 July 1971 records that the Official Receiver had declared the club insolvent the previous day, with debts of nearly £114,000 and assets of £7,226. It had never made a profit. Wolf Mankowitz was no longer associated with the club.
23. *Daily Mirror*, 7 October 1963.
24. *Private Eye*, 38 (31 May 1963), p.16.
25. *San Juan Star*, 1 March 1964.
26. *Observer*, 20 February 2010.
27. Script of *Passion Flower Hotel*, Act I, Scene 9, p.44, Mankowitz Family Archive.
28. Rosalind Erskine, *Passion Flower Hotel* (London: Jonathan Cape, 1962), p.17.
29. Script of *Passion Flower Hotel*, Act I, Scene 9, p.42, Mankowitz Family Archive.
30. *Daily Mail*, 7 October 1965; *Guardian*, 8 October 1965.
31. Chapman, *Licence to Thrill*, pp.106–8.
32. Ed Sikov, *Mr Strangelove: A Biography of Peter Sellers* (London: Sidgwick & Jackson, 2002), p.247.
33. *Guardian*, 14 April 1967. See also reviews quoted in Chapman, *Licence to Thrill.*
34. *Guardian*, 5 October 2009.
35. John Cottrell and Fergus Cashin, *Richard Burton: An Intimate Biography* (London: Arthur Barker, 1971); Penny Junor, *The Man Behind the Myth*, (London: Sidgwick & Jackson, 1985); Melvyn Bragg, *Rich: The Life of Richard Burton* (London: Hodder & Stoughton, 1988).
36. Wolf Mankowitz to Richard Burton, 25 July 1967, Mankowitz Family Archive.
37. Bragg, *Rich*, pp.250–1.
38. Cottrell and Cashin, *Richard Burton*, pp.305–6.
39. *Observer*, 22 October 1967.
40. Quoted in Bragg, *Rich*, p.254.

CHAPTER EIGHT

Israel and Ireland (1967–72)

By early 1968, Mankowitz was as concerned with politics as with press reviews. The Six Day War the previous year, between Israel and the massed forces of four Arab countries, had impelled Mankowitz towards a reassessment of his identity as an English Jew. A long essay which prefaces his play, *The Samson Riddle* (1972), is the fruit, he tells us, of four years' speculation about what it means, now, to be a Jew, and what the story of Samson can tell him and us about the historical distinctiveness of the Jews. He reaches the interim conclusion that, as a Jew with an English upbringing, he is suspended, as it were, between an achieved culture and a people remaking itself: 'I knew finally that though England had not entirely made me, I had done nothing to make Israel and therefore had no permanent place there.'[1] In the Davis interview he talks of his earlier enthusiasm for the aims and hopes of this newly recreated Israel. He bought a house for himself and his family in Tel Aviv, and involved himself heavily in the emergent Israeli film industry, but he finished up bankrupt and exhausted by his over-enthusiasm for the project. By 1972 they were all settled in Ireland and Mankowitz would continue to interrogate his Jewish inheritance by way of writing rather than residence.

In the *Samson* essay he records that he came to Gaza, a few days after the Six Day War, to 'make a film about the emergent Israeli identity'.[2] The film, a documentary, was entitled *Israeli – A Right to Live*. Mankowitz recalls in the Davis interview that it was largely financed by Broccoli and Saltzman; that he and John Schlesinger were among the directors; and that filming took place very soon after the war so that footage included corpses decaying in the sun and desert areas strewn with the boots of the fleeing Arab armies. The film company, Lowndes Productions, gained access to these military zones because of the influence of Moshe Dayan's daughter, with whom Mankowitz had worked on several projects. Mankowitz admits that the aim of the film is propagandistic although, following his own family's political tradition, non-Zionist. Through a resume of the Jews' diasporic past and a survey of their success in melding a democratic civil society with their religious inheritance the film makes the case for Israel's 'right to live', which is the film's subtitle.

The film was never shown commercially although the *Jewish Chronicle* for 22 March 1968 records its first public showing, introduced by Mankowitz, in the synagogue hall of the Kingston branch of AJEX (Association of Jewish Ex-Service Men and Women). I have been unable to trace a copy, but there is an 'Outline' by Mankowitz in the Family Archive which confirms the above summary. It finishes with the Narrator, shown against the wreckage of Egyptian tanks, recounting the estimated costs of the past three Arab/Israeli wars to the Arab countries. 'The same money', he says, 'could have provided schools, medical services, homes, roads etc. for the Arab peoples.' The last sequence has the Narrator walking past the desert debris as the overlaid voice of Ben Gurion promises a defiant search for peace and the Narrator promises that the State of Israel exists and will continue to so.

The Family Archive also contains two important letters between Harry Saltzman and Mankowitz. The first, from Mankowitz, is dated 20 February 1968 and reports a successful showing of the picture 'after a large dinner for the Commander in Chief Barlev in Tel Aviv on 17 February'. The copy will be returned to Saltzman when the Prime Minister and others have seen it. Mexico and Argentina would also like copies. The second letter, dated 14 March 1968, also from Mankowitz, says that 'we are wasting out time with ATV and the BBC' and suggests showings be arranged for the other major television companies. These are further evidence to confirm what Mankowitz says in the Davis interview: that the Israeli authorities found the film magnificent, but saw that it could prove politically disastrous. They did not want to be accused of crowing over the defeated Arabs. Their long-term aim was to live in peace with their neighbours so they put an embargo on the film. W.J. Mann, in his biography of Schlesinger, says the film was never completed due to creative differences with the BBC.[3] There is every evidence that it was completed but political pressure may well have been brought to bear on the BBC and ITV to prevent a public showing.

An undoubtedly incomplete film in this period is an unedited interview between Bernard Braden and Mankowitz for an American series called 'Now and Then'.[4] Internal evidence shows it to have taken place around April 1968. By then, Mankowitz, as a founder-member of the Writers for Israel Committee, a Personal Advisor on Films to the Israeli Ministry of Information, and an unambiguous defender of Israel's conduct of the Six Day War, was committed to a revaluation of his Jewishness. He confesses to Braden that, while not renouncing his philosophical materialism, he has discovered great value in the rabbinical, mystical tradition of Judaism. The rituals of orthodoxy, he contends, direct the intelligent mind towards a consideration of the law. His task now is to balance the activist (sabra) and mystical tendencies within himself. He elaborates here on what he said in his address to the Jewish Book Week a month earlier: 'since the taking of the Wall ... I have unpicked the lock to a vast treasure, which is the Torah and everything that has come out of it'.[5]

But the showman activist in Mankowitz could not be denied his moment. He was the principal organizer and writer, along with his old collaborators Monty Norman and Julian More, of a documentary revue, entitled *Israel 20*, to celebrate the twentieth anniversary of the foundation of the State of Israel. It took place on the evening of 28 April 1968, before an audience of some 10,000 at the Albert Hall. It included sketches of significant moments, in both war and peacetime, in the history of Israel; music that covered all the different traditions of the country, both local and diasporic; strong speeches in support of Israel from distinguished representatives of Britain's three main political parties; and a roll call of performers, both Jewish and Gentile, that included Miriam Karlin, Meier Tzelnicker, David Jacobs, Bernard Bresslaw, Roger Moore, Lord Boothby and Gerry Marsden. The evening took place under the auspices of the Zionist Federation but, as with the Braden interview, Mankowitz was at pains to distance himself from a Zionist view of Israel's future. The *Jewish Observer and Middle East Review* (26 April 1968) represented him as someone who wished to live in Israel but 'his views of *aliya*[6] do not necessarily conform to traditional Zionist ideology'.

Mankowitz thought, at this stage, that he could best contribute to the cultural life of Israel by offering his skills and experience to its fledgling film industry. He had now, for almost a decade, been a scriptwriter on films in a wide variety of genres, and *Cockatrice* had demonstrated that he had a clear grasp of the politics and procedures of film-making. With *Israeli* he developed an interest in the documentary film and his next venture in this field was his voice-over commentary to *Cast Us Not Out* (1969), a very moving London-based short on the plight of poor, Jewish old people. The production company was Samaritan Films, the director was Richard Bigham and the cameraman was Walter Suchitzsky. He brings to bear on his subjects – very old people in a variety of homes, private and State-aided – an unwavering camera-eye whose respect for clarity of detail renders beautiful even the aged hands and faces of his subjects. Mankowitz's voice-over is authoritative and solicitous, quoting statistics and carefully distinguishing between charity and welfare. But the film's subjects also speak. One shot pans along a row of very old Jewish women. It closes up on one who groans that she wants to die. The camera solicits us into neither pity nor sorrow. It presents the woman's truth with the astringency of a Beckettian derelict.

But Mankowitz also had ambitions for the Israeli feature-film business. His was the original script for *Bloomfield*, also known as *The Hero*, whose climax was the last great game of Eitan, a 40-year-old fading star of Tel Aviv's soccer team, the disappointment of his greatest fan, the boy Nimrod (Kim Burfield), and the growing indifference of Eitan's long-term fiancée, the sculptress Nira, played by Romy Schneider.

Mankowitz, as he recounts in the Davis interview, envisaged *Bloomfield* as a low-budget, black-and-white Israeli film in Hebrew, a soccer version of the 1931 film *The Champ*. Then Richard Harris, now a star of popular culture with his role as King Arthur in the film version of the musical *Camelot*, saw the role of Eitan as an opportunity to reprise his starring role as Frank Machin in Lindsay Anderson's highly regarded New Wave film *This Sporting Life*. Harris's involvement changed everything. The budget rose to $2 million and Harris invested some £300,000 of his own money in the production.[7] He also, according to another biographer, took over the production and 'unravelled and rebuilt the screenplay to his own liking, changing three-quarters of the dialogue and running sequence'.[8]

The original director, Uri Zohar, was sacked and Harris, with no relevant experience, took over as director. Steve Berkoff, whose production of Kafka's *Metamorphosis* at the Roundhouse had impressed Mankowitz, had been hired as Zohar's assistant. He was also, to his great relief, fired along with Zohar. The film had become, for him, an intolerable ordeal. He had understood that the production was a contrivance to build up Israel's reputation as a film-producing country, but he thought the script was very substandard and the casting of Harris as a Jewish Israeli footballer ridiculous. A reading of the BFI's Release Script does depict Eitan as a pathetic man-child, sticking gum on the nose of one of his girlfriend's sculptures, incapable of doing business with his bank manager and, at the end, pulling a face at the camera as he is left, desolate and destitute, in the Bloomfield stadium.[9] Yet all the principal parties refused to recognize the inadequacy of that script, and, ominously, Mankowitz was happy to be credited as its co-producer.[10]

The film was finished by February 1970 and Harris edited it throughout the spring of that year. It had a successful non-commercial showing in his home town of Limerick but it had little success in either Europe or America. It was entered for the Golden Bear award at the Berlin Film Festival of 1971, but the audience booed it at the end. It opened in London in December of the same year, but the reviews ranged from lukewarm approval to downright dismissal.

Alex Walker for the *Evening Standard* (12 December 1971) was interested to be guided through 'the bohemian fringe as well as the big business centre' of middle-class Israeli society and he appreciated Mankowitz's script with its 'sharp jibe at the get-ahead motive still lingering in the kibbutz doctrine of equality'. But most reviews were unconvinced by Harris's performance as an ageing footballer and debutant director. Ian Christie for the *Daily Mail* (22 December 1971) would have suspended him from his final game, and Derek Malcolm for *The Guardian* (16 December 1971) deplored the film's 'souped-up camera work, trendy score and Wolf Mankowitz's pseudo-sophisticated dialogue'. The American reception was no better, with Roger Greenspun for the *New York Times* (9 March 1973) criticizing Harris's direction as mannered and the film's theme of the Last Big Game as clichéd. Greenspun has a memorable characterization of Romy Schneider's performance as a 'bemused enigma, beautiful, mysterious and unexciting'. Harris never directed again but soon recovered his star status with the lead roles in the films *A Man Called Horse* and *Cromwell*.

Mankowitz left Israel and the Israeli film industry to their own devices and an *Evening Standard* item of 29 April 1971 reported that the lease on his central London home, an Adam house in Dorset Street, Marylebone, was for sale. He was living in an apartment in Simmons Court Castle, Dublin, and now regarded himself as domiciled in Éire. He was taking advantage of a new law introduced by the then Prime Minister Charles Haughey which exempted from income tax the artistic earnings of an Éire resident. Mankowitz's tax affairs in the UK were, and not for the last time, in some disarray. The previous month he had lost an appeal in the High Court against a penalty of nearly £6,000 imposed on him by the tax commissioners for failing to provide documents that related to a Nassau-based company, Alderden Investments Ltd. His battles with the Inland Revenue, together with his battles with Richard Harris over the direction of *Bloomfield*, had left him, he recalls in lengthy detail in the Davis interview, utterly exhausted and virtually penniless.

The slower pace of life in Ireland, particularly in the small town of Ahakista in West Cork, enabled him to recuperate. He was able to write, as he puts it, 'without having to worry too much about the commercial aspects of what I was writing'. He and his wife, while on a holiday stay at a friend's cottage, had been very taken by a view, outside the village, of trees going down to the sea, and had bought and refurbished a derelict house which overlooked the view. He insists in interview that, for all the cosmopolitanism of his career, which included a seven-year summer stint as Visiting Professor of Theatre at the University of New Mexico in the 1980s, he had regarded Ireland, and Ahakista as his real home since settling there. He even started his own press, the Ahakista Press, to publish leather-bound limited editions of his own works. As a writer and a Jew he had always been accepted by the Irish, more so in fact than by the Israelis in his recent stay there, who resented what they perceived as a superiority complex on the part of Anglo-Jews. The Irish, unlike the English, never questioned his class or culture. It was probably his sense of relieved freedom that enabled him, within a year of settling in Ireland, to write two of his shrewdest and wittiest scripts, for the short film *The Hebrew Lesson*, and for the play *The Samson Riddle*.

In 1970, the year before he settled in Ireland, Mankowitz had renewed his collaboration and friendship with one of the wittiest men he knew, Laurence Harvey. Mankowitz had always valued the strong bond that the two Baltic Jews had created during the making of *Expresso Bongo*, but since then Harvey had become, with films such as *Butterfield 8*, *The Manchurian Candidate* and *Darling*, an international cinema star. By the late 1960s, however, despite his marriage to Joan Perry Cohn, the very wealthy widow of film mogul Harry Cohn of Columbia pictures, he was no longer being offered major film roles. His version of stylish, hard-edged bastardy was no longer in favour and his looks were going.

In March 1970, his film company, Laurence Harvey Productions, joined with Mankowitz's Wolfman Productions 'with plans to produce a series of films to be made, for the most part, in Britain and Cyprus'.[11] No traceable films emerged from this collaboration, but perhaps Harvey, already beginning to feel the onset of the stomach cancer which would kill him three years later, needed the lift that Mankowitz's energy could give him. Harvey had begun his career in the theatre and he looked now to the theatre for renewal. In the same month, Harvey, along with Siobhan McKenna, Patrick Magee and Richard Harris, participated in a benefit performance of readings from Samuel Beckett and other modernist writers at the Oxford Playhouse to mark the inauguration of the Samuel Beckett Theatre at Oxford University. During the evening, Beckett's *Breath*, which lasts for only thirty seconds, and is a recording of human cries and breaths, was played five times.

Mankowitz presented the evening, thereby renewing his commitment to avant-garde art, while at the same time he was, among other projects, writing a film adaptation of Anna Sewell's *Black Beauty* and considering a treatment of *Treasure Island*, classics of children's fiction, one of the most enduring genres of popular culture. Later that year, Mankowitz and Harvey presented another evening of readings, *Here Are Ladies*, at the Oxford Playhouse and then at the Criterion Theatre, London. Siobhan McKenna interpreted a range of female characters from Irish literature, including Shaw's St Joan, Beckett's Winnie and women from *Finnegan's Wake*. The show was a great success and became a staple item in McKenna's repertoire.

In 1971, Mankowitz and Harvey set up the Panamanian International Film Company (PIFCO) as a vehicle to produce a documentary on the Kuna Indians, original inhabitants of the 365 islands that surround the mainland and with a history of successful resistance to the Panamanians. Mankowitz's 'Original Treatment' in the Mankowitz Family Archive, entitled *An Mar Tule* (*We Are the People*), is, in the absence of any traceable copy of the film itself, an important guide to its contents. It fleshes out the summary of the film which appeared in the *Times of Malta* (30 March 1971). Its plot, according to Michael Blare, features a young Kuna woman who decides to return to her island birthplace 'to attend the most important event of the Kuna calendar'. The film therefore traces her outsider's view on her culture of origin as well as indicating key events in the history of Spanish colonization. The impetus to make the film came from its producer,

Richard G. Levy, who wished to record what he saw as a self-sufficient culture being eroded by modern civilization. It was directed by the Peruvian Armando Robles Godoy and narrated by Laurence Harvey.

The film was well received in film festivals that summer but it did not cover its costs. Charles Nevin of the *Observer*, in a much later interview with Mankowitz (12 February 1984), says that in 1971 the Republic of Panama appointed him Honorary Consul for Panama in Dublin in lieu of payment for the film. Mankowitz confirms this in the Davis interview and adds that he got preferential parking in the city and, to boost trade between the two countries, got the Panamanians interested in buying Kerrygold butter, and introduced them to the idea of buying Irish whiskey instead of Scotch whiskey. 'I don't know whether they were totally converted', he muses, 'but if they were I think I've made a great contribution to Irish industrial life.'

Mankowitz was profoundly moved by Harvey's death, at the age of 45, in November, 1973. He loved him for the laughter. 'You'll settle for a relationship with someone', he declares in interview 'who gives you a good laugh rather than any other virtue a human being might have.' The 'Elegy for Laurence Harvey' he wrote and distributed to the mourners at the actor's cremation in Golders Green salutes the rackety exuberance of his prime, and an exit worthy of a man of the theatre:

So for the last time
your laughing sardonic face
looked into the pit
and creased with pain,
then,
grinned finally
as with a shrug
you carefully lifted
your elegant bones into the wings.

O demon lover, white wine poet,
Litvak lunatic, little monster,
your positively last appearance
as a man
was so true that
only death could upstage you.

Rest now, lonely friend,
as you never did before,
In utter peace.[12]

The Harvey elegy was written for a specific occasion, but Mankowitz had already resumed the poetry-writing habit of his Cambridge days with the publication of *XII Poems*, first published in the Workshop Poets Series, London, in 1971, then reproduced as one of the first publications by his own Ahakista Press in early 1972.[13] They are dedicated to 'A.M.', presumably his wife, but each of the poems is spoken by an unknown male to an unknown female. Intimate scenes of love and lust are threaded through a range of stanzaic and rhyme models. Feeling is refracted by wit, the outstanding characteristic, according to T.S. Eliot, of the English metaphysical poets of the seventeenth century. There are echoes of John Donne in 'Poem VII' which begins: 'Nothing you and I have been / till nothing we once two became.' But the predominant influence is that of the Cavalier poets, the gentlemen Royalists who succeeded Donne and brought Woman down to earth from the Christian clouds. 'Poem VI' catches with great expertise the jaunty worldliness we would find in a poem by Sir John Suckling:

> When I possess you utterly
> your love reveals immoderately
> such absolute fidelity
> my heart accepts you easily.
>
> Your body's sweet immodesty
> far sweeter by this constancy
> informs by sigh and lip and eye
> that you are mine entirely.
>
> And it was faithful formerly
> and faithful more immediately
> and faithful it will always be
> to you indeed, but not to me.

This is Cambridge Mankowitz, conscious of a poetic tradition and adept at alluding to it in his own work. In a long and important interview with John Hall for the *Guardian* (16 September 1970) he refers proudly to his early poetry and declares that poetry is a young man's game, for then you have the 'tremendous afflatus [and] need to be heard' that can propel you into writing very good work very quickly. He contrasts this speed with the much greater knowledge and discipline required for 'the architecture of a play or screenplay' and remarks, in the case of the latter, that 'the scriptwriter produces the bricks for a pyramid to be projected on. At the top of the pyramid is the face on the film ... and somewhere at the bottom is material from this writer, the other writer, and also from non-writers.' This is Mankowitz the populist, who declares in the same interview that he determined, at the age of 15, to make a living as a professional writer; who has written in every genre; and who decided that 'you can't go on writing Leavisite criticism when you've reviewed everything that relates to the great tradition'.

At the beginning of his article, Hall notes that Mankowitz has recently completed film-script adaptations of the novels *Black Beauty* by Anna Sewell and *Treasure Island* by R.L. Stevenson. They went on general UK release in the summers of 1971 and 1973 respectively and their scripts demonstrate Mankowitz's versatile command of what he disparages as no more than 'carpentry' in the Hall interview. The central conceit of Anna Sewell's 1877 novel is that it is related by the hero-horse Black Beauty, who takes us on a roundabout trip through the kindnesses and cruelties of rural England, the horrors of cities and war, and the recovery of humanitarian kindness to animals back in the countryside. For Sewell it is the ancient hierarchy of lord, gentry and labourer in rural society that guarantees the active exercise of Christian charity towards man and beast.

Mankowitz transforms this moral fable into a picaresque journey from the quiet farm to capture by gypsies, circus-performer, go-between in an aristocratic love story, battle-service in India, service as a coal-merchant's nag, and a final rescue by Anna Sewell herself. Many incidents, such as the circus and the frustrated young lovers, are Mankowitz's invention; others, such as the extended battle-sequences and the villainous young squire, are expanded out of brief descriptions in Sewell's story. Director James Hill and photography director Chris Menges, here at the beginning of a very distinguished career, had as good an eye for visual excitement for a young audience as Mankowitz. Together they produced a film whose wide spectrum of colour and movement is always focussed by the gloss of the black beauty at the centre of it. If this was carpentry it was carpentry by first-class craftsmen.

Some critics cavilled at Mankowitz's adaptation. Derek Malcolm for the *Guardian* (27 May 1971), sneers that Mankowitz has produced a screenplay 'that would make a horse laugh on occasion', and Dick Richards, writing for the *Mirror* (28 May 1971), suggests that the Royal Society for the Prevention of Cruelty to Animals should have 'looked into the case of poor *Black Beauty*'. But Garry O'Connor's appreciation of Mankowitz's rewriting of Sewell's original – 'a glamorous knife-throwing act is rescued from death by a courteous British ambassador' – for the *Financial Times* (28 May 1971) is more representative of the overall critical reaction. Richard Combs for the *Monthly Film Bulletin* (May 1971) finds the film appealing and appreciates the unfussy way in which it takes the switches 'from gypsy romance to circus comedy to frontier-adventure in its animal-loving stride'.

Cecil Wilson, for the *Daily Mail* (24 May 1971) makes a suggestive observation on the film's UK production and distribution company, Tigon, when he notes that the owner, Tony Tenser, is usually associated with more 'grown up films'. Tenser, of Lithuanian-Jewish parents, was brought up in poverty in the East End, won a scholarship to grammar school but, unlike Mankowitz, proceeded not to Cambridge but to a series of menial jobs until he was accepted as a cinema manager with the ABC chain. After experience as a publicity manager for Miracle Films, an independent distributor which specialized in European imports, he opened his own cinema, the Compton Club, with a fellow-Jew, Michael Klinger, in 1961, which featured imported sex and horror films.[14]

They produced their own films, most notably *Naked as Nature Intended* (1961), but they also had their elitist moments, executive-producing and distributing Roman Polanski's *Repulsion* (1965) and *Cul-de-Sac* (1966), starring Catherine Deneuve. Tenser had split from Klinger by the time of *Black Beauty*, but his specialism was horror films, so a children's movie was as out of character as a Polanski movie. It is quite plausible to speculate that, with a slight change in circumstances, Mankowitz and Tenser could have had each other's careers. Tenser was only four years older than Mankowitz. But Mankowitz's father always insisted on the paramount importance of books and, when Cambridge was a possibility, assured his son that ways and means would be found to send him there.

Treasure Island was released at various dates between 1972 and 1973 in German, French, Italian and English versions. The general release date for the English version was August 1973, to catch the school-holiday audience. This script, unlike that of *Black Beauty*, hardly deviates from the text of Stevenson's novel. Mankowitz and Orson Welles, who co-wrote under the pseudonym of O.W. Jeeves and plays Long John Silver with the charming menace of a veteran trickster, begin with a voice-over of the vivid opening lines of Stevenson's classic: 'Squire Trelawney, Dr Livesey, and the rest of those gentlemen having asked me to write down the whole particulars about Treasure Island ... I go back to the time when my father kept the "Admiral Benbow" inn, and the brown old seaman, with the sabre cut, first took up his lodging under our roof.' The voice-over at the end is equally faithful to Stevenson: '[I] start upright in bed with the sharp voice of Captain Flint still ringing in my ears: "Pieces of eight! Pieces of eight!" '[15] The scriptwriters have understood that Stevenson, like Conan Doyle, was, on the eve of the birth of cinema, writing to some extent cinematographically. The sabre cut, the tap of Blind Pew's stick, the heaped gold coins of the treasure, the mad, bearded face of Ben Gunn – it is the economy of these identifying signs that any film director would welcome. Director John Hough certainly did not quibble and although Angel del Pozo gives a wooden performance as Dr Livesey, which may be due to poor dubbing, Kim Burfield's Jim Hawkins is an eager and intelligent young boy and the discovery of the treasure is imaged, more dramatically than in the novel, as a huge cascade of golden coins from behind a large stone high up in the cave wall.

Welles, in his interviews with Bogdanovich, confirms that the writers were loyal to Stevenson's story. He, the consummate professional, says his own contribution was to keep it clear just where people were on the island which is important for a film audience. Stevenson didn't always bother about that. 'It happens all the time in adventure stories', says Welles, 'the narrative carries you along, cloudy geography doesn't show up on the printed page.'[16] It must have been a pleasure for Mankowitz to renew his partnership with Welles and to have had a hand in writing up Long John Silver as a turncoat rogue. Welles himself reprises here the sardonic slur and vengeful twinkle with which he played Falstaff, the supreme anti-hero, in his own film of Shakespeare's Henry plays, *Chimes at Midnight* (1966).

A very different kind of hero features in the war movie *Sutjeska* (aka *The Fifth Offensive*), to which Mankowitz, along with such as Sergei Bondarchuck and Ugo Pirro, made a script contribution. The film won a Special Prize at the Moscow Film Festival in July 1973 and stars Richard Burton as Marshall Tito leading a small group of Yugoslav partisans together with a long caravan of wounded soldiers against Axis forces in a decisive victory on the river Sutjeska, near Montenegro.

Sutjzeska reproduces most war-movie clichés, with brave stands against overwhelming odds, endless explosions and brave but teary nurses. A caravan of the wounded, however, is unusual and prompts, in the opening shots, the most memorable scene in the film – a flimsy wall of white, washed bandages in the partisan camp, drying and swaying in the sun. The fragility of the partisan army and the ghosts many of the fighters will become are thus dramatically symbolized. But a distraught mother in black now appears, weaving and moaning her way through the bandages. She is played by Irene Papas, by now the requisite actress to play crazed European mothers, contemporary or classical.

Burton plays Tito with minimal expression. He is the remote commander who occasionally unthaws to the common soldier. His voice is peculiar. He speaks his Serbo-Croat lines himself, according to an *Evening Standard* piece sent to Mankowitz by Pamela Cridge Hodgson, an old friend and associate in public relations.[17] But when he speaks English he sounds as if dubbed. This makes sense, since Tito is obviously a non-native English speaker, but the contrast is noticeable because the English liaison officers he addresses speak with perfect upper-class clipped accents. This amusing byplay may be Mankowitz's contribution to the script. His job was, according to the *Standard*, to produce a polished English version for the international market, but it doesn't enhance Burton's performance since the booming clarity of his diction was always his strongest gift as an actor. In a 1990 Sotheby's sale catalogue of Mankowitz's manuscripts, there is an extract from a letter by Burton to Mankowitz in which he says he recruited Mankowitz to the script-team in the hope that 'you could save *me* at least from the wreck by making my speeches sufficiently believable and speakable so that I wouldn't end up as a permanent glottal stop'. There is certainly no Estuary English in the film.

They remained friends, however, as can be seen from a long entry in Burton's diary for 20 February 1972, when the film was still unfinished. It is cited in *Rich: The Life of Richard Burton*, Melvyn Bragg's biography of Burton. Mankowitz was, as Burton recalls, at his 'most engagingly cockney', an act which delights both Burton and Elizabeth Taylor, who is always attracted to Jews. Mankowitz's huge belly and double chin may be unprepossessing, but both the Burtons admire his business expertise – 'sold the [Wedgwood] shops owned by his sister and himself for half a million nicker, tax-free capital fuckin' gain ... [to] Fackin' Wedgwood' – and his cultural range. Burton mentions the Ahakista edition of *XII Poems* as very recent and adds that Mankowitz wants Burton to write for it: 'rondeaux, frigging triolets, belles letters, the story of your life, graffiti, anything you like old mate'. Burton is tremendously impressed: 'his mind is astringent. There is no shit about him & he is a Renaissance man.'[18]

Mankowitz's recollections of the Burtons in the Davis interview are warm but not uncritical. His last memory of Burton is of waiting three days in a guest house in Switzerland before the actor is sober enough to discuss a possible role as lead in a film version of *My Old Man's a Dustman*, to be shot in Dublin. That project was never realized, and others that are, such as *Dr Faustus*, are disasters. Mankowitz mentions 'the Tito film' in passing, but his strongest memory of Elizabeth (Taylor) Burton is her birthday present to Richard, a complete set of the Everyman classics, each volume bound in Moroccan leather of a different colour. Here is Elizabeth's idea of culture, but Mankowitz's comment is: 'It was an absolutely insane non-cultural present.' Mankowitz accepts that Burton was highly intelligent, but struggles to define the nature of that intelligence. He detects in Burton the actor a man who had contempt for acting; someone for whom, with his voice and style and panache, the art came all too easily. 'He was a strange man', he concludes, 'who never really materialised as the kind of intellect he could have been.'

Two months before the Moscow Festival award, Mankowitz was the scriptwriter member of the team that won the Grand Prize at Cannes for a very different film, the screen version of L.P. Hartley's novel *The Hireling*. The novel, set in the mid-1950s, charts the slow growth of a chauffer's sexual desire for one Lady Ernestine Franklin, traumatized by the recent death of her husband and finding, so she thinks, nothing more than a friendly ear on the part of Leadbitter, the chauffer. He is a solitary man, an ex-NCO, who prides himself on his self-sufficiency and despises himself for falling in love. He tries to sabotage her forthcoming marriage to Hughie Cantrip, a Bohemian artist of mediocre talent, by sending her an anonymous letter in which he accuses Cantrip of planning to continue his affair with his mistress, Constance Copthorne, after he has married Ernestine. Leadbitter crashes the car in which he is driving Hughie and Connie to a restaurant in Richmond. The men die but Connie survives to tell Lady Franklin that it was true that she and Hughie planned to continue their liaison. Leadbitter sent Lady Franklin the letter because he loved her. Lady Franklin, with exemplary aristocratic sangfroid, replies: 'Thank you. It was kind of you to come, but you must go now.'[19]

Hartley makes frequent use of the narrative techniques of authorial commentary and free indirect speech, particularly when his women characters worry away at the morality of their actions. These are techniques of literary rather than film narrative and are possible reasons why Mankowitz, in effect, rewrites Hartley's fiction for the screen. He recasts the period and location of the novel so that the emotional and class confusions of Lady Franklin and Leadbetter, who is in fact no better than Hartley's bitter hero, are played out in the context of a West Country market town and its ancestral landowners rather than a fashionable London town house and ancient cathedral cities, the settings in the novel. The period is now post-First World War rather than Second World War because, as Mankowitz declares in an interview with Jean Young shortly after Cannes, Hartley was really writing 'some thirty or forty years before the time he was living' when social relationships were much more hierarchic. Hartley, for Mankowitz, was a 'sort of old-fashioned country gentleman, and his mind and observations of situations was pretty well situated post-James'.[20]

Mankowitz might have added that the country setting allowed the director Alan Bridges to draw upon the prestigious cultural capital of the 'Great House' genre. Its landscapes, its interiors, its labour relations, in effect its stock, had all appreciated in the twenty years since Abe Sparta, in *Make Me an Offer*, had espied value only in its demolition. Television, both BBC and commercial, had recently mounted a challenge to cinema's tenure of this valuable cultural site. *Persuasion* and *Sense and Sensibility* (1971) and *Emma* (1972) had all been televised as mini-series; and ITV's 'Upstairs, Downstairs' began its successful run as a soap opera of right and proper relations between aristocrat and worker in 1971. Nigel Andrews, in his review for the *Financial Times* (20 July 1973) discerned the influence of televisual techniques on the production. 'It looks a bit like a BBC classic serial writ large', he wrote. Each bit clicked into place but the film didn't seem a unified whole. This may well have been Mankowitz's intention, successful or not, since he talks in the Jean Young interview of trying to build the Leadbetter–Lady Franklin relationship 'through a montage of scenes between them with enough incident, thus building it up, with physical contact between them developing to a certain extent'.

This contact, as in the novel, is confined to one kiss that Leadbetter forces upon Lady Franklin when they are halted at a level crossing. She is horrified. She has been happy to present the winner's cup at a boxing tournament organized by Leadbetter. But she cannot conceive of him as a lover. She is already falling in love with her social equal, Hugh Cantrip, who, in the film, is a veteran of the First World War and former Liberal candidate for the local parliamentary seat once held by her husband. Lady Franklin is played by Sarah Miles as, at the beginning, a speechless wraith, incapable of social intercourse. By the time Leadbetter – a superb performance of barely curbed anger by Robert Shaw – kisses her she has begun to reintegrate with her class and relearn its conventions. She is moved sexually by this very brief encounter but, as Mankowitz observes to Betty Jeffries Demby in a long retrospective interview the following year, 1974, this doesn't make her rearrange her life: 'My "Lady Chatterley", although she is perfectly responsive, has a mind of her own, and to move her sexually doesn't change the whole of her life.'[21]

Critics praised the performances of Sarah Miles and Robert Shaw and, by and large, endorsed Mankowitz's radical changes to Hartley's novel. Patrick Gibbs for the *Daily Telegraph* (20 July 1973) approves his backdating the period to the 1920s and his relocation of the film's action to a bleak, rural autumn which 'makes for a bleakness which reflects the story, and the great Tudor country house to which Lady Franklin returns, with its grim housekeeper, adds further to the atmosphere of gloomy beauty'. Jan Dawson's *Listener* review of 26 July 1973 sees plot and setting as 'an astutely calculated attempt to cross the most marketable aspects of *Lady Chatterley* with those of both *The Servant* and *The Go-Between*', but Dilys Powell, for the *Observer* (22 July 1973), while admitting that the film is only a short story – in comparison to *The Go-Between* which is a novel – insists that it is a very good short story and also 'the most acute study the cinema has given us not so much of class as of class-feeling'. Even Penelope Gilliatt, whose *New Yorker* review of 16 June 1973 claims that the real hero of the film is the chauffer's 1923 Rolls Royce, admits the power of Elizabeth Sellars's portrayal of Lady Franklin's mother – '[her] face quivers like lake water blown by a breeze' – and the beauty that Sarah Miles's acting layers over her character's 'etiolated breeding'.

The Hireling was to be Mankowitz's last major screenplay that saw production, and the Betty Demby interview cited above, a review of his many experiences, high and low, of commercial film-making, now reads like a valediction to that branch of his creative life. He stresses once more that money usually wins out over quality; that the writer never controls his story; that the making of *Bloomfield* is *the* cautionary tale against the star also becoming director and producer; and that an aspiring screenwriter should learn his trade by writing his stories, not attending classes on scenario technique. He expresses his admiration for Val Guest, a very professional and unflashy director, but makes a fine distinction between his film of *Expresso Bongo*, directed as a 'satirical comedy on the pop music business', and the musical version, which 'used a satirical exposition of the music business as an allegory on competitive society'. He makes another fine distinction between the writer who has a message to communicate, the writer as pure entertainer, and, very perceptively, the writer who, in an interregnum between these two roles, cannot relinquish 'the *habit* of communication without anything particularly pressing to say' (emphasis in the original). This type is the driver of today's social media.

But, elsewhere in the interview, Mankowitz envisages a different kind of working practice for the film industry. He is very enthusiastic about the democratic, even socialistic mode of film-making that produced *The Hebrew Lesson*, a thirty-minute short directed and written by Mankowitz that won the Irish Critics' Award at the Cork International Film Festival in June 1972. A group of technicians, actors and writers formed the Dublin Film Collective, worked for minimal pay and thus bypassed the hierarchical structure of film-making that can 'inflate egos to the stage where they sit on the industry like great lead balloons'. The particular conditions of Irish film-making in Ireland, where you have to 'soft talk someone into the investment of services', forced a democratic collective into existence, but it suits young beginners as well, because they think 'the production of films is too important to be a purely commodity-producing activity'. Here speaks from behind his mask of cynicism the Mankowitz who declared at the end of his life that his intellectual lodestars had always been Marx and Freud; and who has, perhaps, reflected on the consumerist critique levelled at the film industry by Godard and Truffaut as they halted and wrecked the Cannes Film Festival of 1968.

Mankowitz had been campaigning for a viable Irish film industry ever since his relocation to Ireland in March 1971. A long article for the *Sunday Independent* (31 October 1971) shows a clear grasp of current costs in the industry, the politics of State support and the importance of Ardmore Film Studios as a site for Irish film-making. He urges that a bill, currently being considered by the Dáil (Irish Parliament, lower house), should be passed, which would make available up to one million pounds for Irish companies to make Irish-based films. He notes that the current practice in the film industry is for scriptwriters, stars, directors and producers to claim minimal expenses from the budget in return for ownership of part of the film. A unique opportunity is therefore available, if the proposed Film Board advances loans of £50,000, to make high-quality films for minimal cash outlay. He is not in favour of such a Board exercising any censorship role in the choice of film subjects. Its decisions should be made on commercial grounds – the percentage of producer investment, the amount of Film Board money going straight into the finished product – and it should see itself in partnership with private enterprise.

Mankowitz writes here as a man with a mission – to galvanize Irish film-making and to find a space for his own work. The disaster of *Bloomfield* had drained him and, as he says in the *Samson Riddle* essay, he finished feeling like an outsider in Israel. Ireland welcomed him and respected him as an artist. He was written up in the many interviews he gave as a prominent author and intellectual who would enrich Irish cultural life. Des Hickey, for the *Sunday Independent* (16 May 1971), portrays him as a man with a ferocious writing schedule, plans to write for the Gate Theatre, and an astute and cheerful sense of displacement wherever he lives. He reflects that even at the height of his London fame he was never regarded as English. He defines himself as 'first generation Anglo-Russian Jew, and therefore more at home in Ireland than anywhere else'. Kay Kent (*Irish Times*, 13 January 1972) notes his intellectual formation from Marx, Freud and Leavis, and then quotes him as distinguishing between a belief in communism, which he no longer has, and 'a dialectical training [which] is something you don't throw off'.

Ardmore Film Studios, founded in 1958 and with a world reputation for excellent production and post-production facilities, also offered Mankowitz a level of cooperation and technical expertise which was difficult to find in Israel. Its management, although in the middle of a difficult transfer of its ownership from the private sector to the State-run RTÉ (Raidió Teilifís Éireann, Éire Radio and Television), supported the cooperative principles underlying the production of *The Hebrew Lesson*. Dermot Loughry, then Ardmore's general manager, produced the film, and Ardmore's managing director, George O'Reilly, undertook negotiations for the film's sale in the United States. There was widespread press interest in the making of the film.

Elgy Gillespie reported for the *Irish Times* (6 March 1972) on the shooting of an early moment in the film, set in 1921, when a young IRA gunman (Patrick Dawson) on the run from the Black and Tans stumbles on the makeshift synagogue constructed in his attic by the rabbi (Milo O'Shea). 'A synagogue is it?' he asks, 'A Jewman here?' The rabbi replies, 'What can you do – we're a travelling people'.

Des Hickey for Dublin's *Sunday Independent* (2 April 1972) quotes O'Shea, by then one of Ireland's best-known actors, as happy to be paid by way of a share of the profits and convinced that the film could spearhead an Irish film industry. The *Cork Examiner* announced on 10 March that the shooting of the film had finished several days ahead of schedule; and public relations officer Dermot Breen was quoted in the Dublin *Sunday Press* of 12 March as saying that the production team was so pleased with the film that it was ready to commit itself to six more short fiction films, with Milo O'Shea starring in a variety of roles. *Business and Finance (Eire)* reported on 16 March that personal profits would be calculated on a points system which reflected the degree of time and effort contributed by each member of the collective. Its headline refers to the 'Troubles' of 1921, but everyone must have been alert to parallels between 1921 and 1972 with the recent army killings of thirteen Catholics in Northern Ireland's Londonderry.

The Hebrew Lesson opened the Cork International Film Festival, which ran from 10 June to 17 June 1972 and won the Critics' Prize for the Best Irish Film in competition. Mankowitz gave the opening address in which he again laid out his vision for an Irish film industry and closed the festival with thanks for the award and compliments to his fellow-workers. The festival could as well have been called the Wolf Mankowitz Show, since the retrospective tribute was to him as a film scriptwriter with showings of, among others, *The Bespoke Overcoat*, *A Kid for Two Farthings*, *Expresso Bongo* and *The Day the Earth Caught Fire*. There were also outings for the two films made in collaboration with Laurence Harvey, who attended the festival: *We Are the People*, and *Here Are Ladies*. The reviews for McKenna, at that time as beloved in Ireland as Milo O'Shea, were ecstatic. John Stapleton, in his festival round-up for the *Cork Examiner* of 19 June 1972, represented the popular voice when he described her bringing to every role 'the outer communication which can only arise from an intense inner understanding of her material'.

Modes of communication are also at the heart of *The Hebrew Lesson*. The plot is slight. The rabbi is also a pedlar and at several key moments in the film he tries to improve his Gaelic, which he needs to sell his haberdashery goods in the far West of Ireland, by practising it with the young IRA gunman, for whom Gaelic is a political statement. There is a fair exchange of languages, however, when the rabbi, minutes before two Black and Tan soldiers invade the synagogue on the hunt for IRA soldiers, disguises the young man as an earnest Jewish student of Hebrew with prayer shawl and prayer book. He has the IRA man, who has a good ear for languages, repeat over and over after him, the Hebrew 'Im ech-kachach Yurushalayim', which the rabbi translates after the soldiers have gone as 'If I forget thee, O Jerusalem'. The English soldiers, who can only use their language to swear and abuse, are fooled. They depart with curses, followed by the young man who departs with thanks. He recognizes the Jerusalem passage: 'It's in our Bible.' Hebrew has saved Gaelic. The rabbi wishes him well and goes back to his English, his Gaelic and his Yiddish: 'The price is sixpence each, or two for tenpence ... The day isn't good. Nil an la' go mair. The weather is bad ... Oy.'[22]

The festival critics interpreted the film's message as a condemnation of violence and a 'plea for communication between men at the common human level' (*Cork Evening Echo*, 9 June 1972). Mankowitz, in Jean Sheridan's report (*Dublin Irish Press*, 17 June 1972) on the Writer's Forum at the end of the festival, confirmed that the film's message was not only anti-violence but also that 'you can deal with situations of violence by means other than the gun'. One of those means, suggested John Stapleton for the *Cork Examiner* (12 June 1972), was 'a hand held out for the ancient wisdoms of philosophy' and it is true that Mankowitz's world-weary rabbi rates survival above martyrdom on several occasions. 'You think God wants to save the lives of those bastards', shouts the IRA man as he insists on carrying his gun beneath his prayer shawl. 'Let's just hope', replies the rabbi tartly, 'that God wants to save the lives of us bastards.' Dick Cross (*Irish Independent*, *Dublin*, 12 June 1972) praised the skill of the two central actors but criticized the low-key soundtrack which Mary Leland (*Irish Times*, 12 June 1972) also found inadequate, as well as commenting adversely on 'some extraordinary camera angles'.

The film's technical faults were certainly due to a combination of inexperience on the part of the collective and rushed post-production. Mankowitz was aware that, in order to show at the festival, professional standards had been sacrificed and Dublin's *Sunday Independent* (29 October 1972) quotes him as having 'just, just received the final,

final print of his Ardmore film'. Kevin Barry's review six months later for the *Catholic Standard* (13 April 1973) praises how the film's direction 'manipulates the slightest movements and slightest shifts of angles to give life to the simplicity of its plot'. The film, as we now have it, is a most striking essay in chiaroscuro, with light falling only across the aquiline features of the rabbi and the barely formed chin and nose of the very young man. The attic space is opened up to greater light when the Black and Tans enter and turn over the books and cupboards and candlesticks, but this fades away when they exit to leave only the couple illuminated by a light which is now one of greater understanding. O'Shea's eyes, large and piercing, hold the camera whenever they are in focus. Sight has to supplement speech in order to produce knowledge.

But language remains the central theme of *The Hebrew Lesson*. It begins and ends as a medium for the exchange of goods, but the main action of the film proposes that languages exchanged are goods in themselves and that the act of language exchange creates its own value. The rabbi offers English, Yiddish, Hebrew and Gaelic. He is one of Yuri Slezkine's service nomads, on the boundaries between settled cultures and identities. His only homeland is the mythical 'Yurushalayim'. The IRA man is fighting to possess his own homeland and legitimize his own language. The Black and Tans possess everything and will exchange nothing. All value for them inheres in absolute power. When the IRA man intones the Jerusalem quote, the first soldier asks the rabbi what he is saying. 'He made a blessing for you', says the rabbi. 'Bugger his blessing', says the second soldier. Their exchange can only be sterile. The soldiers' use of language cannot give birth to the marvellous myth or the accidental friendship that are engendered when the rabbi and the IRA man play with their languages. Exchange is cunning and creative; absolute power is paranoid and rigid.

Mankowitz's two works for live theatre in this period were less well received. *The Samson Riddle*, whose prefatory essay has been cited earlier, was presented on 19 March 1972 as a rehearsed reading at the prestigious Gate Theatre and published on the same day. It was part of the annual Dublin Theatre Festival and attracted an elegant audience to hear, among others, Susannah York read the parts of The Woman of Timnath and Delilah, and Miriam Karlin take the role of Samson's Mother. The majority of critics found the play's intellectual content engaging but its dramatic impact uneven. Deliberate anachronisms such as references to rabbis and the male menopause, and Yiddish turns of phrase caused some irritation, but Mary Manning's balanced review (*Irish Times*, 1 April 1972) of the essay plus play-script sums up the majority view.

For her the play is too long and too discursive, and the mix of gobbets from the King James Authorised Version of the Bible and colloquial English unsuccessful. If the quotes were cut and the text presented 'in the simplest terms as folk drama' it could succeed as a stage play. Mankowitz himself underlines the indeterminate status of this text when, in the essay, he calls it 'an enquiry in dialogue form' and says that the oddity of the Samson story has led him to consider the philosophical importance of the ethics and aesthetics of the Mosaic Code. In a long and carefully appreciative review of the published text, the *Cork Examiner*'s book critic (11 May 1972) suggests that *The Samson Riddle* is a deliberate departure by Mankowitz from what he calls his 'immediately marketable product'. This, by contrast, is a work that 'has to wait upon many things to achieve its purpose in the theatre', but for now has afforded the critic the delight of witnessing a Jewish artist meddling with Jewish history.

In retrospect, *The Samson Riddle* reads as a debate between history and myth, an important academic preoccupation in the 1960s and 1970s. The resounding periods of the King James Bible counterpoint Samson's father Manoah's complaints about the impact of war upon wool production, or the guilt-free sex training undergone by the priestesses of Dagon, god of the Philistines. Mankowitz invents a Philistine priest, Zoab, who, late in the play, challenges Samson's belief in his divine mission and an all-powerful Jahveh, and proposes an anthropological explanation for this divinity. 'We have established', he tells Samson, 'that your Jahveh is a desert wind-god glorified with the attributes of an Egyptian sun-god. The eyes of his heroes symbolize the heavenly orb. Their trailing hair and bristling beards, his virile rays.' Samson is unimpressed. 'Oh, when will you Gentiles realise', he bursts out 'that for the Jews there is no such thing as comparative theology? There is only our own, fixed immovably.'

Samson continues to play the role of a man chosen by Jahveh for an impossible mission until he too feels forced to contextualize the mythical story within an historical framework:

> We are not a trading people like you Philistines. We are a simple, agricultural, territorially bound federation of tribes united by ten laws, which we break frequently, in the secure belief that we are

> the nominated protestants of an unseeable, unknowable, all-powerful God, who has reserved for us some special purpose in his quite understandable scheme of things.[23]

In the last scene the focus shifts from the tale to the teller. Samson's mother has throughout been the most intransigent and vociferous supporter of her son as a superhuman worrier. Mankowitz here proposes that she also, by way of a scribe, wrote the story which we now have by way of King James's team of translators. The slaughter of thousands with the jawbone of an ass, the heroic lovemaking, the endless wars, these hyperbolic stories are not just typical of primitive folklore; they are also stories constructed by a proud, masculine woman to commemorate, by proxy, a war-lust that she feels but, as a woman, can only express in language. Feminists in the 1970s would come to call this history 'herstory', although it is doubtful if Mankowitz, for all his interest in women and children as topics for journalism, would have validated such a neologism.

NOTES

1. W. Mankowitz, *Wolf Mankowitz: The Plays*, preface by Anthony Dunn (London: Oberon Books, 2006), pp.18–19.
2. Ibid., p.17.
3. W.J. Mann, *Edge of Midnight: The Life of John Schlesinger* (London: Hutchinson, 2004), p.281.
4. Kindly made available by Valerie Bernard of the British Film Institute's Contracts and Copyright Department.
5. *Jewish Chronicle*, 22 March 1968.
6. Non-Israeli Jews who wished to emigrate to Israel.
7. Gus Smith, *Richard Harris: Actor by Accident* (London: Robert Hale, 1990), p.124.
8. Michael Feeney Callan, *Richard Harris: Sex, Death and the Movies* (London: Robson Books, 2003), pp.206–13.
9. Release Script, no. 5640, BFI Scripts, BFI National Archive, Berkhamsted.
10. Steve Berkoff, *Free Association: An Autobiography*, paperback edn (London: Faber & Faber, 1997), pp.124–30.
11. Anne Sinai, *Reach for the Top: The Turbulent Life of Laurence Harvey* (Lanham, MD, and Oxford: Scarecrow Press, 2003), p.337.
12. Mankowitz Family Archive.
13. All subsequent quotations from *XII Poems* are from the Ahakista Press edition.
14. Details from Tony Tenser's obituary, by Gavin Gaughan, *Guardian*, 13 March 2008.
15. Robert Louis Stevenson, *Treasure Island* (London: Penguin, 1999), pp.3, 190.
16. O. Welles and P. Bogdanovich, *This is Orson Welles*, paperback edn (Cambridge, MA: Da Capo Press, 1998), p.269.
17. Letter from Pamela Cridge Hodgson to Wolf Mankowitz, 6 September 1971, Mankowitz Family Archive.
18. Melvyn Bragg, *Rich: The Life of Richard Burton* (London: Hodder, 1988), pp.406–7.
19. L.P. Hartley, *The Hireling* (London: Hamish Hamilton, 1957), p.247.

20. Jean Young, 'The Hireling: The Scriptwriter', *Film*, 5 (August 1973), p.23.
21. Betty Jeffries Demby, 'The Art of Screenwriting: An Interview with Wolf Mankowitz', *Filmmakers Newsletter*, February 1974, pp.26–9.
22. This and subsequent quotes have been transcribed directly from the film. The film script differs, in minor details, from the stage play, first performed at the Almost Free Theatre, London, and directed by Ed Berman on 22 January 1978. A version of the stage play is reproduced in *Wolf Mankowitz: The Plays*, cited earlier in this study. The Oberon edition has mistakenly reversed the titles of the film and the play.
23. Mankowitz, *Wolf Mankowitz: The Plays*, pp.89, 91.

CHAPTER NINE

The Eclectic Professional (1972–81)

Mankowitz's second work for the theatre in 1972 presented a very different hero with a very different history. *Stand and Deliver*, subtitled *A Bawdy Ballad*, was a musical based on the life of the eighteenth-century thief Jack Sheppard. He was born in Spitalfields, escaped prison for theft four times, was a folk-hero to the London poor and was finally hanged at Tyburn, aged 22. The old East End team of Mankowitz (book) and Monty Norman (music and lyrics) reunited to give audiences, first at the Edinburgh Festival (Royal Lyceum Theatre, 20 September), and then for a short run (24 October to 4 November) at London's Roundhouse, their latest venture into popular culture. The show wasn't popular, although as Roundhouse documentation at the Victoria and Albert Museum's Theatre and Performance Collection confirms, it didn't close early because the contract for its London run was only for two weeks and attendance, while poor, was not disastrous.[1]

The London critics called it 'unbearably vulgar', according to Mankowitz in interview with the Dublin *Sunday Independent* (29 October 1972). He didn't think it would get a West End transfer – 'what they seem to want these days are Jesus freaks' – but he also thought that the Roundhouse was not a suitable venue for a classical musical. Martin Esslin's review for the December number of *Plays and Players* comprehensively damns the whole show. It is a 'witless pastiche of Gay's *The Beggar's Opera* centred on cardboard reproductions of historical characters ... bereft of any good lines of dialogue or witty repartee, but stuffed with puerile naughtiness and revolting *double-entendres*'. But he does wonder if the bare, open spaces of the Roundhouse have overexposed the musical's limitations. A proscenium arch might have presented 'a far more coherently pretty picture'.[2] The production was a joint venture between John Gale for Volcano

Productions Ltd and Bernard Delfont Ltd. So Mankowitz was not guilty, at least, of producer hubris on this occasion.

The *Sunday Independent* interview finishes with Mankowitz looking forward to a quiet family Christmas in their new home in Ahakista, west of Cork and facing the Atlantic. This would be their permanent home for the next twenty-five years and, as has been already noted, would afford Mankowitz a necessary place and pace to recuperate from his manic activism of recent years. He would continue to write, with a particular emphasis on novellas and biographies, and, in his last years, would take up painting and collages. But Mankowitz was a son of the city. London had bred him and the metropolis had been the setting and source of his earliest triumphs. He was still, at heart, the man who belonged to damp and fog and for whom, to repeat, 'London at four o'clock in the morning with a wet pavement is a natural environment.'[3] The repose of the west coast of Ireland probably saved him from an earlier death, but his fictions now would be largely historical, as if his current environment offered little stimulus to his imagination. His next major commission, a multi-part series for Yorkshire Television entitled 'Dickens of London', was perhaps a way of living the city again through his historical imagination.

But, before Dickens, he summoned back his own London. He made a selection from his numerous short stories describing the deals, the clubs, the atmospheres and the girls which he had published in the *Evening Standard*, *The Mendelman Fire* and other outlets in the late 1950s and early 1960s. The title was *The Blue Arabian Nights*, published by Vallentine Mitchell in 1973, with the book launch at the appropriate venue of the London Eccentrics Club on 12 June. He published the collection under the imprint of his own Ahakista Press in the same year. What the BBC had rejected some fifteen years earlier as a cynical series set in a louche venue would be read as a lively account of a now démodé moment in London's post-war life. But it had been a formative moment for Mankowitz as a London Jewish writer and he wanted, at this moment of definitive change to his life, to put it on record and to define himself within it.

Des Hickey for the *Sunday Independent* (25 November 1973) gives an accurate summary of the protagonists of these 'slightly acidulent stories' as a rag-bag of 'ten-per-cent agents, gown salesmen, shop-lifters, agony columnists, neurotic taxi-drivers, old-gold dealers and the inevitable theatrical colony'; and Linda Talbot for the *Hampstead and Highgate Express* (20 July 1973) commends his 'knack of fabricating semi-fantasy round a simple idea' but criticizes the 'superficially inflated sense of humour'. Much more accomplished, however, than the tales, which are not much more than quick takes on a swiftly moving scene, is Mankowitz's 'Introduction', where he places himself within 'a lost decade, somewhere between the middle of the fifties and the end of the sixties' and lists, among his numerous activities, film-writer, television performer, writer of any verbal commodity that would sell, ceramic encyclopaedist and inveterate night-walker. He describes himself as a child of the war who had known no youth, and as a young man eager to play all the many roles on offer.

His immediate playground was 'the square mile of multicoloured neon between Park Lane and Piccadilly before they sank beneath the glistening superstructure of up-thrusting, Europe-facing, post-War London'. He operated

> out of an office with a Moroccan harem door, the walls papered with theatrical posters, its great bay-window looking both up and down Piccadilly, down and up which my chauffeur-driven racing car used to nose through the always increasing traffic, stopping for material at the still slightly heart-warm townships between O. Henry and Damon Runyan in the Far West and Sholom Aleichem in the Far East.[4]

One perspective slides the reader down from lofty to ground level, but without any necessary correlation between height and power, since the racing car noses along one of the richest streets in London and the counter-perspective, a horizontal line from East to West London, affords equal cultural space to such dissimilar writers as O. Henry, Runyan and Sholom Aleichem. The office decor is both exotic and local. The narrator, like the protagonist in a Henry James novel, overhangs the scene. He is central and he has choices, but, unlike a James hero, he also has the drive and energy to make himself anew through those choices. This patch of the city was then fertile ground to breed multiple selves. All you had to do was act.

A year earlier Mankowitz had written an ill-tempered piece for *Punch* (15 March 1972) on Piccadilly past and present. He translates his sense of loss into anger at that loss. The Piccadilly of his boyhood, he writes, 'was the centre of a world in which artists and bohemians had their own class preserves, privileges and limitations'. To qualify for that class you had to 'disown the one you came from and demonstrate some sort of talent professionally' which was then judged on the basis of its commerciability. Present-day Piccadilly, the one he has just left for the green hills of Erin, is, during the day, a 'booking office for far-off places, by night a car-park for trendy cowboys and androgynous pirates, the hair-dressers, rag-sellers, real estate-promoters, and disco-bashers, the sub-culture vultures'. There is, in fact, no great difference between this catalogue of shady citizens and the dramatis personae of *The Blue Arabian Nights*. But now, a year later, Mankowitz perhaps felt committed to Ireland and its cultural opportunities and could view his London past through a more objective lens.

During his first two years as a resident in Éire, Mankowitz certainly established a commanding intellectual presence. If the late 1950s were his *anni mirabiles* as a new, impressive voice in all branches of London-centred media, the range of his output in the early 1970s confirms him as the epitome of the professional writer. He traffics back and forth, with seeming ease, between the worlds of elite and popular culture. He writes metaphysical poetry; the book for a musical based on the life of an eighteenth-century East End thief; a Cannes-winning adaptation of a respected middlebrow novel; and publishes a valedictory collection of stories and sketches from his earlier West End period. His scripts for the films of *Black Beauty* and *Treasure Island* reach the screen. He polishes up the English subtitles for an odd film starring Richard Burton as Marshal Tito. He renews his exploration of his Jewish inheritance with an intellectually challenging play. He scripts and directs *The Hebrew Lesson*, a miniature masterpiece, and tries to create the basis for an independent Irish film industry. He was no more successful here than in Israel. He had given of his best in many fields, but he now realized he had to reduce the frantic pace of his commitments.

Mankowitz described his work habits to Des Hickey in an interview for the *Sunday Independent* (16 May 1971) soon after settling permanently in Ireland. A writing stint from eight in the morning until two in the afternoon would be followed by an hour's sleep. 'He calculates', said Hickey, 'that he writes 40 weeks out of 52. For the rest of the time he's probably trying to promote something to write about.' He certainly maintained this writing regime. Brendan Lehane, interviewing him five years later for the Ulster edition of the *TV Times* (23–29 October 1976), cites a routine of early rising, work throughout the morning, a walk after lunch, some cooking and a lot of sleep. Self-promotion, however, is not mentioned. Although loquacious on a wide range of subjects, including the Roman, Etruscan and Persian antiques that furnish the restored farmhouse in Ahakista, this interview presents a man whose focus is on writing not politicking and whose environment, living with his wife and youngest son, is essentially domestic.

The *TV Times* interview marked the transmission, on 26 October 1976, of the fifth hour-long episode in a series of thirteen, of 'Dickens of London', his next significant work for the public and scripted for Yorkshire TV. Three years was a long break between works by Mankowitz but the Sotheby's catalogue attributes to him at least six unproduced film-scripts in this period; and, during his toast to the Dickens Fellowship at the London Birthday Dinner in the summer of 1976, he said he had been living with Dickens's works and biographies for the last eighteen months.[5] In the Lehane interview, Mankowitz acknowledges a fascination with London and a driven professionalism as common ground between Dickens and himself. Dickens was a 'sort of Harold Robbins for mass appeal, Orson Welles for the charisma of his personal appearances, Laurence Olivier for his presentation of classic theatre; and, say, a Nye Bevan for his standing in the country'. Mankowitz declares they are very different writers – 'He overwrites. I underwrite' – but he also asks the interviewer and the reader to realize the size and scope of his TV scripting achievement (twenty-six episodes in the original commission), which is to have created the largest portrait of any artist in any medium in any period: 'It would have made a lesser man a basket-case.'

Mankowitz kept his head and, in addition to the TV series, wrote a biography of Dickens, which was published by Weidenfeld on 9 September 1976, to coincide with the transmission of the first TV episode on 28 September. Christopher Falkus, managing director at Weidenfeld, had already written to Mankowitz in March congratulating him on the choice of the forthcoming biography as a main selection for the Book Club Associates, who would accordingly take around 45,000 copies.[6] The Book Club members, however, would have received a biography which, despite its twelve pages of colour, including a double-page reproduction of Phoebus Levin's *Covent Garden* and W.P. Frith's *Many Happy Returns*, and 100 black-and-white illustrations, was more than a coffee-table book. Dickens's complex relationships with his chief publishers, Chapman & Hall and Richard Bentley, and his battles to tilt existing copyright law in favour of the author, are narrated with a scholarly attention to detail. The book has no endnotes but, with the exception of some minor instances, its dates and presentations of Dickens's finances accord with those cited in Michael Slater's magisterial biography of Dickens, published in 2009.

Slater says in his preface that he has focused 'primarily upon his [Dickens's] career as a writer and professional author' and makes space for a detailed consideration of the 'truly prodigious amount of *other* writing that he was constantly producing' (emphasis in the original) at the same time as his famous novels.[7] Mankowitz has neither the space nor the time to consider in detail Dickens's many essays, sketches and social polemics, although he does pay attention to his theatre pieces and, in the TV series, frames every episode with Dickens preparing and presenting very theatrical readings from his novels during his second American tour in 1867. But he is as fascinated as Slater by Dickens's iron will to succeed after his unhappy childhood and Maria Beadnell's cavalier rejection of his devoted love. 'All these sorrows inflicted upon him', writes Mankowitz, 'formed a character that, to defend its self in future, would assert its will ... What was necessary, then, was the independence and esteem of success'.[8]

The Book Club readers might also have been startled to encounter the beginnings of a psychoanalytical reading of Dickens's marriage and of one of his most popular novels, *David Copperfield*. Mankowitz notes that Dickens was surprised when John Forster, his business colleague and first biographer, pointed out that the initials of the novel were Dickens's own in reverse, as is the case with many of the character-pairings in the novel. Mankowitz sums up the novel as 'like a dream of his life [which] works as a dream works, by dislocation, symbol, reversal, compression'. At the same time, in his TV script, he was suggesting that Mary, Dickens's wife Catherine's sister, who died suddenly at the age of 17, was the permitted focus of the erotic energy his wife could no longer arouse. 'Kate', concludes Mankowitz in the biography, with her plump, lethargic and fecund body, 'did not serve any neurotic need'.[9] Peter Ackroyd concludes, in his biography of Dickens, that 'All the engagement of his nature, all the idealism and veneration, were elicited only by the innocent young girl or young woman.'[10]

Mankowitz also makes much, as have all Dickens biographers, of Dickens's 'Autobiographical Fragment', first recorded in Forster's biography, with its horrified recollections of the 12-year-old boy's employment in Warren's Blacking Factory at Hungerford Stairs on the Thames; his lonely and often surreal peregrinations through London to and from the factory and the Marshalsea prison where his father was imprisoned for debt; and his shame and despair that this, the life of a vagabond without education or family, was to be his fate for the rest of his life. Mankowitz, as we shall see, writes up the blacking factory as a 'primal scene' for Charles's humiliation by his inferiors, elements of which are then recombined into an imagined scene of erotic submission to the dead Mary Hogarth.

But he might also have explored the equally fraught relations that Dickens establishes in the 'Autobiographical Fragment' between his life, writing, and writing his life. The fragment enacts a repeated pattern of negation and affirmation of its own writing: 'No words can express the secret agony of my soul as I sunk into this companionship'; 'how much I suffered it is ... utterly beyond my power to tell'; '[this] does not seem a tithe of what I might have written, or of what I meant to write'. At the same time, the writing-up of London detail in the 'Autobiographical Fragment' is confidently Dickensian. Only Dickens could have recalled the title of a coffee-room, seen by a hungry boy from inside, as he drank his meagre coffee, as MOOR-EEFFOC. Only Dickens, ashamed and miserable when visiting his family in the debtors' prison, could have stored up in his memory, for no purpose he could then have anticipated, 'their different peculiarities of dress, of face, of manner'.[11]

For Dickens, therefore, writing is here, and always would be, a precarious site of self-definition. Yet it was only through writing that he could define himself. He had neither a university education nor a classical training. His family was constantly in debt. He was not a gentleman, although he moved, from his late twenties, in gentlemanly and aristocratic circles. Writing was not yet a profession. Dickens was what he wrote, hence his frantic output, his battles over copyright and with publishers, and his love affair with his readers.

Allan Grant, writing for the *Hampstead and Highgate Express* (24 September 1976), was disappointed that this biography added no new facts nor advanced any new interpretations to the established reading of Dickens's life, but he does draw attention to the central paradox of a life full of paradoxes: 'the spectacle of the young man's instant extraordinary success and continuous international fame and his delight in these giving way to an unappeasable restlessness and sense of loss'. Grant also wonders whether Dickens's constant theatricalization of his own and others' lives is a mask to hide the absence of a real self. Dickens's compulsive peformativity is one of the major themes of the TV series, where Dickens's father, John, and Dickens as an adult are played by the same actor, Roy Dotrice, throughout. The first episode, where an exhausted Dickens confuses a man dressed as Pickwick with his fictional creation who, Dickens acknowledges, created Dickens the writer, is entitled 'Mask'.

C.P. Snow's review of the biography for the *Financial Times* (16 September 1976), which also covers an academic study, *The Dickens Myth* by Geoffrey Thurley, reminds his readers that Mankowitz was once a high-class literary critic 'before he took to entertaining us', and considers the biography a welcome work of 'literary' writing. It has no startling revelations to make but the text is clear and sensible, with 'occasional unobtrusive stabs of original judgement'. With its magnificent array of illustrations, Mankowitz 'hasn't much space to spread himself' but Snow concludes he is close to Thurley – whose book he praises – in spirit, an association with academe that must have pleased Mankowitz. Gerda Charles's review in the same month for the *Jewish Chronicle* praises Mankowitz's scholarship and insights without reservation and finds the study 'a fully composed picture of an enormous and original and in the end mysterious genius'. She believes that Mankowitz, with his achievements in so many different fields and with all the qualities 'to become the Jewish Dickens', will deserve as good a book to be written about his literary life; but she fears that he lacks not Dickens's talent and energy, but 'the development of some kind of stubborn resistance to the temptations of diversity'. Ireland – 'a cork-lined country' – may be the Proustian retreat he needs.

The TV series was as skilful a selection and assemblage of biographical data as the biography itself. But its aim, as well as its medium, was different. His problem, as he says at the London Birthday Dinner, is to 'ensure that the fictitious Dickens I attempt to create is as nearly as possible parallel with the real Dickens'.[12] The result is that Dickens the hard-headed businessman cohabits with Dickens the fantasist. He is always renegotiating, with publishers, printers and theatre managers, the exchange rate at which he will sell his talents and, as with the biography, Mankowitz's script always includes prices, profits and details of contracts. He is always, in the framing scenes in New York, monitoring, with the help of his manager Dolby, the amounts of energy he can offer his audiences during his readings in return for their adulation and their ticket revenue. In Episode 5 he declares to Mr Hogarth, his future father-in-law, that, unlike Scott who considered himself a gentleman who happened to write, he considers himself a writer who happens to be a gentleman. In the next episode, entitled 'Fame', he declares to the Hogarth family that he never commits thoughts to paper unless he is obliged to write because of a commission.

As an efficient manager of his waking self, Dickens Junior finds himself constantly in demand to bail out his spendthrift father.

Mankowitz's John Dickens is an actor manqué, full of rotund phrases and grandiose claims to fame, but his use of language entrances his son as a boy, and their rambles round the Kent countryside and the streets of London create an unbreakable bond between them. Mankowitz invents a mode of mock formal address between them, where the father calls his son 'Sir' and the young Dickens calls his father 'Guv'nor', which expresses very movingly their mutual pleasure in each other's company. In the 'Autobiographical Fragment', Dickens recalls that his father wanted to take him away from the blacking factory, but that his mother was keen for him to stay on and that he could never forgive her for her action. To have Roy Dotrice, in an acting tour de force, play both John and Charles Dickens accentuates the central importance, in Mankowitz's view, of his father, the fantasist and trickster, in Charles Dickens's life. In the very last scene of the TV series, John Dickens, on his deathbed, asks his son to confirm that Mr Micawber is based on him. Charles says he is and his father dies with a happy smile.

Dickens Senior takes every opportunity to praise, in rolling periods, the virtues of marriage and domesticity, but contrives to leave his wife to deal with their practical aspects. Dickens Junior regards with pride and affection his blossoming family, with his wife Catharine (played with a lolling sensuality by Adrienne Burgess) and her sister Mary as its fulcrum. But he also needs to explore the dark underside to this world of happy light, a sub-world of prisons, prostitution and poverty. Episode 11, entitled 'Nightmare', is Mankowitz's invention of a visit Dickens makes, under the guidance of Edgar Allen Poe, to the bed of a man whom Poe has mesmerized just at the point of his death. He is therefore in a state of suspended animation, which is a torture to him. When Poe breaks the spell, the man withers into a skeleton and then subsides into a carpet of dust. In Episode 12, 'Angel', Dickens is twice confronted, in London and Manchester, by three wolfish, yellow-fanged children who advance on him with outstretched hands and the cry: 'Gi us sumfin!' The children have been preceded by a dark vision of the blacking factory by Hungerford Stairs, by now a visual leitmotif in the series.

In Episode 3, entitled 'Blacking', the young Dickens is not only treated with contempt by most of the rough, uneducated lads he has to work with, but, in an incident invented by Mankowitz, he is stripped down to his underpants by the two biggest bullies, Smelly and Tucker, his mouth is stuffed with the oiled paper used to seal the pots of blacking and he is thoroughly blacked all over with the polish. The association of blacking polish and humiliation thus established, in another invented scene in Episode 8, 'Possession', his sister-in-law, Mary, tires of being treated as a child by Dickens, and takes off on a hectic horse-gallop across the Kent countryside to prove she is a grown woman. Dickens pursues her, they come to a halt, he is angry, she refuses to play the penitent and demands that he apologize. 'How should I apologise to my little Mary?', he simpers. 'You may kiss my boot', she concedes. The camera looks down on Dickens as he does so with a look of puzzled pleasure, then up to Mary's face from below, suffused with a guilty, fierce joy before her eyes close in ecstasy. Incest taboo and public censure would forbid actual sex between the two, but Dickens can play out the fantasy of a dominatrix by way of the fetish.

This scene is repeated on two further occasions, in Episode 9, entitled 'Dreams', which also dramatizes Dickens's fascination with Mesmerism, and is not so implausible an invention as it seems. Mary died unexpectedly of heart failure at the age of 17. She died in Dickens's arms and he venerated her forever after as his ideal of virginal, self-sacrificing girlhood. His wife, a fecund mother, could not play that role in his imagination. He wore a ring of Mary's, preserved her clothes and wanted to be buried in the same grave. Neither his wife nor her other younger sister, Georgina, who assumed Mary's role in the household, thought Dickens's attitude in any way unusual. The only vocabulary they all had to describe their feelings in such a situation was the traditionally religious one of purity and innocence. At the conclusion of Episode 9, Dickens's confession to his mesmerist of his recurring dream of kissing Mary's riding-boot occasions no moral anguish on either side. Dickens the businessman comes to the fore. Dreams, he implies, are good source material for a writer. His job, after all, is to put them down, to fix them so that others may catch and hold them.

Press reviews deal with the early episodes. James Murray is deeply impressed by Dotrice's doubling up as Dickens Senior and Junior and praises the performance of Simon Bell as the young Dickens, 'soaking up the characters of childhood and storing them away for the classic books' (*Daily Express*, 29 September 1976), but Nancy Banks-Smith (*Guardian*, 6 October 1976) finds the decor too consciously theatrical – 'Everyone acted away like anything' – and the dialogue extremely mannered. Stanley Reynolds's review for *The Times* (6 October 1976) also criticizes the staginess of Marc Miller's direction and production, 'as if the viewer were seeing a production meant for the theatre', and 'the sugary glue of Mr Mankowicz' [*sic*] well-known sentimentality'.

The theatricality is surely integral to the series' presentation of Dickens as an inveterate performer, and what sentimentality there is will soon be countered by Mankowitz's linkage of the blacking factory trauma with Dickens's obsessive idealization of young, female purity.

At an early stage in his interview, Gerald Davis comments on Mankowitz's considerable engagement with Dickens as a man and a writer and asks him if there were any remnants of Dickens's London when Mankowitz was a child in the East End some sixty years before. Mankowitz says there were a few traces and gives a brief description of his family's housing facilities at that time in the two-room flat in Fashion Street. As for Dickens, Mankowitz says he never liked him as a character and his engagement with him was purely commercial. Dickens, however, more than any other English writer, moved between different social worlds and devised plots and languages that bared undiscovered relations between these worlds of the rich and the common people. It may be that Mankowitz's own trafficking between the elite and popular cultures of his time had some unadmitted resemblance to Dickens's journeyings back and forth between the light and darkness of Victorian society.

Mankowitz's next biography, which appeared in June 1978, would be of Edgar Allen Poe, whose ecstasy was for deathly pale young maidens, but, while researching yet another richly illustrated life for Weidenfeld, he produced two very different works. The first was *The Day of the Women & the Night of the Men*, with illustrations by Charles Raymond and published by Robson Books in July 1977. It is a mixture of apothegms and mini-stories which propose a modern reading of classical and religious myths, or replay, with sardonic humour, such perennial topics as sex, art and money. In 'The Devil and the Entrepreneur', the businessman successfully bargains back his soul from the Devil in exchange for 1,000 other souls. 'The world is over-populated and souls are marked down accordingly', argues the businessman and 'eventually a deal satisfactory to both parties was concluded.'[13] 'The Day of the Women' and 'The Night of the Men' contrast a world run by women who are refugee aliens from a dying planet and an all-female earth run in extraordinary amity until some of the women begin to grow beards.

'The Truth about Orpheus' here is that he was a traveller for a publisher of popular music and his search for Eurydice gives him a good living and an attractive social position. In Mankowitz's powerfully evocative phrase, he finds Eurydice in 'a bare suburb, an empty artery of the city which had seen better times', a modern version of Hell, and they fall into each other's arms. But Orpheus then reflects upon what he will lose if he commits himself to this beautiful woman and it is when he glances away from her that he loses her. What he retains, however, is the respect of his employers. 'Socrates and the Hemlock' is a witty parody of Socrates' heuristic method of eliciting philosophical truth from his interlocutors, while the male lover in 'The Acme of Romantic Love' only wins the love of his beloved when he has so mutilated himself as to be incapable of making love to her. Raymond's line drawings are elegantly simple, whether of female breasts or zombie-like businessmen. The collection reads like an exercise in that classical and early modern genre 'the character study', and thus acts as proof that Mankowitz has lost nothing of his professional versatility, despite his 'exile' to a remote province of Ireland.

Mankowitz's contribution to the second work, *The Day God Laughed*, published by Robson Books on 7 July 1978, with illustrations by Cecily Ben-Tovim, was to act as interlocutor to Hyam Maccoby in a series of discussions on Maccoby's selection of passages, as the subtitle describes them, from the *Sayings, Fables and Entertainments of the Jewish Sages*. In his introduction, Maccoby makes it clear that these selections from the Gemara section of the Talmud have been chosen to demonstrate the flexibility of rabbinical interpretations of sacred texts and to distinguish the role of the rabbi as a lay leader from the role of the priest in Christianity. The Talmud, he claims, because it is more concerned to lay down an appropriate procedure than give a final answer, 'consecrates the process of argument itself'. Maccoby also claims that the parables of Jesus in the Gospels are examples of a Talmudic genre practised by the Pharisees and that Jesus himself was a Pharisee.

Mankowitz plays, for the most part, the role of interested layman who prompts Maccoby into providing further examples of rabbinical debate: for example, over how many times per week sexual intercourse between a man and his wife is required, depending on his occupation. The consensus is twice per week for labourers and once every thirty days for camel-drivers. Wives therefore have distinct conjugal rights as well as rights in property and dowry. A detailed discussion ranges over contrasting attitudes to the naked body as between the classical Greeks who exalted its beauty (Mankowitz) and the Jews who 'lived inside their bodies' and 'didn't put them outside as something to worship' (Maccoby). Mankowitz agrees: 'I think Jews respect the power of the body. It contains such power that you can't make an easy thing of it ...

you can't separate yourself from it in order to admire it.'[14] This rational discussion forum contrasts with the dramatic scene described in the *Samson Riddle* essay, the midnight Brooklyn court of a Chassidic rabbi in 'a nicotine-stained room of books and fading photographs of sublime rabbinic ancestors',[15] but the aim is the same, to explore how congruent religious scepticism is with a Jewish identity.

Mankowitz himself assumes multiple identities as a writer in this period. A fortnight before the publication of *The Day God Laughed*, on 22 June 1978, Weidenfeld published *The Extraordinary Mr Poe*, a biography which traces in detail the dipsomaniac and manic-depressive career of the poet, tale-teller and editor who was, with publication of *The Raven* in early 1845, for that moment, 'a success in the adored and homely American overnight tradition'.[16] The lugubrious bird of ill-omen was an apposite familiar for the man who had conjured out of his drinking bouts, opium addiction and obsessions with consumptive young women such macabre tales as *The Murders in the Rue Morgue* and *The Masque of the Red Death*. His satanic reputation thrilled refined ladies with artistic pretentions, the 'starry sisterhood', but they shrank from his manic protestations of love because they realized Poe could only love a woman who was dead or dying. By the age of 20 he had suffered the loss, from consumption, of three older women: his mother, his stepmother and the mother of a schoolboy friend. His cousin Virginia was 13 when he married her and she died of consumption twelve years later.

As with the Dickens biography, Mankowitz favours a psychoanalytical approach to Poe's life and texts. He makes extensive use of Marie Bonaparte's analysis of Poe's obsession with ethereal femininity,[17] and notes recurring preoccupations with the dying mother-sister, the red phantom of tuberculosis and womb-like tunnels of darkness and light in Poe's stories and poems. But he also constructs a clear narrative of Poe's often erratic journeyings up and down the east coast of America and into the mid-west, and elucidates Poe's complex and often multiple relationships with adored women. Mankowitz also produces convincing evidence to show that Poe, when sane and sober, was a shrewd editor with a good sense of the emerging American market for literary magazines. He quotes at length from a letter by Poe to the young owner of a weekly newspaper in Oquawka, Mississippi, called the *Spectator*, in which he gives precise calculations for the price and volume of copies needed to break even or to make a profit, and cites the rise in circulation figures when he was editor of the *Southern Literary Messenger* and *Graham's Magazine*. But he also requested an advance of $50 on his appointment as editor and, when it arrived, squandered it on drink and drugs.[18]

Mankowitz quotes extensively elsewhere, sometimes to the extent of several pages, from primary sources. These extracts certainly help him complete his contracted word-count, but they are also worth quoting for their style and the sense of period they give the reader. The lengthiest account is a recollection, in an interview for *Harper's*, by Mary Devereaux, of a summer of passionate flirtation with Poe when he was living in Baltimore and beginning to make a reputation for himself as a local Byron. She recalls that Poe was a very passionate wooer and when, one evening, Mary's mother refused to call down her daughter to see him, Poe declared that he had the right to see her because she was now his wife 'in the sight of heaven'. Mary's uncle James wrote Poe a severe letter to cut off future contact with his niece. Poe's response was to cowhide the uncle in his store and throw down the whip in front of Mary declaring, 'I make you a present of that.'[19]

Mankowitz is cautious about the details of this relationship. He thinks that it had some physical basis but that the extent of their intimacy must remain speculative. He always puts inverted commas around their 'affair' and notes Poe's drinking and tendency towards hyperbole could well have accounted for his grandiloquent statement about marriage in the eyes of heaven. Julian Symonds, however, in his review for the *TLS* (8 July 1978), criticizes Mankowitz for accepting that Devereaux and Poe had a love affair; and that, upon the flimsy evidence of a minor poet, Susan Archer Talley, the Rev. Rufus Griswold was charged by Poe with the supervision of his literary affairs after his death. Symons admires the illustrations, particularly those by lesser-known artists such as Harry Clarke and Edmund Dulac, but launches, at the end, into a philippic against Mankowitz's slovenly scholarship. His bilious critique is unbalanced and may well have been induced by the publication of his own biography of Poe in the same month as Mankowitz's.

Other critics were more temperate. Francis King for the *Sunday Telegraph* (25 June 1978) has some quibbles about the book's scholarship, but he finds the psychoanalytical approach convincing and the author's accounts of Poe's many attempts at marriage to his 'starry sisterhood' both funny and sad. Deborah Maccoby, for the *Jewish Chronicle* (28 July 1978) is convinced by the relationships Mankowitz establishes between Poe's disordered life and the hallucinated distortions which are his major poems and stories, but regrets he did not devote more space to Poe the proto-Symbolist.

Paul Zwieg, in his long article, 'Literary Terrorist', for the *Saturday Review* on the Symons and Mankowitz biographies, finds that both books provide excellent resumes of the life, based on previous scholarship. Mankowitz emphasizes Poe's addictions while Symons underplays them; Symons's narrative is fairly circumstantial and he devotes more time to literary analysis than Mankowitz who, with his reliance on Bonaparte's study, provides persuasive links between the life and the works. For Zweig, Mankowitz is 'especially good on the decay of Poe's love life' as he 'butterflied from one pallid poetess to another'. Zweig, without comment, calls the Mary Devereaux relationship a 'possibly consummated affair'.[20]

Raspberry Reich, Mankowitz's next novella, published in April 1979, derives its title from a statement by Ulrike Meinhof, a member of the left-wing terrorist group the Red Army Faction that performed robberies and political assassinations in West Germany throughout the 1970s. For Meinhof the Federal Republic was still fundamentally Nazi but that ideology of steel and violence had been overlaid by the gloop of consumerism. It is a Raspberry Reich 'which stifles us with its rich sweet goo'. Mankowitz's principal character, Princess Lorelei, is a teenage aristocrat at a Swiss boarding school which is full of rich girls. Lorelei has another persona, Lorry, who is another Ulrike, head of the self-styled Red Army Faction at the school whose most radical action is to dress as punks at the annual school concert and climax their song 'Death to the Raspberry Reich' by stabbing their fake balloon breasts and releasing purple streams of raspberry juice.

Steel is revealed beneath the juice when Lorolei, with her sidekick from school, Clio, who is part-Jewish, explore a secret study which Lorolei has discovered in the ancestral castle of Boschkampf where they are guests of Lorelei's grandfather, the Count von Widdenburg. Photographs show the Count on very friendly terms with Hitler and other members of the Nazi high command. The Count explains the relationship away by saying that, as a Swiss banker, he was called upon by all sides to provide finance during the war.

Lorelei is convinced but her alter ego Lorry-Ulrike is not. She holds him at gunpoint and denounces him as a Nazi and demands a huge ransom for his release. Clio is scared and wants to opt out of the ransom plan. Lorry kills her – the Jews always get it in the neck – but then reverts to Lorelei, who runs for protection into her grandfather's arms. He reassures her that he will protect her and, in an internal reverie, assures himself that everything will continue as before. He and his fellow Nazis will remain 'the Knights of Eternal Fire and Ice', absolved from all morality and conscience 'for they were free of the restrictive enslaving taboos which the weaker masses of Man, that joke of the gods, had evolved to conceal weakness and cowardice'.[21]

Mankowitz reconciles very different registers – schoolgirl bickering, Nazi dreaming, popular culture notation – with casual expertise. The ending shifts the plot from being a sport at the expense of the Left to being a warning critique of the Right. The shift of narrative voice, from omniscient narrator to free indirect, acknowledges this change. Norman Shrapnel, for the *Guardian* (14 June 1979), only acknowledges the posh school setting 'where they fit in political assassination between deportment and music'. But this is a midnight feast where 'once the original excitement is over, the jam spreads a bit thin'.

Abracadabra!, published by Macmillan on 3 July 1980, intertwines two very different voices, those of a querulous old man, called Ben Abarbanel, stuck in a London geriatric ward in 2013, who recounts his memories of his schoolboy evacuation from the East End to Sodbury, a Wiltshire town with a railway history. The present-day Abarbanel inveighs into his tape recorder against the impersonal bureaucracy of the hospital, only one facet of a Britain that has converted to Islam and is policed by agents of the Inland Revenue.[22] His sentence structures are ornate and his tone of voice orotund: 'the question to which you require an answer is mine to answer, and answer it I will in the course of the statutory thousand and one days ahead, of which this shall be computed the conclusion of the fifth'.[23] The reference to the *Thousand and One Nights* casts the old man as a narrator who is telling tales to save his life. He is, as Gay Firth comments in his review for *The Times* (3 July 1980), a 'beguiling, hilarious Scheherezade with chutzpah ... desperately joking to win a private way to life and death'.

His main tale is one of love and magic. The pain of his evacuation – separation from his family and bullying from their temporary headmaster – is mitigated by the abstruse and eccentric researches of his landlord, who claims his name is Solomon Hakoen and that he is descended from a long line of alchemists. Hakoen is convinced that Ben is a descendant of the Spanish Abarbanels, famous for their intertwining of magic and finance. He asks Ben to get obscure alchemical treatises from his father who is a dealer in rare books and finally allows Ben into his secret laboratory, the Chamber of Transmogrification. But this turns out to be another Mankowitz tale of tricksters and conmen. Hakoen is not Jewish but an Old Etonian called Hopkirk and Ben, far from being an alchemical adept, is such an incompetent scientist that he only succeeds in blowing up the Transmogrification Chamber. Ben, however, knows his literature. With his last line, he sighs 'Ah, Mephistopheles', and Mephistopheles replies: 'It is the thousandth night. You must begin again.'[24]

The correspondence between Ben and father is not literary. Ben asks for books and explains why, but the tone of the letters is unaffected love and respect. Ben describes his father as a bad businessman but a very shrewd bookman, a distinction that his mother, trying always to balance the household finances, fails to appreciate. Ben recalls with nostalgia his childhood, living above their shop called Mile End Books, and his father's love for tales of fantasy and exploration, particularly Richard F. Burton's *Pilgrimage to Meccah*. There are further biographical allusions here. The Abarbanel Senior who emerges is very similar to the Mankowitz Senior whom, as noted earlier, his son describes in the Davis interview. Mankowitz was evacuated with his schoolmates at East Ham Grammar School to the Commonweal Secondary School in Swindon, the fictional Sodbury, in 1939. He would be 14 at the time but there is no record of his being billeted with such a bizarre figure as Solomon Hakoen; and there is not and never has been any London hospital named after Barbara Castle. *Abracadabra!* is as truthful as its title.

Martyn Goff, writing for the *Daily Telegraph* (10 July 1980) was not much impressed by the fiction, finding it whimsical and far-fetched and, like David Wilson for the *TLS* (1 August 1980), trying too hard to amuse. Nicolas Shrimpton's *New Statesman* review (25 August 1980) also finds the political satire laboured, but Ben's tale 'has a good deal of zany charm' and he concludes that the book 'would be much better if it were a little less miscellaneous'. Thomas Hinde (*Sunday Telegraph*, 6 July 1980) was less censorious than his colleague and concluded that the novel was an example of humour by exaggeration, a specific kind of Jewish writing in which Mankowitz is a specialist: 'The geriatric's father, a seller of comics in the Mile End Road, is particularly splendid.' The *Jewish Chronicle*'s reviewer, Sharon Wallach, for their issue of 1 August 1980, gives a resume of the plot, where she explains that Ben is confined forever to hospital, to old age, as a result of the botched experiment in Sodbury. She points out the distinguished Spanish heritage of the family name Abarbanel and concludes that fantasy and realism are expertly balanced in the novella.

In the third section of *Abracadabra!*, Ben, a victim of race-baiting by his head teacher, reflects that a Jew becomes a man at 13 'in order to have longer to try and find out what being a man is for'.[25] This could be the motto for Mankowitz's last significant work of this period, a twenty-five minute talk at 7.45 pm, preceding a BBC2 production of *The Merchant of Venice* on 15 December 1980. His slightly amended text, along with others which introduce a range of Shakespeare plays, is reproduced in a collection edited by Roger Sales.[26] He is shot walking in and around Lincoln Cathedral and Lincoln Castle, and commenting on them as sites of anti-Jewish hysteria and expulsion in the mediaeval period. The opening shots show him entering a bookshop near the cathedral, pausing by a pile of books, and declaring: 'I am a Jew, and I am a writer, but I am also a man.'[27] He then quotes briefly from Shylock's famous speech in Act III: 'Hath not a Jew eyes ...', which is given in full later on. Mankowitz considers that this speech, uniquely for the period, acknowledges that Jews are human beings and that they reflect the societies in which they live. Christian society is vengeful and villainous; Shylock is part of that society; why should he not follow its customs?

'Men are', Mankowitz concludes, 'what they make of themselves and of one another.' Judas cannot exist without Christ, nor Shylock without Antonio. But Mankowitz hesitates as to whether Jews need to exist for anti-Semitism to exist. Shakespeare probably never met a Jew, but he is able to represent very accurately the traditional tropes of Christian anti-Semitism. Mankowitz concludes: 'I wonder if *The Merchant of Venice* proves that this Christian disease persists whether we are there or not. If so, it is their problem, not Shylock's or mine.' The television production, which followed on from the talk, portrays, according to John Naughton's review for the *Observer* (21 December 1980), a vicious, Hobbesian society. The Venetian Chamber of Commerce displays 'the menacing unity of a pack of ravening wolves' and Jack Gold's direction 'casts a baleful eye on the wider society outside the tragedy'. Nobody, it would seem, escapes whipping in this production.

Mankowitz's own productions in this period, from the mid-1970s, read as an eclectic collection of subjects and genres. Biographies and aphorisms keep company with fantasy novellas and an academic disquisition. He had, however, to keep writing for financial reasons. The Inland Revenue was still pursuing him for unpaid taxes, and the following year (1981) he, or the Inland Revenue, petitioned for his bankruptcy with total debts of £69,161. He put on a brave front at the hearing, declaring that, as an artist who spends his life 'running around the world inventing fantasies for the public', it was unlikely that he would also be a gifted mathematician. His accountant had let him down and his papers were in disorder. But the Inland Revenue still demanded that he pay off tax claims of £53,000.[28] It is likely that he was discharged by 1989 under the terms of the Insolvency Act of 1986.[29]

This somewhat random output of writings also seems typical of a man in the first years of retirement. He keeps going as before but his activities do not cohere as before because the supporting structures are no longer there. A major role in the development of the Irish film industry might have focussed his writing and publicity skills but there was no sequel to the triumph of *The Hebrew Lesson*. He would, however, recover his equilibrium, despite declining health, by accepting a visiting academic post at the University of New Mexico, and by devising new narratives with which to represent his old themes of exchange and the trickster.

NOTES

1. Ref. THM/271/2/1/41, Theatre and Performance Collection, Victoria and Albert Museum, London.
2. Cited in Adrian Wright, *A Tanner's Worth of Tune: Rediscovering the Post-War British Musical* (Woodbridge: Boydell Press, 2010), pp.190–1.
3. *Jewish Chronicle*, 19 December 1958.
4. Wolf Mankowitz, *The Blue Arabian Nights: Tales of a London Decade* (Dublin: Ahakista Press, 1973), p.9.
5. Alan Watts, 'The London Birthday Dinner Party', *The Dickensian*, 72–3 (1976–77), p.124.
6. Letter, Christopher Falkus to Wolf Mankowitz, 22 March 1976, Mankowitz Family Archive.
7. Michael Slater, *Charles Dickens* (New Haven, CT, and London: Yale University Press, 2009), p.xiv.
8. Wolf Mankowitz, *Dickens of London* (London: Weidenfeld & Nicolson, 1976), p.44.
9. Ibid., pp.162, 150.
10. P. Ackroyd, *Dickens* (London: Sinclair-Stevenson, 1990), p.916.
11. All the quotes and references in this paragraph are to Forster's quoting from the 'Autobiographical Fragment', *The Life of Charles Dickens*, vol. 1 (London: J.M. Dent, 1966), pp.19–33. (Originally published 1872–74.)
12. Watts, 'The London Birthday Dinner Party', p.124.
13. All quotations and references to this work are from Wolf Mankowitz, *The Day of the Women & the Night of the Men* (London: Robson Books, 1977).
14. Hyam Maccoby and Wolf Mankowitz, *The Day God Laughed* (London: Robson Books, 1978), pp.11, 204.
15. Wolf Mankowitz, *Wolf Mankowitz: The Plays*, preface by Anthony Dunn (London: Oberon Books, 2006), p.16.
16. Wolf Mankowitz, *The Extraordinary Mr Poe* (London: Weidenfeld & Nicolson, 1978), pp.181–2.
17. Bonaparte, Marie, *The Life and Works of Edgar Allen Poe: A Psycho-Analytic Interpretation*, trans. John Rodker (London: Imago, 1949; reprinted 1971). (First published 1933.)

18. Mankowitz, *The Extraordinary Mr Poe*, pp.230–1.
19. Ibid., p.85.
20. Paul Zweig, 'Literary Terrorist', *Saturday Review*, 6 January 1979, pp.50–2.
21. Wolf Mankowitz, *Raspberry Reich* (Dublin and London: Macmillan, 1979), pp.206–7.
22. There is a biographical element here, in that Mankowitz, according to an *Observer* note of 11 November 1979, was the subject of an Inland Revenue writ in the High Court to recover £50,787 of unpaid taxes between 1962 and 1969.
23. Wolf Mankowitz, *Abracadabra!* (Dublin and London: Macmillan, 1980), p.55.
24. Ibid., p.165.
25. Ibid., p.25.
26. Roger Sales (ed.), *Shakespeare in Perspective*, vol. 1 (London: Ariel/BBC Publications, 1982), pp.208–14.
27. This and all subsequent references and quotes are from the script of the TV production, courtesy of the Mankowitz Family Archive.
28. *Daily Telegraph*, 19 August 1981.
29. My thanks to Chris Bolger for these legal details.

CHAPTER TEN

The Final Flare (1982–91)

The first lecture in a summer series under the auspices of the University of New Mexico was given by Mankowitz on 14 June 1982. The *New Mexico Daily Lobo* reported in its edition of 17 June that 'this big man with the wit and sophisticated charm of an English gentleman' had offered his audience a deliberately unromantic version of the acting profession. Most actors' lives, he concluded, were sad and empty when the performance was over. To cope with their inevitable psychological stress they committed themselves early on to one of three archetypes of acting – the actor-as-fool, the actor-as-king or the actor-as-god. Mankowitz then selected Peter Sellers, Richard Burton and Orson Welles as prime examples of each category, and paid particular attention to Welles who, he contended, had both intuitive acting intelligence and an analytical intelligence about the world at large. This 'great white whale' could always see the big picture. He was never impounded within any current production because 'he is an ongoing spirit of all the production ... even if the smallest production is a commercial'. Mankowitz's close association with these famous actors would have added weight to his analysis of their survival strategies. His sardonic undermining of the heroic illusionisms of theatre and cinema might well have caused a frisson among the more idealistic members of his audience.

The press report finishes by publicizing Mankowitz's recently published biography of the actress Ada Mencken (*sic*) and giving advance notice of a satirical work in progress, *The Devil in Texas*. The full title of the biography is *Mazeppa: The Lives, Loves and Legends of Adah Isaacs Menken* and it was published in Britain in August 1982. Mankowitz subtitles the volume *A Biographical Quest*, but after reviewing all the available evidence he is unable to pronounce definitively where she was born, when she was born and what her maiden surname was. His tentative conclusion is that she may have been born in 1839, near New

Orleans, with the name of Bertha Theodore; that she may have been of mixed race; and that the birth year of 1835 that she gives at the time of her first marriage, to Alexander Isaac Menken, heir to the dry goods business of a wealthy Cincinnati Jewish family, probably overstated her age by four years in order in order to comply with State laws about minimum marriageable age. She certainly died in August 1868, either of peritonitis or a cancerous abscess, and was buried in the Jewish section of Père Lachaise cemetery on 10 August.

The Menken, as she became known to her audiences and many admirers in America and Europe, was, in a very literal sense, a one-trick pony. She had had some limited success playing breeches parts in obscure spectacle dramas such as *The Enchanting Songstress* and *The Female Soldier*. One Captain John B. Smith had revived at the Green Street Theatre in Albany an old three-act drama based on Byron's poem *Mazeppa*, a dashing tale of a young aristocratic hero and heroine separated by the heroine's forced engagement to a terrifying count. The climax was a ride across, above and back down onto the stage of the hero strapped to the back of a black stallion.

Captain Smith decided to raise audience expectations by having a woman play Mazeppa, and for her to be strapped to the horse wearing a body-stocking covered by a short, flimsy tunic. From a distance and with careful lighting she would appear to be naked. Smith offered the part to Menken, who at first refused it, but then, when Smith described the fame and fortune she would amass as the first female Mazeppa, she accepted. She was a good horsewoman and, by nineteenth-century standards, had a fine figure and good legs. Her astute agent, Ed James, organized a press conference before her debut, in which the journalists were dazzled by her short cropped hair, simple dress and femme fatale suite: 'There, in careful light, waited Menken, reclining on a tiger-skin, sipping champagne, feeding bon-bons to a French poodle and smoking a cigarette.'[1]

The first night of Menken's *Mazeppa* in Albany was on 7 June 1861. It was a great success. Captain Smith's extensive pre-publicity, including a parade through the streets of Albany of thirteen trained stallions carrying placards describing them as 'The Menken Stud', had created high expectations of an erotic theatrical experience which were fully satisfied. Androgyny, nudity and female vulnerability were all on show. Menken would go on, in her short career of only some seven years as a star of the theatre, to play other roles, in equally undistinguished plays, but audiences always associated her with Mazeppa. The role was a co-production, before, during and after the performance, in which actress, agent and manager constructed what Mankowitz calls the first Great American International Star. When Menken gave her press conferences she was, as we have seen, already on stage. Mankowitz presents her as the first actress in theatre history to make extensive use of photography to build her reputation and to keep herself constantly before the public gaze. When she made a bid, late in her career, for literary fame, she released pictures of herself and her latest lover, Alexander Dumas the Elder, with Menken nuzzling into the portly chest of the great author. Mankowitz calls this a photo of 'the lovely Menken', but to our eyes she looks more like a dumpy laundress.

Mankowitz makes another large claim for her. He reads her free-loving, performative life as an early example of feminist liberation. The debate about whether women should use their beauty or their intelligence to gain equality with men is as undecided now as when Mary Wollstonecraft made the case for intelligence in 1792. Mankowitz's preface declares his fellow-feeling for Bohemians, tough and tender 'iron butterflies' like Menken, but he later admits, when tracing her multiple marriages, that there is a tension in Menken's life and career between the reckless Bohemian and the 'little middle-class girl from the South West' who never lost her belief that 'true love should lead to marriage'.[2]

At the end of her life Menken consorted with literary figures such as Dumas, Swinburne and George Sand, not for reasons of respectability, but because literature was a less ephemeral art than the stage and she was trying to 'produce a convincing atmosphere of high poetic class'[3] around the most important project of her life, her collection of thirty-one poems, entitled *Infelicia*. She died a week before the volume was published. The critics savaged it. Mankowitz reproduces a selection of the poems. They are mournful exercises in outworn romantic themes of despair and desertion. The printed word needed different illusionist skills to those practised by the greatest 'flesh artist' of her day.

Mankowitz makes another claim for Menken, that her informal and ad-libbing style in comedy dramas foreshadowed the soubrette style in American musicals. With only press reports, however, of her performances it is difficult to judge her musical ability. She is probably best seen as a distinctively American descendant of such eighteenth-century English actresses as Mary Robinson and Kitty Clive. They manipulated the newly emergent print market for gossip columns and theatre puffs, and posed for somewhat risqué portraits. But they were careful to maintain a reputation for sexual propriety. As Amanda Vickery remarks in her preview of the National Portrait Gallery's 2011 exhibition, *The First Actresses: Nell*

Gwyn to Sarah Siddons: 'Being a lofty vehicle of erotic fantasy was one thing, a whorish backstory was quite another.'[4] Menken determined to make the two stories one, to reveal herself to the public as both a fake stripper and a highly sexualized woman. She was a real fake, an adept performer within both popular and high culture, and a most distinguished addition to Mankowitz's gallery of tricksters.

Reviewers were as captivated as Mankowitz by the exuberant career of La Menken. They understood that this biography had engaged him at a deeper level than those of Dickens and Poe. For Brian Masters of the *Evening Standard* (18 August 1982), no one had told Menken's story with such vitality and wit, and for David Holloway of the *Daily Telegraph* (12 August 1982) this is a 'hard but affectionate look' at a lady who raises important questions about Jews and Jewishness which Mankowitz is well placed to debate. His considered review, the length of which is a compliment to Mankowitz's scholarship, sees Menken more as a star than a lover and sees clear parallels between her last days and those of Marilyn Monroe. Even Francis King – a hostile reviewer, as we have seen – admits in the *Daily Telegraph* (15 August 1982) that, although Mankowitz's text is 'hectic, flamboyant and slapdash', he weaves together the multiple narratives of Menken's life in a most entertaining manner.

Mankowitz's scholarship exposes one such narrative – by a previous biographer, Noel Gerson, who wrote under various pseudonyms – as a complete invention. Gerson claimed to have discovered an early diary by Menken which recorded her experiences as a prostitute. Academic libraries had no record of the diary and Mankowitz came to believe that it was a complete fabrication by Gerson. He challenged Gerson to admit, as one experienced professional writer to another, that the diary was 'an achievement in fable-building which should be acknowledged for its creative force'.[5] John Stokes, in his very favourable review for the *TLS* (20 August 1982), notes that Gerson was flattered by this approach and confessed that the diary was a hoax. The great trickster had her male avatars even 100 years after her death.

The wide range of favourable reviews for the Menken biography was evidence that Mankowitz, despite his exile in Éire, was still considered a significant writer in English cultural circles. Charles Nevin, in a genial interview for the *Guardian* (12 February 1984), casts him as a professional writer and teacher who moves with ease through a number of very different worlds. He presents him as the Panamanian Consul in Dublin who is also a bankrupt Jew from the East End who spends much of his time lecturing New Mexico youth in Santa Fe. But he is also, for this occasion, the author of the outline for *Almonds and Raisins*, a ninety-minute documentary compilation of fragments and extracts from what remain of the more than 300 Yiddish-language films made in New York or on location in Poland between 1927 and 1940. Mankowitz is most enthusiastic about this archival preservation of a culture which was effectively killed off by Jewish assimilation into American English-speaking culture and the Nazi occupation of Poland. He is also moved by the 'simple emotional scenes [the film] presents'. Nevin suggests they are schmaltzy, to which Mankowitz replies that what the British find sentimental 'constitutes a low-key minimal and muted display of emotion to other nations'.

The film, written and produced by David Elstein and Russ Karel and directed by Karel, had a release in 1983, but its general UK cinema release was in February 1984, its television showing for Channel 4 on 20 September 1984 and its New York release in August 1985. Orson Welles's linking narrative is, as Lucy Hughes-Hallett describes it in her television review for the *Standard* (21 September 1984), 'sharply funny as well as affectionate'; but she also points out that the film is a record both of the agony suffered by families exiled from their homes and of Jewish Americans eager to assimilate into American affluence: 'Wives with hairdos as stiff and shiny as a Cindy Doll's boasted about their husband's business successes.' The style of acting is highly melodramatic, but no more so than in the bulk of silent and early sound films, which inherited that style from nineteenth-century popular and classical theatre. The Menken would have exploited all its opportunities.

Alexander Walker's review for the *Standard* (23 February 1984) on the occasion of the film's general release at the Phoenix cinema, East Finchley, focuses on the way the compilation plots the two-way stretch of Jewish tradition, looking forward and back, through a selection of archetypal movie scenes, including 'the first generation's sweatshop days, [and] the second's Park Avenue penthouse achievement'. David Robinson for *The Times* (24 February 1984) mentions the testimony of the 'surviving witnesses of this lost history', including the bearded patriarch Zvee Scooler; and John Pym for the *Financial Times* (24 February 1984) alludes to the mixture of pleasure and grief felt by another witness (in fact Miriam Kressyn) as she views pre-war Polish films and sees again colleagues, most of whom were subsequently murdered by the Nazis. Julian Petley's review for the *Monthly Film Bulletin* distinguishes between the numerous films from Hollywood, from *The Jazz Singer* to *Fiddler on the Roof*, about Jews or Jewish subjects and the films preserved in *Almonds and Raisins* which addressed 'such a *specifically* Jewish audience'. The film's commentary emphasizes, he claims, that these films occupy 'something of an ideological battleground between the forces of assimilation and isolation'.[6]

Mankowitz was proud to have been involved in making the film and its combination of archival scholarship and popular culture would appeal to him, but he was cautious about such high-sounding claims for its significance. Russ Karel talks, in a *Time Out* interview, about its 'universal story of immigrants trying to retain a culture'; Mankowitz says it will only be attractive to 'film buffs interested in a curious episode in the history of cinema'.[7] The subject, however, has been of recent interest to theatre buffs, with a run at the National Theatre from 18 January 2012 of Nicolas Wright's *Travelling Light*, which proposes the discovery, by chance and by a genius of instinct, of the principles of moving pictures by a group of villagers in an East European shtetl in the early 1900s. The play moves back and forth between the shtetl and 1930's Hollywood and highlights, as does *Almonds and Raisins*, the importance of community tales of love, death and money as the bases for archetypal Hollywood narratives.

Mankowitz's next novella, *The Devil in Texas*, published in September 1984, is another curious episode, this time in the history of the 'campus novel'. This genre, in its English version, features a weedy, undistinguished academic in the humanities or social sciences who wins the most beautiful woman on campus. These are realist novels with unrealistic plots and therefore their predominant mode must be satirical. This anti-hero is a kind of holy fool whose pratfalls and gaucheries expose the venal pomposity of his colleagues and superiors. The prototype is Jim Dixon, the maladroit history lecturer in Kingsley Amis's *Lucky Jim* (1954), while spineless, paunchy James Walker, Fellow in Creative Writing at the mid-western Benedict Arnold University, emerges as the improbable lover of the delicious student Julie Snowflake in Malcolm Bradbury's *Stepping Westward* (1965). Bradbury situates his fictional university town of Party at the very middle point of the mid-west itself ,'where the middle west meets the far west and the southwest the northwest',[8] a non-place and an analogue to the narrator's neutral vantage point from which he satirizes both English prostration and American dynamism.

Sefton Goldberg, the Jewish protagonist of Howard Jacobson's *Coming From Behind* (1983) and a lecturer in English at Wrottesley Polytechnic, has no doubts about sexual prowess. 'His race', after all, 'had its sexual pride to protect', as he observes towards the end of a novel which begins with him having sex on his office floor with a mature student just prior to the graduation ceremony. Jacobson shifts this anti-hero's sense of failure and inadequacy from sex to career. Goldberg is a Cambridge English graduate who finds himself teaching in a Midlands polytechnic. His private research project is 'a sort of history and vindication of the will to failure in art'. The novel culminates in a fantasy sequence, where he is interviewed for the Disraeli Fellowship at the Cambridge college of Holy Christ Hall by a panel of dons with names from English novels and, despite very minimal qualifications, he eventually gets the post and flees the Midlands. The beautiful job would be more important to him, as a Jewish outsider, than the beautiful girl. He still remembers the embarrassing scene after his own graduation when his father, an amateur conjuror, set up his little collapsible table on the college lawn and, before an interested crowd, produced a large, white, new-laid egg from the ear of F.R. Leavis.[9]

This is minor magic compared to the Texan devil, the arch-demon Lilith, whom Dr Oliver Stanley, expert in 'Gnostic heresies and diabolistic cults', inadvertently summons up in the Bean Memorial Library, Longhorn University City, when he mutters an ancient invocation to Lilat/Lilith which he has found in an obscure sixteenth-century publication, the *Mysterium Arcanum.* Dr Stanley, a bachelor on a year's sabbatical from Cambridge to study histories of vampirism in a local Hungarian emigrant settlement, fulfils all the criteria of the campus anti-hero. He is 40 years old, of unprepossessing appearance and in a low-key relationship with his secretary, whom he shares with two other lovers. Mankowitz puts him in a range of comic situations – lost trousers, drunkenness, bashful lover, sudden fatigue – which are not only typical of the academic holy fool, but also representative of the antics of the two famous cinema clowns, Stan and Olly.

To this paragon of English weediness, almost female in the shadow of the giant-booted Texans, who are overshadowed only by their city-centre building of towering pink granite, appears Dr Amorian, supervisor of the Rare Books Section, with peaches-and-cream skin, violet-azure eyes, and a mass of radiantly blonde hair. Dr Stanley will later notice her free, swelling breasts beneath a fine, silk shirt and, much later, her roseate nipples and milk-white thighs after strenuous lovemaking on piles of uncatalogued magazines in one of the library's garrets. After one ecstatic session Dr Stanley admits to himself that he is in love with this incarnation of femaleness whom, on her instructions, he calls Lupa. He wonders if she has the same passion for him and if this sudden affair is typical of more relaxed sexual mores in Texas than in England. He decides he will live for the moment in this new land of plenty, but England and his campus hero archetype immediately pull him back: 'Dr Stanley had become a man in a man's country; almost, anyway.'[10]

Dr Amorian is the shape-shifter of female and male myth. She is a calm, middle-aged librarian, a prickly feminist and the concupiscent lover of Rare Books. She is a hard-drinking Texan girl who rampages through the bars of Longhorn, and Miss White Ranch at the birthday party for Admiral White, one of the leading figures in the county. She is Daddy's girl and The Lady of Situations. She entrances and exhausts Dr Stanley, who takes refuge in their out-of-town cabin with a gay couple – Billy, the manager of a local clothes-shop and Lyndon White-Bean, a lawyer and renegade member of the White clan. But Dr Amorian has a single-minded goal. She wants Dr Stanley to destroy his paper on Texan vampires. She is a descendant of the Hungarian Czerny family who settled in Texas in the nineteenth century, changed their surname to Cherny, married into the White family and now run the county as the Cherny Whites. She makes him an offer he daren't refuse. He will destroy his research and the university will provide him with a research post with all expenses paid and his servicing needs directly supervised by Dr Amorian.

He agrees the deal and signs the contract in the blood from an accidentally cut hand. The last line commits him to the deal in body, mind and soul. Dr Amorian transforms herself into her most terrifying avatar, a vast, white, bat-like angel whose claws scoop up Dr Stanley and carry him off high above the city where he can see 'the Lone Star of Texas shining red over the dark pyramids of the Campus'.[11] Dr Stanley, however, turns out to be something of a trickster himself. He tires of his cosseted life and the gradual draining of all his energies by Lupa. He reveals to Lyndon White-Bean that he has Native American ancestry through a marriage between a nineteenth-century Indian fighter and a woman from the local Obibi tribe. Lyndon advises him that he probably has a claim to land now owned by the Cherny Whites. He negotiates the second deal of the novel, a simultaneous marriage and divorce with Dr Amorian, a renunciation of all claims to Cherny-White territory and a generously funded professorship in Reborn Christianity at his Cambridge college. The last scene of the novel has Dr Stanley about to resume comfy lovemaking with his secretary Imogen when he notices she is wearing the same ring as Dr Amorian and smells a familiar scent of juniper, pinon, desert air and falling redbud blossoms.

The campus novel is a satirical novel and *The Devil in Texas* has several set pieces of high comedy: the musings on the need for the Devil by Stanley's Professor White, author of the *Simplistic Gospels*; the Texan Clothes Hoss, a giant store consisting of 'several acres of boots, hats, belts, jeans and a vast range of fetishistic leather gear'; and the parade of beauty queens in rhinestone tiaras with Vaseline-coated lips of hot, pink lipstick and mouths of identically white teeth.[12] David Montrose, for the *TLS* (19 October 1984) finds some of the 'soft-edged satire' overwritten and concludes that the closing escalation of plot 'never quite recaptures the novel's earlier impetus'. There are passages that drag, particularly a potted history of the State of Texas, but, within the context of this study, *The Devil in Texas* marks an important stage in the evolution of key themes in Mankowitz's later fictions.

Montrose, in an admittedly short notice, makes no reference to Mankowitz's further elaboration here of his interest in esoteric, kabbalist interpretations of Jewish religious texts. Mankowitz's Stanley is as atheist as his creator but both are fascinated by the struggle between belief and interpretation of religious texts and the scholarly ingenuity brought to bear on this vocation. Woman is often the enigmatic sign in these patriarchal texts, and Lilith or Lamia is construed, on various readings, to be Adam's first wife or a demon. To accommodate such a mythical protagonist within the realist convention of the campus novel, Mankowitz inverts its traditional plot. In *The Devil in Texas* the most beautiful woman on campus wins the weedy academic through a Faustian deal. 'There's nothing but magic at the top', as tycoon Barney Kelley observes to his academic son-in-law, Stephen Rojack, at the end of Norman Mailer's *An American Dream*.[13]

In a wide-ranging interview the following year for the *Guardian* (9 February 1985), Mankowitz, with reference to *The Devil in Texas*, wonders what a don would sell his soul for. 'A knighthood from Mrs Thatcher', suggests the interviewer, and Mankowitz agrees that that is probably a realistic exchange. He outlines future projects, including a play about the pilgrims who visit D.H. Lawrence's grave in New Mexico, but he also reveals that his illness is a rare cancer of the pancreas which produces the equivalent of battery acid. It seems ghoulish that his adaptation for Anglia Television, broadcast the previous year (2 June 1984), of a slight story by Antonia Fraser about the humiliation of a chauvinist novelist by his lesbian wife and his publicist, should be entitled *Have a Nice Death*. But Mankowitz seems, throughout his illness, to have appraised it with a pragmatic irony. The medical expertise available in New Mexico tempts him to extend his two-year stay at the university and, in the event, he had a Visiting Professor post at the University of New Mexico until 1988. His dramatization of the Menken's relationship with Swinburne, entitled *Iron Butterflies*, was performed to local appreciation at the university's Rodey Theatre in the summer of 1984. It is more an expository than a dramatic two-hander, with Swinburne's cries of anguish sounding very Billy Bunterish, and, despite interest from Bill Kenwright and Susan Hampshire, the piece did not receive a professional London performance.[14]

The interview also looks back on his career as a scriptwriter, where he considers his best work to be *The Day the Earth Caught Fire*, with its two alternative newspaper headlines at the end. He regrets the passing of the 1960s ambiance when only creativity mattered and changes could happen very swiftly. Susan Hampshire, he recalls, began as an assistant stage manager on the stage version of *Expresso Bongo*, but her posh debby voice made her ideal casting for the debutante daughter Cynthia and so began her very distinguished acting career. He reminisces about his days in the 1950s as a tyro columnist on Hugh Cudlipp's *Sunday Pictorial*, which gave him valuable material for his exposition of the process of news-making in *The Day the Earth Caught Fire*. He paid his dues at El Vino's but he recalls this younger self as no more than a fascinated onlooker at these giant elephants of the newspaper industry. He retells the tale behind his exotic post as Panamanian Consul in Dublin but notes there are very few traffic wardens around his home in South-West Cork to check his CD (*corps diplomatique*) plates.

* * *

In the course of an interview he gave to John Walsh for the *Evening Standard* (19 March 1987), Mankowitz comments on the gentrified Whitechapel cottages near his birthplace in Fashion Street and remembers how much he enjoyed the colourful life of the local markets when his grandfather had a cap shop in Slater Street. But he also remembers that hard upbringing in two rooms in a tenement block and concludes that it was no fun to be poor and much better to be rich. Walsh describes his interviewee as a 'furious-looking bear of a man' wearing an oatmeal greatcoat and sporting a beard 'that might have been hewn from granite'. He was ill, but he is presented as a man for whom medical help in New Mexico and his professional commitment to writing enable him to face out his predicament with wit and courage. He talks of having too much energy to be satisfied with achievements in just one genre and lists, once more, F.R. Leavis, Carol Reed and Orson Welles as major mentors in his intellectual development.

The occasion for the interview is the publication, on the same day (19 March 1987), of *Gioconda*, his novel which recreates the theft and restitution of the *Mona Lisa* to the Louvre in 1911–13 as the ground for his most intricate reflections to date on exchange, production, illusionism and the art market. He admits in the Walsh interview that it has been his hardest book to write because he wanted to establish several levels of reality 'where the most preposterous details might happen to be true'. This entailed him extending his habitual novella form into a full-length novel. The Parisian Bohemia of Picasso and Apollinaire, with its geniuses, mistresses and conmen, is described in detail, as are the very different worlds of Daniel Lavine, junior partner in his Uncle Julius's Lavine Galleries in Old Bond Street, London; James Peacock, RA, last of the Pre-Raphaelites, living out his alcoholic days in a vast, leaking studio in St John's Wood; and Sigmund Freud, who interrupts his summer vacation pursuit of hunting mushrooms to provide the Prefect of the Paris Police, Louis Lepine, with a psychoanalytical portrait of the man who has stolen the *Mona Lisa*. He is, Freud concludes, a latent homosexual, fixated on his mother, intellectual, artistic and of Mediterranean origin. Lepine's superiors are unimpressed by this information and he is forcibly retired from his post.

In Mankowitz's tale the thief has many aliases but does not conform to Freud's description. He presents himself to Lavine as Gery Pieret, an intimate of the Picasso/Apollinaire circle and an anarchist dedicated to the overthrow of bourgeois society. Any monies he can extract from Lavine in exchange for the portrait will be 'converted into good pamphlets, bombs of words, and perhaps a few of dynamite'. Lavine argues that the *Mona Lisa* is unsaleable and therefore any price they might agree will be arbitrary. Her true value can only be realized within the Louvre: 'The only home she has to go to is the one from which you have so cleverly removed her.' As the novel proceeds and the *Mona Lisa*, through copies which are themselves works of art, multiplies herself threefold, Pieret, who now calls himself Vincenzo Peruggia, finds his Mona Lisa is sapping his energy and making him dull and stupid. His 'mercurial gleam' is gradually fading: 'The longer he held her captive, the more captive he became to her. Her magic overwhelmed his; instead of having her in a box, he was her prisoner.'

Pieret's Mona Lisa has something of Dr Amorian's vampiric power in the *Devil in Texas* but, unlike the shape-shifting academic, she remains always the same. Two other women, Cleo de Marande, beautiful model, whore and art gallery owner, and Marie Laurencin, obsessed mistress of Apollinaire, have minor but important roles in the tangled relations between Lavine, Pieret and the international art market. They try, through haughty beauty or domestic retreat, to insulate themselves from the ravenous commodification of the market, but they cannot escape. They are valued for their sex, and it is their sex for which they have to obtain the best exchange rate. Marie, calm and self-possessed in her mother's home in Auteuil, reminds herself fiercely that 'she was her own woman, it was her own cunt, and she would paint whatever she wanted in any fucking way she liked', but she comes running when Apollinaire calls. The narrator points out that *mona* is Venetian slang for 'vagina'. The implication is that only the work of high art, distinguished by what Walter Benjamin called its 'aura',[15] can transcend market evaluation. Only the *mona* of the *Mona Lisa* is not for sale.

Mankowitz's tale, however, gives us three Mona Lisas. At one stage, Lavine, who profits so much from his dealing in rare pictures and tapestries that he dies as the most renowned dealer on both sides of the Atlantic, possesses all three. He has marked the original and its copies with distinctive chalk-marks on the back. The chalk has rubbed off and even his expert eye cannot distinguish between them. He therefore picks out one at random which, by way of the curators at the Uffizi Gallery, is returned to the Louvre; he sells one to a rich Texan collector and hangs the third over the bed in the room adjoining his Bond Street office. Here he hopes once more to entertain Cleo 'with Mona Lisa smiling down upon the erotic elegance of his bed as she had upon that of another lover of the lovely ladies of Paris, that awful cad and art thief, Napoleon Bonaparte'.[16]

Mankowitz seems here, with his concern for copies and mirrors, to edge into the critical world of the French theorist of postmodernism, Jean Baudrillard. 'Simulation' is the key term in his critical vocabulary. It designates a contemporary development of the image which is central to Baudrillard's vision of our post-Marx world. Seduction, in his analysis, has now replaced production as the goal of consumer society. A world where an object and its reproduction routinely dissolve into each other would seem an appropriate description of Lavine's three Mona Lisas. Baudrillard was a great admirer of Andy Warhol, whose serial reproductions of a Campbell's soup can or a Marilyn Monroe photo could be read as the logical development of Mankowitz's three Monas.

Life, as so often, has recently imitated art. A composite photograph of three Mona Lisas accompanies a feature by Mark Brown, the *Guardian*'s art correspondent, on the restoration of a copy of the painting made at exactly the same time as Leonardo was painting the original. The original, the copy prior to restoration, and the cleaned-up work are the three Mona Lisas that accompany the article of 2 February 2012. But now it appears that distinctions between the original and its copies have been further blurred. Brown quotes the art critic Martin Bailey who declares that, with this cleaned-up copy, 'we are seeing the Mona Lisa herself for the first time, as she really looked because the painting in the Louvre is covered with layers of dirt and varnish'. This Mona Lisa is younger and more attractive than the painting in the Louvre.

The experts' emphasis on technique and process is more akin to Mankowitz's procedures in *Gioconda* than Warhol's multiple reproductions. As with *Cockatrice*, it is the ways in which the art object comes into being that interest him more than the finished product. Chapter 7, 'Old Masters', is a masterclass by the ancient Pre-Raphaelite, James Peacock, on the sfumato technique for catching light and shade on wood, and the exact temperatures needed for the mixture of pigments to reproduce the dryness of a painting of around 1500. The passage is highly technical and draws upon Mankowitz's own detailed knowledge of such procedures from his art-dealing experience. It is not photography, it is manual craft, as is another, later passage where Pieret, during a one-year sentence for hotel burglary, learns techniques for pickpocketing which enrich him at the Armory Show. He is amazed to hear from the conversation of such as John Quinn and Alfred Steiglitz that works by his old Bohemian mates Picasso and Duchamp are worth hundreds of dollars. He determines to hunt down Lavine and extract more money from him for the *Mona Lisa* sale. Pieret the thief counterpoints the creative artists, but he also complements, at a lower level, the great dealers such as Henry Frick, Joseph Duveen and their heir apparent, Daniel Lavine.

Gioconda is overloaded with themes and narratives, as Mankowitz admits in the Walsh interview. The central relationship between Lavine and Pieret can get obscured by the proliferation of adjunct scenes such as the description of Freud on holiday, the case notes of the psychiatrist who interviews Pieret (now known as Vincenzo Peruggia), or the cast of famous real live artists and dealers at the Armory Show. Fictionalizing the famous is always problematic. It is only acceptable if presented with the irony and lightness of touch that Woody Allen, for example, brings to his portrayals of Fitzgerald, Stein, Bunuel and Hemingway in *Midnight in Paris* (2011).

Mankowitz is more convincing when he allows us to see the Show through the eyes of Pieret or, in a strong authorial voice, renders – with an attention to detail worthy of Theodore Dreiser – the rhythm, atmosphere and routines of a grand hotel such as the Waldorf Astoria:

> Pieret had discovered long ago that the more expensive the hotel, the less suspicion was entertained of those who strolled its foyers looking expensive; systematic casual strolling with curt nods to commissionaires, desk-clerks, head-porters, major-domos, maîtres d'hôtel, and other lackeys, was all that was necessary to make one an acceptable character in the daily and nightly theatre of grand hotel life.[17]

Critics recognized *Gioconda* to be a most accomplished work. Two long reviews, by, respectively, John Melmoth for the *TLS* (27 March 1987) and Linda Taylor for the *Listener* (26 March 1987), give full details of what Taylor calls a 'wondrous factual/fictional/historical/romantical tapestry', a picaresque novel whose mode of address is, as Melmoth puts it, 'robust, loud-mouthed, pugnacious and unequivocal'. He is also impressed by Mankowitz's scholarship and calls his selection of extracts from *Paris-Journal* and *Le Matin* 'scrupulous and engaging'. Melmoth is less certain about the novel's emphasis on the mystery of women, the wearisome 'principle of the eternal female', as he calls it, and considers dubious the etymology of *mona* meaning 'cunt' rather than 'madonna'. Linda Taylor, however, has no doubt about its vulgar meaning and even suggests that, viewed sideways, the *Mona Lisa*'s famous smile does indeed resemble a vulva. For both critics the novel is a successful combination of a popular fictional form and arcane research – what Melmoth calls 'an erudite smock-ripper'.

The schmucks connoted by the title of Mankowitz's next novel, *The Magic Cabinet of Professor Smucker*, published on 17 March 1988, are the egotistic victims of the professor's skills as a magician and illusionist. After a lifetime of tricks, learnt from his Uncle Teddy and then his great mentor, Howard Thurston, he finds himself, at the age of 75, beached in West Hollywood, his hands arthritic and his only clients a bunch of self-obsessed babblers. Smucker now advertises himself as the founder of the Lost-Life Foundation which is about to launch a series of cassette tapes entitled *Lost Life Journeys*.

His slogan is 'Find Your Lost Life and Live Again', but, towards the end of the novel, he has become the victim of his own publicity. At the launch party for the tape series, held at the Final Gig club, the owner, Mephisto

Green, gradually turns into his Uncle Teddy, and he suffers a series of fainting fits and later hallucinates that his own lost lives are returning. He is, in particular, bedevilled by one Alice V. Syms, whose seances he exposed as frauds many years before, but who now returns to haunt him, speaking through the medium of a barely literate child, Maria-Inconcepta, whose mother is employed by one Principessa Janni San Marco. Smucker is terrified by the child, not because of eerily delivered threats of death and revenge, but because he might now have 'the great misfortune to encounter an actual authentic case of mediumistic possession'.[18]

His entire career, from circus acts as a boy, through mesmerizing vast crowds in Latin America, to performing before the Queen, has been based on the conviction that his skill lies in creating illusions and that people will believe anything. 'There is no magic', he remarks in one of his many monologues to his pet toad, 'only tricks.'[19] He has only contempt for his few remaining clients: Mrs Redman, who burbles on about her lost life as an omnivorous spider woman; Shmerz, his diminutive Jewish accountant, to whom he offers access to a past life as a nomad Cossack-like king; and the Principessa, who turns out to be one of his former assistants and wants to relive days of delirious sex in his dressing room. Dreams, for Smucker, have never been anything more than the irrational flotsam of the mind and irrelevant to what he considers the serious business of life, 'the contriving of well-controlled illusions for a paying public'.[20]

His cynicism is challenged by Maria-Inconcepta's ventriloquism of Alice V. Syms, so it is with a mixture of fear and relief that he finds himself, in the latter part of the novel, suffering his own hallucinations. The voices, the out-of-body experiences, the neighbour's boy Oscar speaking with the pedantic precision of his father – they are all the products of a disordered brain. Oscar leads him to his favourite play-area, a zone of tar pits on the edge of the city where a city benefactor has created a series of prehistoric animals in stone. It is here that Smucker, mad and exhilarated, imagines he can conduct his last great magic performance, to turn his pet toad into a 10,000-pound elephant. Smucker is wise to all the tricks of his trade but neither he nor Howard Thurston ever divined how Houdini made a 10,000-pound elephant disappear before a packed audience at the London Hippodrome in 1918. Here is Smucker's moment to equal the master. He focuses all his forces and feels himself at the epicentre of great energy; the stone mastodons come alive; slowly an elephant rises from the black pit and Smucker dies a happy magician.

Smucker is a kind of 'sport' and it is clear that Mankowitz enjoyed writing it. Smucker is the knowing professional who explains the procedures behind such tricks as the megaphonic trumpet, the hat-and-coin trick and the woman sawn in half. Mankowitz's concentration on process over product finds an apt analogy in this exposé of the magician's illusory effects. He makes Smucker an old man because, I suggest, he wants to examine the condition and mentality of someone facing death. He certainly recounts, in the Davis interview, an out-of-body experience at London Airport very similar to the one undergone by Smucker at the tar pit. His monologues to his toad are the least successful inventions of the novel. The toad's silence affords Smucker too much licence for orotund and obvious critiques of the inanities of West Coast culture. But Mankowitz's evocation of the bizarre world outside his crumbling flat – an area, as Willis Hall says, 'more ghastly than glitzy and not so much tinsel-town as downright tawdry'[21] – is cheerfully satirical. Robert Nye, for the *Guardian* (13 April 1988), wonders if there a split between the style of the narrator and the character of Smucker but decides that 'the final chapters convinced me that [Mankowitz] is well aware of what he is doing'. It is a very knowing fiction.

Leo Lhooq, main protagonist and one of two chief narrators in Mankowitz's next novel, *Exquisite Cadaver*, published on 19 July 1990, spends all his time out of his body. His speaking consciousness, looking down from the ceiling of a ramshackle ranch on the outskirts of Capital City in New Mexico, gradually comes to understand that the corpse on the bed beneath him is his own cadaver. His cadaver reminds him of the game, 'Le Cadavre Exquis', that he and his Dadaist and Surrealist comrades, Breton, Tzara, Picabia and Duchamp, used to play in a café in Paris in the 1920s. Each draws, unknown to the others, a portion of a body. The drawings, when put together, represent 'an exquisite creation of the subconscious of all'.[22] Soliciting chance and the unconscious to rule their lives seems to this group, the next wave of modernist artists, an affirmation of creative life after the maniacal, deadly order of the First World War. Lhooq adopts his name from the retitling Duchamp gives to his moustachioed Mona Lisa – LHOOQ, which stands for 'Elle a chaud au cul' or 'She has a hot arse.'

Women circulate among the artists. Lhooq's obsession is one Carlotta, another shape-changer, sometimes a common whore, sometimes a fine lady. The centre of the novel is a magnificent sequence where Picabia, wealthy in his own right, takes Lhooq on a trip to the South of France where they stay at his villa and have endless English teas on his manicured lawn. Carlotta, whom Lhooq obsessively draws as a cat-woman, appears to be Picabia's mistress in residence and presents herself to the artists as 'a new delicate creation in white, [who] behaves with elegant maturity'. Lhooq is jealous but Picabia is calm and says that Carlotta is either a friend or merely a woman. In any case she is a very bad fuck. Lhooq dismisses Picabia as a mere playboy, not a true Bohemian like himself, but his passion for Carlotta cools as he grows more into the role of Senor Risotto, his persona for the visit.

Lhooq and Picabia work together on their projects. Lhooq tries to draw Carlotta with one scorpion-leg, and Picabia is designing a kind of perpetual-motion clock. The teas and lunches, long and heavy, keep appearing: 'Fruit and plum cakes will soon be upon us. Seed-cake will be served in due course. Cucumber sandwiches, thin as spliced parchment, will fly about us, while silver urns steam below decorated teapots awaiting freshly infused Darjeeling, China or best Cylon.' The servants are impeccable, the women guests and their escorts – 'bankers, immaculate thieves of the Bourse' – elegant and sophisticated, and Carlotta a pale princess, until they smell the noxious smoke from the studio where Picabia is burning huge canvases. The servants, hired from the local lunatic asylum and encouraged by Carlotta, now transformed into a mad maenad, start hurling cakes and sandwiches at each other and at the guests. It is mayhem, the Marx Brothers in Marienbad, and, for Lhooq, Carlotta remains no more than 'the impression, barely perceptible, of her absent frozen body upon the sheets beside me'.[23]

There will be other women, notably Devorah Mannlein, daughter of Jewish Trotskyists, whose dark eyes, blood-red lips, bottomless purse and total fidelity threaten indeed to reduce the Bohemian hero to a domestic manikin. She is a pure product of Greenwich Village and, as her devotion grows, so – to Lhooq's eyes – does her body. She towers over him, with breasts like perfectly formed dead volcanoes and buttocks like smooth desert hills. He beats her, robs her, insults her, but nothing, he finds, can loosen the grip of the love of a good woman. Lhooq is at this time working closely with Duchamp, who is reassembling his shattered version of *The Bride Stripped Bare by Her Bachelors, Even* or *The Large Glass*. He translates the Devorah affair into his modern language of electricity and conductors. He reminds Lhooq of 'the mysterious female power, both passive and permitting, active and desiring' which leads on the bachelors of his famous artwork, servants of her desire 'which transmits an order releasing illuminating gas which flows intro the malic moulds in the Bachelor Machine'.[24] Lhooq now understands the vampiric nature of the never fully ravished bride, and the freedom which a promiscuous

Carlotta offered him. He was, he tells Duchamp, satisfied by neither, but Duchamp has tired of the discussion and wants to return to their chess game.

The novel's alternate, impersonal narrator records the impact of Lhooq's cadaver on the cultural politics of Capital City. An ambitious cub reporter on the *Express*, Jack Justin, scents a story in the solitary death of this foreigner, surrounded by vaguely artistic junk. If no one claims Lhooq's property it reverts to the State, which can put it up for auction. But, as Justin discovers, Lhooq has a certain fame in art-historical circles, as a minor member of the post-war Parisian avant-garde. Influential members of Capital City's cultural elite, who see themselves as promoting the work of the western realist Frederick Remington and lesser-known figures, might be equally interested in claiming the Surrealist Lhooq as one of the city's sons.

Mankowitz studs his text with plausible press reports by Justin which chart the growing campaign to honour Lhooq. The director of a local art gallery, the local Expert, draws in one Dr Masson, a young, ambitious academic from the East, to authenticate Lhooq's estate; art dealers in New York begin to show an interest; a local millionaire, Allan Glendale, is persuaded to exchange his rare Remington for Lhooq's surrealist art. The State Governor, who cares nothing for art but who is running for re-election, has to activate his Arts Committee. Mankowitz reproduces, as Chapter 9 of Part 3, the minutes of that meeting, which record the waspish alliances and genteel manoeuvres which lead to the committee recommending Glendale's exchange.

There is an engaging satirical edge to Mankowitz's depiction of the process by which art is authenticated and given value. The key figure is Masson, who discovers among Lhooq's artistic remains a rat-chewed manuscript which records all his transactions as the forger and vendor of many of the best-known and richly prized works by such as Kandinsky, Klee, Duchamp and Breton. Many of these works have been listed and catalogued by Masson himself. If he reveals their inauthenticity, their value, in whatever market, plummets and Masson's career is at an end. He struggles briefly with his conscience and then burns the manuscript. Lhooq's fame therefore will be authentic to the extent that subsequent exhibitions and auctions of his work include only a few fakes, catalogued as genuine Picabias, and to the extent that market price is, in the case of the art object, an index of true value. Mankowitz, however, presents the art market as a closed system where any value might be assigned to any product provided that the constituent parts of the system – the scholars, the dealers, the media and the millionaires – so interlock as to repel external criteria. But what criteria could be applied to such anti-art movements as Dada and Surrealism is the question posed by the very structure of *Exquisite Cadaver*, with its alternating chapters of clear-eyed reportage and fantasy reconstructions.

Roger Lewis, in a laudatory review for the *Financial Times* (4 August 1990), recognizes the quality and importance of Mankowitz's concerns. He notes that his main subject here is 'the equivocation of moral and artistic rates of exchange' and calls the novel 'a box of marvels'. He gives a full and accurate account of the complementary information given to the reader by the novel's twin voices and underlines how its varied sources of information create 'a carefully devised collage of styles and documents'. Lewis himself, as we have seen, was an invaluable source for the documentation of the disastrous production company formed by Mankowitz and Sellers. He must have retained a high regard for the former because he twins him with Anthony Burgess as two writers who are 'uncompromisingly eclectic and colourful' with a love of 'the odd and the anarchic ... outlandish words and erudite or crackpot digressions'. Lewis is himself a highly idiosyncratic and entertaining writer, so he must have warmed to a novel peopled by surrealists and Dadaists.

John Clute is less enthusiastic about the novel in his *TLS* review for the week of 17–23 August 1990. He recounts its intertwining plots, and comments that when Lhooq gazes on the blank desert outside his ranch he sees a Breton-like '*tabula rasa* for the workings of the unconscious'. Nothing is new in this version of America: 'It is all bought or borrowed (or stolen) from the old unending *amour fou* of elsewhere.' But for Clute the novel is also derivative. It is an example of fantastic fiction, already practised by Flann O'Brien and John Crowley, although Mankowitz gives his own twist to the genre by setting this tale of a spirit coming to terms with its past life on the surreal stage of the American West. Christopher Walker for the *Observer* (22 July 1990) is more enthusiastic about 'Mankowitz's fascinating piece of fictional archaeology' which exposes the double standards of an avant-gardism which never forgets its bourgeois support-structure: 'The truth revealed by Mankowitz's perceptive and entertaining novel is that anti-art is highly marketable.'

Sarah Caudwell brings an art-history perspective to bear on her review for *Modern Painters*.[25] She points out that when Lhooq is buried, to the great acclaim of local worthies, the corpse is that of an unknown vagabond, since Lhooq's cadaver has already been incinerated. This, however, is irrelevant. LHOOQ was a name invented by Duchamp to be used as a generic signature for any art product. Lhooq never existed. He is a composite, like the group compositions of exquisite cadavers. Lhooq, therefore, is, 'the only artist to have achieved the Dadaist ideal of being no-one and painting nothing'.

Caudwell is less sure about what she perceives as the central contention of the novel, that the market place will always corrupt the integrity of the work of art, but Mankowitz's own artistry, of language and structure, forces the reader to take seriously such a thesis. *Exquisite Cadaver* is at the opposite pole to a Dadaist creation. If Mankowitz's intention was to write a Dadaist novel, then, concludes Caudwell, 'I can only apologise for any pain that these remarks may cause him and congratulate him on his failure.' A review by Mankowitz himself of a recently published history of Dada precedes Caudwell's review and finishes by claiming that Dada is still a vital force 'for all who are tired of the expected and weary with the established'. It is, for him, a modern movement which is 'undateable and ongoing'.

Exquisite Cadaver is the most finely achieved fiction of Mankowitz's last period. Here he comes to terms with modernism, on his own terms. Its reflexive plot, mix of registers and subtle parodies acknowledge the respect for Joyce that he insists on in the Davis interview. But its central problematic – the economic and cultural balance between production, exchange and value – had been his central preoccupation from the start of his career as a professional writer in post-war Britain. He was also, as we shall see in more detail later, beginning to test his own abilities as an heir to Surrealism and Dada, with the first exhibition of his own collages held at The Davis Gallery in Dublin in May 1990. Patrick Skene Catling, in a lengthy interview-cum-résumé of his career (*Sunday Times*, 11 August 1991), quotes him, now diagnosed with terminal cancer, as saying: 'Making collages is so much easier than writing. The only physical suffering is the battle with glue. With writing the idea comes first, followed by long, hard work. I can give a collage its meaning after it's done, with an insane caption.'

But Mankowitz was not quite done with books. The Catling interview marks the publication, on 12 August 1991, of Mankowitz's last novella, *A Night with Casanova*. The reader is invited in to share the great lover's memory of a night of discussions and visions with a shape-shifting stranger in a run-down inn near the chateau of Dux in Bohemia. It is 1797 and Casanova has been employed as librarian at the castle, chief residence of the Count von Waldstein, for the last ten years. He is 72 years old, decrepit and broke, and this employment is his last refuge from the armies of creditors, State officials and police in pursuit of the legendary trickster. The moment for him and his like, elegant rogues who delighted the dull courts of petty princes, has passed.

They had formed, as Stefan Zweig observes in his brief, brilliant biography of Casanova, 'in conjunction with the Jesuits and the Jews, the only International that as yet exist[ed] in the eighteenth century'. But Count Waldstein 'took pity on him, charmed by the derelict's cynical volubility' and bought him 'as he would have bought any other curio'.[26] The Casanova of Mankowitz's novella has had enough of the Count's, and his servants', contempt for him. He waits for the six o'clock coach to whirl him away to his rightful world of glittering balls and beautiful women.

He never leaves. Another guest, rather like the Ancient Mariner, holds him spellbound. His shoes need repairing and the innkeeper, Stichka, recommends the services of another traveller, a Jewish cobbler. His workmanship is outstanding and, since this master craftsman will take no payment, Casanova joins him in the kitchen. This tall, bearded man in a reddish caftan and a short, woollen cloak, who has a command of at least three languages, is clearly a man of erudition and, in Casanova's estimate, a fit audience for his tirades against the count and the story of his escape from the infamous Leads prison in Venice. Casanova insists to the tall stranger that he is a rationalist and a deist, but also admits to knowledge of the Jewish Kabbalah. The cobbler now reveals himself as an expert in this field, and the two men exchange references and citations from key texts. Casanova has no belief in magic, nor in an afterlife, but he has a professional interest in trickery and is nostalgic for the audacious adventures of his youth.

The Jew's incantations transport him back to Venice in a period of two particular triumphs. He relives his seduction of a beautiful young nun and savours once more a particular night when he had an audacious win at the gaming tables. But the bloom has gone from this replay of former successes. He now realizes, or remembers, that his innocent novitiate was the promiscuous daughter of a ducal family, whose sexual fetish was to be despoiled in a nun's habit. His gambling triumph is now devalued by memories of the foul breath of the players, the pox-ridden cheeks of the women, and his imprisonment once more in the Leads for theft and magical practices. When he returns to the present he curses the Jew for his magic, but the Jew observes that a return to the past is always inflected by the experience of the present and that Casanova's claim on immortality will be his memoirs, which will write his life as he wishes it to be remembered. Casanova is enraged: 'A multiple pox upon my future readers ... A curse upon all living follies! Must I return to a life of pissed-upon polenta? Never! I will not do it! I will die first!' The Jew is immediately interested: 'What method of despatch would you favour?', he enquires.[27]

This Jew has a very personal involvement with death. He is Ahaseurus, the Wandering Jew of Christian mediaeval legend, the man who called on Christ to hurry to his death at Golgotha and was cursed to walk the earth until Christ's Second Coming. This Jew seems dead after drinking Casanova's poison, but revives as a virile 30-year-old. Casanova is profoundly impressed by what he regards as a masterly deception, but parades his scholarly credentials by recounting the story of Ahasuerus. This Wandering Jew rejoins that the tale is a case of mistaken identity. He is a Greek, whose real name is Cartophilus, and he was one of a band of Jesus devotees. He only encouraged Christ to hurry to Golgatha in order to shorten the period of his suffering. But Christ, beaten and disorientated, confused the cobbler's kindly advice with the vicious sneers of his neighbour, an Edomite rug-seller, and the legend was born.

Casanova is delighted by this tale, which he assumes is part of the repertoire of a professional confidence man, but he is unimpressed by the melancholy tone and mien of the narrator. Casanova, in all accounts of him, is always represented as an ebullient and optimistic adventurer, a man devoid of spirituality who 'made a great many women happy, but ... made no woman hysterical'.[28] He offers to take the Wandering Jew under his wing and help him escape the tedious prison of his legend, just as he escaped from his Venetian prison. The Jew is grateful, then asks him the key question in any Mankowitz fiction: 'What can I offer you in exchange for your admirable advice?' Casanova is ready. He has remembered from his library researches that the Wandering Jew can transfer to a human being some portion of his own stock of years. Casanova knows that he cannot be young again, but he does want to live longer. 'I will trade you a new persona for a handful of years. Speak! How does such an exchange attract you?'[29]

The Jew is reluctant to disturb the pattern of his destiny but Casanova insists. He wishes to learn from one whom he considers a master magician, a most distinguished member of the Mercurial academy, so Casanova is transformed into an eternal traveller. He is always moving on, since he cannot stay more than twenty-four hours in any one place. He finds himself drawn to church services, where he makes oracular statements about Christ's mercy, or to endless theological discussions with Jews about the imminent arrival of a Messiah. Casanova recounts these adventures with the utmost contempt for the beliefs and observances of both Jew and Gentile. He continues his cobbler's work and his testimonies to Christ's coming salvation but finds it tedious work without intellectual satisfaction. He decides, after coming upon yet another Jewish village destroyed by the pious, that the Jews' unspeakable agony is the only immortality available in human history, and that he, the Wandering Gentile, can now testify that there is no benefit of any kind in such immortality.

The panorama of such human unintelligence forces him to demonstrate his own intelligence. He devises a credo which is faithful to his principles of enlightened materialist reason: 'Man, feeling good, projects his emotions beyond himself and calls them God, but when feeling bad, denominates his long shadow a Satanic Force. It is matter exteriorized, and that is all.'[30] He concludes that the world is God's but that man belongs to the Devil. There are, he muses, practical possibilities in this new cosmogony. He could found and lead a sect. His followers would heap bounty before him. He cries out to return to being Casanova, to live and die the meaningless life of a man. 'Life is meaningless', he cries, 'but more than enough.'[31]

This is the cry of Rantz in *Laugh Till You Cry*, published some forty years before. It is also a reaffirmation, by Mankowitz, of the enduring influence on his generation of existentialist absurdism. The rest of the novella reviews key moments in Casanova's life as a man in his epoch: his accurate estimation of himself as an old gallant, his rancours and hatreds, and his record of his times, his memoirs. Writing, not religion or magic, will enact his triumph over death. He pays tribute, after a long catalogue of his conquests, to the one woman for whom he truly cared: 'the sweet and complete Henriette, the darling French spy'. Stichka tells him the carriage can wait no longer, but Casanova replies that it cannot take him anywhere he has not already visited. He has to return to the detested *Schloss*. He has to finish his memoirs.

Writing, then, becomes, in the end, Casanova's life, as it had been Mankowitz's from the beginning. Casanova, unlike Mankowitz, is no professional. He is, as Zweig notes, 'a chance intruder in world literature' but his genius consists 'not in the way he tells the story of his life, but the way in which he has lived it'.[32] The attraction of his memoirs for Mankowitz, however, probably lies in what Tom Emery of Dickinson College detects in his entry for Casanova in the *Encyclopedia of Erotic Literature*: that in his autobiography, 'happiness and well-being are guaranteed by the constant circulation of desire'. If the multiple exchanges – between men and women, between men and men, between women and women – are blocked, then 'frustration, despair and thoughts of death' ensue. It is, finally, this 'joyous *exchange* of pleasure, both within the text, and between text and reader, that distinguishes Casanova's *History of My Life* from the work of libertine thinkers such as Sade and that constitutes the source of its enduring popularity'.[33]

Critics recognized the valedictory status of the novella and several combined a critical review with an overview of Mankowitz's writing career. David Nathan, for the *Jewish Chronicle* (16 August 1991), begins by quoting Mankowitz on the close links between Casanova's reflections on his old age and Mankowitz's steady acceptance of his own imminent death. His cancer, he informs Nathan, is malignant, incurable, terminal and slow; but he accepts it as an organic part of his life and makes the best of it. The rest of the piece covers his university years, success in the 1950s, support for Israel in the 1960s, scriptwriting successes and a summary of the main events of the novella. His cancer has increased his disrespect for religion – 'It would be an insult to whatever deity one believes in to be influenced by the prospect of dying' – but it is also what Nathan earlier calls Mankowitz's irreverent wit that is 'pure East-End auction room' which prevents him from taking seriously the religious solemnities. Nathan's shrewd summary of his writing quality is that its Beckettian precision is streaked through with a commercialism from which Sam would have recoiled in horror.

T.P. O'Mahony's interview for the *Cork Examiner* (7 August 1991) focuses more on Mankowitz's love for the views and the peace of Ahakista, which the interviewer interprets as a quasi-religious awe in the face of natural beauty. The discussion then moves onto the future of fiction, indeed literacy itself, about which Mankowitz makes gloomy prognostications; the genius of Joyce and Beckett; the religious tolerance of Eire as compared with the sectarianism of the North; and an astute analysis of Somerset Maugham's talent: '[He] is a bad writer but a good storyteller.' Mary Leland's interview for the *Irish Times* (20 August 1991) reprises the usual curriculum vitae but it also elicits from Mankowitz a harsh critique of Dickens: 'He didn't know things about himself: there was a kind of creeping hypocrisy and he worshipped the adulation of the crowd.' With *Casanova* now published, its author is more interested in the collages which he builds up, fragment by fragment, on his studio easel. He tells Leland that after a lifetime composing rational storylines he enjoys the odd narratives that emerge by chance.

Shaun Whiteside, for the *TLS* (16 August 1991), concentrates on the content and structure of what he calls Mankowitz's odd little novel. A brisk summary of the main topics of conversation between Casanova and the Wandering Jew categorizes their exchanges as 'increasingly wild conjectures' about immortality and women. But when Casanova actually experiences the immortality he desires, 'the book's central conceit makes a kind of sense'. Whiteside finds this a bitter book, a book which smells of latrines and rot: 'Casanova's voice throughout is a single long, belching, irritable sneer.' Michael Wright, for *The Times* (1 August 1991), although he shares something of Whiteside's disgust at 'the farty bile directed at a variety of targets', praises the book as a micro tour de force and admires the 'tricksy provocativeness with which [Mankowitz] flirts with the age-old problem of the relation between fiction and reality'. Is the whole episode a trick or a dream? The novella, for Wright, is 'kid gloves deconstruction'.

Patrick Skene Catling, for the *Sunday Times* (11 August 1991), gives us familiar details of Mankowitz's life and professional career but, as a colleague of long standing, he is able to compare appearances between the urbane man of scathing wit whom he knew in the late 1960s and the present man, somewhat diminished by illness, but now an august, bearded, patriarchal figure. Mankowitz's style in this novella is 'as vigorously bawdy as ever' but, by the end, it is clear that 'Thanatos has become more alluring than Eros.' Catling gives a more detailed account of the novella's plot in his *Evening Standard* (8 August 1991) review, where he remarks that the writing of what is a short disquisition on death is 'so vigorous that it seems to be about life'. He provides generous textual quotes in what is a short review, cites several of the paradoxes that Casanova and the Wandering Jew debate, and concludes that, after their esoteric discussions, Casanova 'is enabled to experience the tedium of wandering forever. I wish only that the account of it were longer.'

Peter Guttridge provides the fullest and most succinct account of Mankowitz's career to date in a summary article for the *Independent* (3 August 1991) entitled 'Face to Face with a Wolf'. He tells a good story about Mankowitz being mistaken for Joseph Mankiewicz – 'but nobody ever mistakes me for you, Wolf', says Mankiewicz – and gives a vivid sense of the enormous range of his cultural activities from young manhood onwards. He quotes Mankowitz's view that his most serious work dates from *Abracadabra!* and pinpoints his interest in the trickster and the conman as central to his fictions. Mankowitz's interest in Casanova derives, he says, from their opposing views on death. He thought of the ageing process as a total insult: 'I'm the complete opposite – I am very well aware of the ageing process.' He says that he completed *Casanova* two years ago, but now doubts whether he has to energy to write any more. As with other interviews, he mentions the pleasure he takes in his collages and in the surreal titles – *Snakes etc. and Two Balls* – that he awards them.

NOTES

1. Wolf Mankowitz, *Mazeppa: The Lives, Loves and Legends of Adah Isaacs Menken: A Biographical Quest* (London: Blond & Briggs, 1982), p.11.
2. Ibid., p.154.
3. Ibid., p.227.
4. Amanda Vickery, 'Beauties in Breeches', *Guardian*, 15 October 2011.
5. Mankowitz, *Mazeppa*, p.189.
6. Julian Petley, 'Almonds and Raisins', *Monthly Film Bulletin*, 51 (April 1984), pp.111–12.
7. Russ Karel, 'Almonds and Raisins', *Time Out*, 706 (1 March 1984), p.45.
8. Malcolm Bradbury, *Stepping Westward* (Harmondsworth: Penguin, 1968), p.9. (First published by Secker & Warburg, 1965.)
9. Howard Jacobson, *Coming From Behind* (London: Vintage Books, 2003), pp.167, 19, 183. (First published 1983.)
10. W. Mankowitz, *The Devil in Texas* (London: Robert Royce, 1984), p.60.
11. Ibid., p.92.
12. Ibid., pp.63ff, 106, 146.
13. Norman Mailer, *An American Dream* (London: Paladin, 1992), p.217. (First published by André Deutsch, 1965.)
14. The two-act version of *Iron Butterflies* is available in *ADAM International Review*, 449/451 (1984), pp.84–112.
15. See W. Benjamin, 'The Work of Art in the Age of Mechanical Reproduction', in W. Benjamin, *Illuminations* (London: Fontana, 1973), pp.219–53.
16. W. Mankowitz, *Gioconda* (London: W.H. Allen, 1987), pp.47, 238, 77, 272.
17. Ibid., p.183.
18. W. Mankowitz, *The Magic Cabinet of Professor Smucker* (London: W.H. Allen, 1988), p.107.
19. Ibid., p.129.
20. Ibid., p.108.
21. Willis Hall, *Yorkshire Post*, 21 April 1988.
22. W. Mankowitz, *Exquisite Cadaver* (London: André Deutsch, 1990), p.6.
23. Ibid., pp.120, 134, 136, 138.
24. Ibid., p.171.
25. *Modern Painters*, 3, 4 (1990), pp.107–10.
26. Stefan Zweig, *Casanova: A Study in Self-Portraiture*, translated by Eden Paul and Cedar Paul (London: Pushkin Press, 1998), pp.36, 110.
27. W. Mankowitz, *A Night with Casanova* (London: Sinclair-Stevenson, 1991), p.61.
28. Zweig, *Casanova*, p.88.
29. Mankowitz, *Night with Casanova*, p.105.
30. Ibid., p.122.
31. Ibid., p.123.
32. Ibid., pp.13, 16.
33. Gaetan Brulotte and John Phillips (eds), *Encyclopedia of Erotic Literature* (London: Routledge, 2006), pp.206–10.

Conclusion (1990–98)

Mankowitz had already had a public exhibition of his collages, at The Davis Gallery in Dublin in May 1990, by the time *A Night with Casanova* was published. It was entitled *Events in the Fiendish Park* and the ten collages which make up the signed edition are representative of his themes and procedures. Selected titles include: *The Bishop and his Bodyguard Visit the Hospice in the Fiendish Park*, *Writer's Dream Induced by Rare Plant Found in Fiendish Park* and *Cockroaches Attacking Beautiful Women in Fiendish Park*. The Bishop, bottom right and with back to the viewer, is balanced by two well-dressed thugs with tommy guns and between them is a juxtaposed selection of cuttings of church balconies, tombstones and a cornice top left. This writer's dream is a plume of blank sheets of paper, from the writer's cross-sectioned brain, which winds across and round a background of already printed sheets, in different fonts, from *Gioconda*. The beautiful women are not much more than an eye and lashes in the centre and a stone nose on the right of a collage which is almost entirely composed of shiny red-and-black-backed cockroaches.

Conventional representations of religion, art and beautiful women were all challenged by the Surrealists through techniques of juxtaposition, mixed media and, in the case of women, dismemberment and displacement. Mankowitz catches the wit as well the desperation of these male attempts to corral the beautiful female body in two other collages in the *Fiendish Park* series, *Clues in the Case of the Theft of the Duchess of Devonshire* and *Socrates*. Onto the slim body of a blonde bathing-beauty he superimposes, round her face, an aureole composed of exotic leaves and a portion of wire-fencing; and onto her stomach and upper thigh a cut-out of the eighteenth-century portrait by Gainsborough. The 'clues' down the right-hand side include a photo of a police-type photo with the eyes blanked out, a postcard from Austria to Mankowitz in Ireland and a pay-in slip to one E. Breckenridge of Paradise Island for £340,000.

Socrates is a modest bust of the aged philosopher that is held delicately between the thighs of another blonde bathing-beauty as she sits on her haunches on the beach. Where her bust and stomach would be is an enlarged reproduction of her face and neck, and springing from her forehead is a smaller reproduction of that face and neck. Her lips are full and her hair swept back and combed through as if held in place by Brylcreem. Her face is her body, her full and slightly parted lips are all over her, she is calm and composed. The calm and composure of the philosopher, who through questions elicited truth, are dwarfed by the already existent truth of the female body. The girl is, at most, in her early twenties but the implication is that she already knows a truth, as a female body, that no exercise of dialectic could reveal.

Mankowitz, of course, knew the truth about his own failing body, and other collages and photographs, in his family's private collection, demonstrate that he continued to handle his situation with grace and humour. *The Last Days of Thermidor* has a lobster clinging to the lower lip of a red-faced, bearded, sunken-cheeked self-portrait. He may have consumed the lobster but, as the title implies, his own ambitious plans for radical change have had, as with that stage in the French Revolution, to mutate into more conservative activities. *Construction Attacked by Aubergines* is scholarly fun as the thick-fleshed plants smear a design of black, sharp-edged angles across an off-centre plate, a heterodox genesis of Constructivism from Naturalism. *Portrait of the Artist as an Old Man* is more sombre. Multiple copies of a head-and-shoulders photo of him as a gaunt, bearded patriarch are scattered across a yellow background on which are pasted random strips of a sealant called 'SecurSeal', overlaid by criss-crossing strips of film. The patriarchal beard and commanding stare reappear in *Wolf and Fork* (2), a close-up of Mankowitz in a high-collar white shirt against a background of cardboard plates, but he deliberately undermines his authority by the knife and fork he holds up in his right hand. He presents himself as a simultaneous parody of a surgeon and Neptune.

The prelude to this succession of life-affirming constructions is a much more sombre and reflective creation, dated December 1989, and entitled *Diminishing Identity*. It is a layered ensemble of different types of printed material – letters in different fonts, a reproduction of the *Mona Lisa* with a moustache, his Panamanian Consulate identity card, an image of the Portland Vase, two citations of his wife and her qualifications, several notations of 'boys' and 'father' – which narrows to a funnel-exit right of his photo, stamped with 'boys' and 'Obit', from the collage frame. There are also allusions to his theatre co-productions with Lewenstein of plays starring Olivier and Scofield and a page, painted green, which lists some of his many prose works. It is not just the round-up of a life in letters, it is an affirmation of the value, the use-value, of his life as a whole. His insistence, in the Davis interview seven years later, that the narrative of his life was one of chance encounters, haphazard events, is here enacted by the chance encounter, in one flat frame, of the *Mona Lisa*, his wife, Panama and *The Bespoke Overcoat*.

If with these collages he was renewing his allegiance to the Surrealists, he did not lose faith in the literary masters of Modernism. The date of the Breton's first Surrealist Manifesto, '1924', is prominently imprinted on the *Identity* collage, but Mankowitz, in this early 1990s period, has not forgotten 1922. This is the date of the first publication of James Joyce's *Ulysses*, and Joyce was, as Mankowitz insisted in the Davis interview, 'the greatest verbal genius of anyone in our time'. Mankowitz retells the complex story of the book's publication in Paris by Sylvia Beach and its gradual escape from the claws of the American censors in an unpublished film script in the Family Archive entitled *Dirty Book*. The script is credited to one Seth Linder, from an original screenplay by Wolf Mankowitz, but Daniel Mankwiz assures me that the script is almost entirely his father's work and that the family holds the copyright.

The script presents the publication story of *Ulysess* through a series of flashbacks from Bloomsday, 16 June 1962, on the occasion of the dedication, by Sylvia Beach, of the Martello Tower as a Research Centre for Joycean Studies, to the travails of its first edition by Beach's imprint, Shakespeare & Co., and its trials in various American courts. The most important, which is the centrepiece of the script, is the book's trial for obscenity before Justice Woolsey in 1933. It reads like a forerunner of the trials on similar charges of *Lady Chatterley's Lover* in 1959 and Hugh Selby, Jr's *Last Exit to Brooklyn* in 1967. Freedom of speech, especially sexual language, in literature was a defining issue for writers of Mankowitz's generation and it is not surprising that the trial scenes are the most successful in this film script. Council for the defence, Morris Ernst, first shocks the audience by arguing that, although 'fuck is not a word currently used in parlours ... yet it is an honourable word, an ancient word of solid Anglo-Saxon heritage relating to the process of planting. The farmer fucks seeds into the soil.'

He then changes tack and admits that he found the book very difficult to read, but that he came to understand its method during a church meeting in Nantucket. Justice Woolsey says he fails to see the connection. Ernst replies:

> Though I was absolutely intent on the lecture I was giving, I was at the same time observing the long windows, the clock, the eagle, the painted dome above, the grey old lady in the front row, a baby in the sixth, and innumerable other details. Suddenly it occurred to me that that very comprehensiveness is the essential achievement of *Ulysses*.

The book is acquitted, legitimate sales can now take place in the United States, and Mankowitz devotes much of the rest of the script to the copyright machinations, by Joyce and others, that leave Sylvia Beach hurt and disappointed by the financial ruthlessness of someone she considered a dear friend as well as a great writer. A book of genius is also a product. Beach, nonetheless, remains faithful enough to that genius to take great pride and pleasure in opening the Martello Centre for Joycean Studies.

Mankowitz was also faithful to the memory of his old friend and producer partner Oscar Lewenstein in his obituary notice for the *Guardian* (28 February 1997). He recalled their co-production years at the Royal Court in the 1950s, and added that there was another Jewish theatrical enthusiast involved, Joe Wingate, the owner of the theatre, who helped to make the Royal Court '*the* theatre of the 1960s'. He praised Lewenstein as a man who only considered the theatrical quality of the plays he produced: 'consequently he made a lot less money than he would have if his motivation had been less romantic and idealistic'. They had never, during all their collaborations (including the mounting of *Expresso Bongo*, the musical), had any falling out, 'even under the pressure of providing cigars for Orson Welles'. Lewenstein remained, for him, a strong, charming and courageous man, and 'if production costs are not too high he could still come up with something interesting'.

In the summer of the same year (1997), Mankowitz, as we have seen, gave a long and comprehensive survey of his life to Gerald Davis. He characterizes himself, at the start, as a forgotten writer, 'an elephant's graveyard of old stories', living out his last days in a remote corner of Ireland. There is some asperity, but no self-pity, in this self-portrait. He then narrates the essence of a life, in and out of writing, of great curiosity, energy and talent. But he was right about the graveyard and he died the following year, on 20 May 1998, in Durrus, County Cork, a few miles up from Ahakista. He was cremated in Dublin and there is a plaque at Golders Green Crematorium, in North London, which commemorates him, his wife Ann and their second son Jonathan who died at the early age of 43.

The obituaries were respectful but all noted the decline in his popularity from the late 1960s. John Calder, who remembered him well from the Edinburgh Writers' Conferences in the early 1960s and the battles over censorship in that period, gives the most sympathetic summary of his life and work. He describes him as a man with a voracious appetite for knowledge and an 'underlying interest in philosophy which developed particularly during his illness from cancer in his last years'. His work was distinguished by 'an ironic sense of humour, an understanding of human motivation and weakness, and a compassion for those unable to rise from the underside of society'. Calder concludes that he will probably be best remembered for the early plays and *The Irish Hebrew Lesson*.

The obituarist for *The Times* provided a more comprehensive list of Mankowitz's works than Calder, although the verdict on his contributions to many different cultural fields is that his abundant talent 'never translated into sustained artistic achievement'. Mention is made of *Raspberry Reich* as 'an excellent idea marred by being relentlessly overworked' and of *A Night with Casanova* as 'a sardonic fantasy on the theme of mortality' which had been praised as 'a bawdy miniature *tour de force* and a suitable vehicle for Mankowitz's personal philosophical summing up'. The *Daily Telegraph* also gives comprehensive coverage of his output but considers his most impressive works to be those of the 1950s, 'when he helped to lighten the gloomy post-war years'. The obituarist notes his 'infallible ear for the sound of Yiddish as uttered in English' and estimates him to be 'the best Anglo-Jewish writer since Israel Zangwill but he took his talents too lightly and spread them too thinly'.[1]

Obituaries, by their very nature, have to reach condensed conclusions about the worth and standing of their subjects. This study, which has placed Mankowitz's oeuvre within the extensive variety of cultural and political contexts that its subject matter demands, has also aimed to provide the bases for more nuanced readings of his fictions than either academic or journalistic critiques have hitherto provided. He worried away at the value of art throughout a prolific career; but there is no necessary correlation between the volume of his writings and their aesthetic value.

He was always a London writer: a Jewish writer he was always. We remain to enjoy his many fictional worlds.

NOTE

1. *Independent*, 23 May 1998; *The Times*, 22 May 1998; *Daily Telegraph*, 22 May 1998.

Bibliography

ARCHIVE SOURCES

BBC Written Archives Centre, Caversham Park, Reading.

BFI [British Film Institute] Scripts, BFI National Archive, Berkhamsted, Herts.

The British Library Sound Archive, St Pancras, London.

Downing College, Cambridge.

Lord Chamberlain's File, The British Library, St Pancras, London.

Mankowitz Family Archive.

The National Archives, Kew, Richmond, Surrey.

Theatre and Performance Collection, Victoria and Albert Museum, London.

Westminster Council Archives, London.

LIST OF MANKOWITZ'S PRINCIPLE WORKS

Mankowitz, Wolf, *The Portland Vase and the Wedgwood Copies* (London: André Deutsch, 1952).

Mankowitz, Wolf, *Wedgwood* (New York: E.P. Dutton, 1953).

Mankowitz, Wolf, *Majollika and Company* (London: André Deutsch, 1955).

Mankowitz, Wolf, *Make Me an Offer and A Kid for Two Farthings* (London: André Deutsch, 1955).

Mankowitz, Wolf, *The ABC of Show Business* (London: Oldbourne Press, n.d, probably 1956).

Mankowitz, Wolf, *My Old Man's A Dustman* (London: Barker Dragon Books, 1958).

Mankowitz, Wolf, *Make Me An Offer, Expresso Bongo and Other Stories* (London: Hutchinson Educational Ltd, 1961).

Mankowitz, Wolf, *Cockatrice* (London: Longman, 1963).

Mankowitz, Wolf, *Five One-Act Plays* (London and New York: Evans, 1964). First published 1956.

Mankowitz, Wolf, *The Penguin Wolf Mankowitz* (Harmondsworth: Penguin, 1967).
Mankowitz, Wolf, *The Blue Arabian Nights: Tales of a London Decade* (Dublin: Ahakista Press, 1973).
Mankowitz, Wolf, *Dickens of London* (London: Weidenfeld & Nicolson, 1976).
Mankowitz, Wolf, *The Day of the Women & The Night of the Men* (London: Robson Books, 1977).
Mankowitz, Wolf, *The Extraordinary Mr Poe* (London: Weidenfeld & Nicolson, 1978).
Mankowitz, Wolf, *Raspberry Reich* (Dublin and London: Macmillan, 1979).
Mankowitz, Wolf, *Abracadabra!* (Dublin and London: Macmillan, 1980).
Mankowitz, Wolf, *Mazeppa: The Lives, Loves and Legends of Adah Isaacs Menken: A Biographical Quest* (London: Blond & Briggs, 1982).
Mankowitz, Wolf, *The Devil in Texas* (London: Robert Royce,1984).
Mankowitz, Wolf, *Gioconda* (London: W.H. Allen, 1987).
Mankowitz, Wolf, *The Magic Cabinet of Professor Smucker* (London: W.H. Allen, 1988).
Mankowitz, Wolf, *Exquisite Cadaver* (London: André Deutsch, 1990).
Mankowitz, Wolf, *A Night with Casanova* (London: Sinclair-Stevenson, 1991).
Mankowitz, Wolf, *Wolf Mankowitz: The Plays*, preface by Anthony Dunn (London: Oberon Books, 2006).
Mankowitz, W. and Haggar, R. (eds), *The Concise Encyclopedia of English Pottery and Porcelain* (London: André Deutsch, 1957).

PUBLICATIONS

Ackroyd, P., *Dickens* (London: Sinclair-Stevenson, 1990).
Ackroyd, Peter, *London: The Biography* (London: Vintage Books, 2001).
Anderson, Lindsay, *The Diaries*, paperback edn (London: Methuen, 2005).
Barker, Denis, Wolf Mankowitz obituary, *Guardian*, 23 May 1998.
Benedict, Ruth, *Patterns of Culture* (London: Routledge, 1935).
Benjamin, W., 'The Work of Art in the Age of Mechanical Reproduction', in W. Benjamin, *Illuminations* (London: Fontana, 1973), pp.219–53.

Berkoff, Steve, *Free Association: An Autobiography*, paperback edn (London: Faber & Faber, 1997).

Bonaparte, Marie, *The Life and Works of Edgar Allen Poe: A Psycho-Analytic Interpretation*, translated by John Rodker (London: Imago, 1949; reprinted 1971). First published 1933.

Bottomore, T.B. and Rubel, M. (eds), *Karl Marx: Selected Writings in Sociology and Social Philosophy* (Harmondsworth: Pelican, 1963).

Bradbury, Malcolm, *Stepping Westward* (Harmondsworth: Penguin, 1968). First published by Secker & Warburg, 1965.

Bragg, Melvyn, *Rich: The Life of Richard Burton* (London: Hodder & Stoughton, 1988).

Broccoli, Albert R. and Zec, Donald, *When the Snow Melts: The Autobiography of Cubby Broccoli* (London: Boxtree, 1998).

Brown, Norman O., *Hermes the Thief* (New York: Vintage Books, 1969).

Brulotte, Gaetan and Phillips, John (eds), *Encyclopedia of Erotic Literature* (London: Routledge, 2006).

Brunsdon, Charlotte, *London in Cinema: The Cinematic City since 1945* (London: BFI Publications, 2007).

Caine, M., *What's It All About?* (London: Century, 1992).

Callan, Michael Feeney, *Richard Harris: Sex, Death and the Movies* (London: Robson Books, 2003).

Callow, Simon, *Hello Americans* (London: J. Cape, 2006), 2 volumes.

Chapman, James, *Licence to Thrill: A Cultural History of the James Bond Films*, 2nd rev. edn (London and New York: I.B. Tauris, 2007).

Cheyette, Bryan (ed.), *Contemporary Jewish Writing in Britain and Ireland: An Anthology* (London: Peter Halban, 1998).

Christie, Anne, *First Act* (Loughton: Judy Piatkus Books, 1983).

Cottrell, John and Cashin, Fergus, *Richard Burton: An Intimate Biography* (London: Arthur Barker, 1971).

Demby, Betty Jeffries, 'The Art of Screenwriting: An Interview with Wolf Mankowitz', *Filmmakers Newsletter*, February 1974, pp.26–9.

Donnelly, K.J., *Pop Music in British Cinema: A Chronicle* (London: BFI Publications, 2001).

Editorial, 'Culture and Crisis', *Politics and Letters*, 2–3 (Winter/Spring 1947), p.8.

Elam, Keir, *The Semiotics of Theatre and Drama*, New Accents series (London and New York: Methuen, 1980).

Empson, William, 'Rochester', in J. Haffenden (ed.), *Argufying, Essays on Literature and Culture, William Empson* (London: Chatto & Windus, 1987), pp.273–8.

Erskine, Rosalind, *Passion Flower Hotel* (London: Jonathan Cape, 1962).
Evans, Peter William, *Carol Reed* (Manchester: Manchester University Press, 2005).
Findlater, Richard (ed.), *At The Royal Court* (Ambergate: Amber Lane Press, 1981).
Forster, J., *The Life of Charles Dickens*, vol. 1 (London: J.M. Dent, 1966). First published 1872–74.
Freedland, M., *Michael Caine*, paperback edn (London: Orion, 2000).
Gillett, Charlie, *The Sound of the City* (London: Sphere Books, 1971).
Gogol, Nicolai, *Plays and Petersburg Tales*, edited and translated by Christopher English, World's Classics series (Oxford: Oxford University Press, 1995).
Guest, Val, *So You Want To Be in Pictures* (London: Reynolds & Hearn, 2001).
Hall, W., *70 Not Out: The Biography of Sir Michael Caine* (London: John Blake, 2003).
Harper, S. and Porter, V., *British Cinema of the 1950s: The Decline of Deference* (Oxford: Oxford University Press, 2003).
Hartley, L.P., *The Hireling* (London: Hamish Hamilton, 1957).
Heilpern, John, *John Osborne: A Patriot For Us*, paperback edn (London: Vintage Books, 2007).
Hemingway, E., 'Fiesta (The Sun Also Rises)', in E. Hemingway, *The Essential Hemingway* (London: Arrow Books, 2004), pp.3–202.
Hickey, D. and Smith, G., *The Prince: The Public and Private Life of Laurence Harvey* (London: Leslie Frewin, 1975).
Hoggart, Richard, *The Uses of Literacy* (London: Chatto & Windus, 1960). First published 1957.
Hoggart, Richard, *An Imagined Life: Life and Times 1959–91* (London: Chatto & Windus, 1992).
Howarth, H., 'Wolf Mankowitz: In the Zangwill Tradition', *Jewish Affairs* (March 1955), pp.37–40.
Howe, I. and Greenberg, E. (eds), *A Treasury of Yiddish Stories*, introduced by Wolf Mankowitz (London: Deutsch, 1955).
Hunter, I.Q., 'The Day the Earth Caught Fire', in I.Q. Hunter (ed.), *British Science Fiction Cinema* (London and New York: Routledge, 1999), pp.99–111.
Inglis, Fred, *Raymond Williams* (London: Routledge, 1995).
Jacobson, Howard, *Coming From Behind* (London: Vintage Books, 2003). First published 1983.
James, Henry, *Henry James: Selected Tales*, edited by John Lyon, Penguin Classics series (London: Penguin, 2001).

Junor, Penny, *The Man Behind the Myth* (London: Sidgwick & Jackson, 1985).

Kael, Pauline, *Kiss Kiss Bang Bang* (Boston, MA, and Toronto, ON: Little, Brown & Co., 1968).

Leach, Robert, *Theatre Workshop: Joan Littlewood and the Making of Modern British Theatre* (Exeter: University of Exeter Press, 2006).

Leaming, B., *Orson Welles: A Biography* (New York: Viking, 1985).

Leavis, F.R., *The Common Pursuit* (Harmondsworth: Peregrine Books, 1962).

Leavis, F.R., 'Literary Criticism and Philosophy', in Leavis, *Common Pursuit* (1962), pp.211–22.

Leavis, F.R., 'Sociology and Literature', in Leavis, *Common Pursuit* (1962), pp.195–203.

Lewenstein, Oscar, *Kicking against the Pricks* (London: Nick Hern Books, 1994).

Lewis, Roger, *The Life and Death of Peter Sellers* (London: Century, 1994).

Maccoby, Hyam and Mankowitz, Wolf, *The Day God Laughed: Sayings, Fables and Entertainments of the Jewish Sages* (London: Robson Books, 1978).

Mailer, Norman, *An American Dream* (London: Paladin, 1992). First published by André Deutsch, 1965.

Mandler, Peter, *The Fall and Rise of the Stately Home* (New Haven, CT: Yale University Press, 1997).

Mankowitz, Gered, 'Introduction: Mason's Yard', in Gered Mankowitz, *The Experience: Jimi Hendrix at Mason's Yard* (San Rafael, CA: Insight Editions, 2010), pp.18–25.

Mann, W.J., *Edge of Midnight: The Life of John Schlesinger* (London: Hutchinson, 2004).

Marx, Karl, *Capital*, vol. 1, introduced by G.D.H. Cole, Everyman's Library series (London: J.M. Dent, 1962).

Maschler, Tom (ed.), *New English Dramatists 3* (Harmondsworth, Penguin, 1961).

Mayhew, Henry, *Mayhew's London*, introduced by Peter Quennell (London: Spring Books, n.d., probably 1956). First published 1851.

McAleer, Dave (ed.), *Hit Singles: Top Twenty Charts* (London: Carlton Books, 2007).

McLuhan, Marshall, *Understanding Media* (London: Sphere Books, 1967). First published 1964.

Meikle, Denis, 'Fisher's Folly or The One That Got Away – The Two Faces of Dr Jekyll', *Little Shoppe of Horrors*, 19 (2007), pp.82–9.

Metcalf, John, 'Wolf Mankowitz', *Atlantic Monthly*, October 1956, p.868.

Moss, Robert F., *The Films of Carol Reed* (Basingstoke: Macmillan, 1987).

Oldsay, Bernard (ed.), *Dictionary of Literary Biography, 15 (Part 2): British Novelists 1930–1959* (Detroit, MI: Gale Research Co., 1983).

Osborne, John, *Look Back in Anger* (London: Faber, 1979). First published 1957.

Osborne, John, *Almost a Gentleman: An Autobiography, Vol. 2, 1955–1966* (London: Faber & Faber, 1991).

Osborne, John, *Plays 2* (London: Faber & Faber, 1998).

Pearson, John, *The Profession of Violence* (London: Panther Books, 1973).

Pinter, Harold, *The Birthday Party* (London: Eyre Methuen, 1980). First published 1960.

Pinter, Harold, *The Homecoming* (London: Methuen, 1966).

Rebellato, Dan, *1956 and All That: The Making of Modern British Drama* (London and New York: Routledge, 1999).

Reisz, Matthew, 'Eastenders – but not as we know it', *Guardian*, 16 September 2006.

Rigby, Jonathan, *English Gothic: A Century of Horror Cinema*, 3rd edn (London: Reynolds and Hearn, 2004).

Ronay, Edina, 'When George Harrison Came To Supper', *Observer*, 7 December 2003, p.35.

Sales, Roger (ed.), *Shakespeare in Perspective*, 2 vols (London: Ariel/BBC Publications, 1982 and 1985).

Sandbrook, Dominic, *Never Had It So Good: A History of Britain from Suez to the Beatles*, paperback edn (London: Abacus 2006).

Sandhal, Linda J., *Encyclopedia of Rock Music on Film* (Poole: Blandford Press, 1987).

Shellard, Dominic, *Kenneth Tynan: A Life* (New Haven, CT, and London: Yale University Press, 2003).

Sikov, Ed, *Mr Strangelove: A Biography of Peter Sellers* (London: Sidgwick & Jackson, 2002).

Sinai, Anne, *Reach for the Top: The Turbulent Life of Laurence Harvey* (Lanham, MD, and Oxford: Scarecrow Press, 2003).

Sinyard, Neil, *Jack Clayton* (Manchester: Manchester University Press, 2000).

Slater, Michael, *Charles Dickens* (New Haven, CT, and London: Yale University Press, 2009).

Slezkine, Yuri, *The Jewish Century*, paperback edn (Princeton, NJ, and Oxford: Princeton University Press, 2006).

Smith, Gus, *Richard Harris: Actor by Accident* (London: Robert Hale, 1990).

Spencer, C.S., 'Wolf Mankowitz', *Menorah* (June 1954), pp.21–6.

Spicer, Andrew, *Typical Men: The Representation of Masculinity in Popular British Cinema* (London and New York: I.B. Taurus, 2001).

Stevenson, Robert Louis, *Treasure Island* (London: Penguin, 1999).

Taylor, John Russell, *Anger and After* (Harmondsworth: Pelican Books, 1963).

Vickery, Amanda, 'Beauties in Breeches', *Guardian*, 15 October 2011.

Walker, Alexander, *Peter Sellers: The Authorised Biography* (London: Weidenfeld, 1981).

Weaver, Tom, *Attack of the Monster Movie Makers: Interviews with Twentieth Century Genre Giants* (Jefferson, NC, and London: McFarland, 1994).

Welles, O. and Bogdanovich, P., *This is Orson Welles*, paperback edn (Cambridge, MA: Da Capo Press, 1998).

Williams, Raymond, 'The Idea of Culture', *Essays in Criticism*, 3, 3 (July 1953), pp.239–66.

Williams, Raymond, *Culture and Society 1780–1950* (London: Chatto and Windus, 1958).

Williams, Raymond, 'Culture is Ordinary', in N. Mackenzie (ed.), *Conviction*, (London: MacGibbon & Kee, 1959), pp.74–92. First published 1958.

Williams, Raymond, *Politics and Letters: Interviews with New Left Review* (London: New Left Books, 1995).

Wilmut, Roger, *Tony Hancock – 'Artiste': A Tony Hancock Companion*, paperback reprint edn (London: Methuen 1985).

Wright, Adrian, *A Tanner's Worth of Tune: Rediscovering the Post-War British Musical* (Woodbridge: Boydell Press, 2010).

Young, Jean, 'The Hireling: The Scriptwriter', *Film*, 5 (August 1973).

Young, Michael and Willmott, Peter, *Family and Kinship in East London* (London: Routledge & Kegan Paul, 1957).

Zweig, Paul, 'Literary Terrorist', *Saturday Review*, 6 January 1979, pp.50–2.

Zweig, Stefan, *Casanova: A Study in Self-Portraiture*, translated by Eden Paul and Cedar Paul (London: Pushkin Press, 1998).

Index

Please note that the letters 'CWM' stand for Cyril 'Wolf' Mankowitz.